BERKELEY'S THOUGHT

Berkeley's Thought

GEORGE S. PAPPAS

CORNELL UNIVERSITY PRESS

ITHACA AND LONDON

First published 2000 by Cornell University Press

Printed in the United States of America

Library of Congress Cataloging-in-Publication Data

Pappas, George Sotiros, b. 1942
    Berkeley's thought / George S. Pappas
        p.   cm.
    Includes bibliographical references and index.
    ISBN 0-8014-3700-8
    1. Berkeley, George, 1685–1753.   I. Title.
B1348 .P36 2000
192—dc21   99-088432

Cornell University Press strives to use environmentally responsible
suppliers and materials to the fullest extent possible in the publishing
of its books. Such materials include vegetable-based, low-VOC inks,
and acid-free papers that are recycled, totally chlorine-free, or partly
composed of nonwood fibers. Books that bear the logo of the FSC
(Forest Stewardship Council) use paper taken from forests that have
been inspected and certified as meeting the highest standards for
environmental and social responsibility. For further information, visit
our website at www.cornellpress.cornell.edu.

Cloth printing   10 9 8 7 6 5 4 3 2 1

FOR CHRIS

Contents

Preface

My aim is to give an interpretation of some of the core ideas in the thought of Bishop George Berkeley. This book focuses on three core elements: Berkeley's rejection of abstract ideas and the arguments he gives in support of that rejection; Berkeley's notion of immediate perception and of what he takes the objects of immediate perception to be; and Berkeley's defense of common sense. Selection of these three themes to be investigated and developed has been guided mainly by the fact that Berkeley himself stresses the importance of them to his overall thought.

The rejection of abstract ideas is connected by Berkeley to other important parts of his philosophy, and I investigate a number of these in some detail. Among these are the connection that the rejection of abstract ideas has to Berkeley's famous thesis *esse is percipi* as applied to non-perceiving things; the relation between Berkeley's theory of vision as articulated in the *New Theory of Vision* and abstract ideas; the connection between abstract ideas and what Berkeley has to say, negatively, about the primary quality–secondary quality distinction; and the relationship Berkeley finds between abstract ideas and scepticism. Although these connections are extremely important to Berkeley, they have been largely neglected in commentaries on his work.

The concept of immediate perception in Berkeley's thought has been studied by others, but few have been willing to follow A. A. Luce and T. E. Jessop in holding that Berkeley consistently accepts the thesis that physical objects are among the objects that are immediately perceived.

Fewer still would accept their contention that Berkeley is best understood as a defender of commonsense realism. I try to show in chapters 6 and 7 that there is a great deal that is correct in the Luce–Jessop interpretation of Berkeley, and in that sense I aim to resuscitate and breathe new life into their reading of Berkeley. Not that I agree with all of their respective attributions; Berkeley is not, after all, a realist about the existence of physical objects. But many of the other key elements included in the notion of commonsense realism were consistently accepted by Berkeley along with his defense of an idealist metaphysics.

Among other things, I try to explicate what Berkeley takes common sense to be, and to assess the role it plays in his overall philosophy. This role, I argue, is actually rather less than his various comments on common sense would suggest. Agreement between one's philosophical theory and the dictates of common sense, I claim, makes up just one factor among many which can be used to gauge the acceptability of the theory. Agreement with common sense occupies no special, privileged position on this matter.

The other side of Berkeley's defense of common sense, so to speak, is his rejection of scepticism. In the last chapter Berkeley's case against scepticism is examined, and I maintain that it is Berkeley's account of immediate perception and the objects thereof that ultimately underwrites his rejection of scepticism. It is not, as Berkeley himself would have us think, the rejection of abstract ideas, nor the acceptance of the *esse is percipi* thesis, that does this work.

My interest in Berkeley was sparked years ago in a class taught by Chan Coulter and further spurred by spirited discussions with Jack Bailey. Later, extensive discussions on Berkeley with James Cornman proved to be invaluable. I have also learned a great deal from discussions with Alan Hausman and Wallace Anderson in the years when we were colleagues. I have also benefited much from conversation or correspondence with many people: Margaret Atherton, Martha Bolton, Tom Lennon, David Drebushenko, Jody Graham, Ernie Sosa, David Armstrong, Georges Dicker, Phil Cummins, and Ken Winkler. Those whose writings have influenced my thinking the most are George Pitcher, Ken Winkler, Douglas Jesseph, Julius Weinberg, Colin Turbayne, Ian Tipton, Margaret Atherton, and Phil Cummins. I have also profited from many useful suggestions and criticisms from two anonymous reviewers, most (but not all) of whose advice I have tried to follow. My daughters, Christina and Sara, persevered through many discussions of Berkeleyan themes and deserve special thanks and commendation. My wife, Chris, has been an especially valuable and patient resource, in ways too numerous to mention, and I am pleased to dedicate the book to her.

Some parts of the book are based on earlier publications of mine. Parts of chapter 5 are based on two papers: "Ideas, Minds, and Berkeley," *American Philosophical Quarterly*, 17 (1980), and "Berkeleyan Idealism and Impossible Performances," in Robert Muehlmann, ed., *Berkeley's Metaphysics* (University Park: Pennsylvania State University Press, 1995). Part of chapter 6 is based on my "Berkeley and Immediate Perception," which first appeared in Ernest Sosa, ed., *Essays on the Philosophy of George Berkeley* (Dordrecht: Reidel, 1987), reprinted here with kind permission from Kluwer Academic Publishers. Material in chapter 7 is based on my article "Berkeley and Common Sense Realism," in *History of Philosophy Quarterly*, 8 (1991). Chapter 9 is based on "Berkeley and Scepticism" in *Philosophy and Phenomenological Research*, 59 (1999). All of these materials are used with the kind permission of the editors of the journals or presses to whom I extend my thanks.

GEORGE S. PAPPAS

Columbus, Ohio

BERKELEY'S THOUGHT

CHAPTER 1

Scope and Method

In the chapters that follow I discuss many of the major themes in Berkeley's philosophy: abstract ideas and the process of abstraction; perception, particularly immediate perception and its objects; and common sense. I single out these themes because, I think, so much else of importance in Berkeley's thought depends on what he says about them. In approaching Berkeley's philosophy, I do not deny that one might profitably approach the same subject by concentrating instead on some other key doctrine, such as, what Berkeley says about God. Indeed, I am inclined to think that a number of different avenues into Berkeley's philosophy might be pursued, each with valuable insights. Stressing the three themes above is but one of these avenues, no more, but one which promises to illuminate how disparate elements of Berkeley's philosophy are connected.

To illustrate the importance of these three themes, and to briefly anticipate more detailed treatment to be given in later chapters, a few words about each of the themes is in order. Concerning abstract ideas, it is well known that Berkeley opposed admission of such entities into his philosophy. He also opposed the process of abstraction, i.e., the procedure by which we are supposed to acquire abstract ideas. His arguments against both the procedure and its alleged products occur in the introduction to the *Principles of Human Knowledge*, and the context makes it quite clear that Locke is one of his principal targets. However, almost no attention is paid to abstract ideas or abstraction later in that book, despite the fact that these matters are the main topic of the introduction. It looks very much as

1

if Berkeley raises the topic only to completely drop it in the body of the work. Moreover, a close look at books he published after the *Principles* reveals even less attention to abstract ideas and abstraction. These topics are virtually absent from the *Three Dialogues*, and they are but infrequently mentioned, and then only briefly, in still later works such as *De Motu*, *Alciphron*, and the works on mathematics, *The Analyst* and the *Defense of Free Thinking in Mathematics*.

These two facts about Berkeley's actual treatment of abstract ideas and abstraction—detailed examination of the topic in the introduction to the *Principles* and but scant and seemingly desultory reference to the same topics in other parts of the same book and in later works—suggest two conclusions one might draw about the role of this topic in Berkeley's larger philosophy. The first, suggested by the introduction to the *Principles,* is that the rejection of abstract ideas is connected closely to the other matters Berkeley there discusses, namely, language learning and language use—topics explicitly addressed by Locke—and to nominalism. On the latter point, Berkeley expressly denies that any of our ideas are *general* and proposes an alternative account of how we make use of ideas which are in themselves wholly particular to make reference to a range of objects sorted into the same class. To be sure, these issues of nominalism and language use and learning are of great interest and importance; but it looks as if the question of abstract ideas is confined to these two issues. This impression is reinforced when we take note of the other fact, namely, the very infrequent references *en passant* to abstract ideas in later work. From this infrequency one gains the impression that abstraction and abstract ideas have no real connection to the larger themes argued for in those later pages. Thus, one arrives at the conclusion that though important to Berkeley's views on nominalism and on language, the relevance of his negative attitude on abstract ideas ends just there. Nothing else in his philosophy depends on that negativity.

This conclusion is a natural one to draw, and I think some commentators have done exactly this. Yet I think such a conclusion is actually in error since Berkeley himself did not view matters this way. On the contrary, he thought that the rejection of abstract ideas played a far greater role, so much so that practically everything that is distinctive about his philosophy depends on the success of the attack on abstract ideas. For example, Berkeley maintains that the supposition that objects exist independently of all perception somehow depends on the assumption that there are abstract ideas and so, by implication, his famous thesis that for non-perceiving entities, to be or exist is to be perceived, also has some dependence on abstract ideas. In turn, this principle of *esse is percipi* surely qualifies as one of the most central and vital elements of Berkeley's philosophy, one which is itself connected to many other parts of his metaphysical and epistemological positions.

The exact nature of the dependency that Berkeley finds between abstract ideas and his metaphysical views will be explored more fully in later chapters. Here it will be helpful to give another example of the important role Berkeley sees for the rejection of abstract ideas, one connected not to his metaphysical views but rather to the theory of visual perception he works out in the *Essay Towards a New Theory of Vision*. In that work, Berkeley argues that a consequence of his theory is a certain sort of heterogeneity of the ideas of sight and touch. Such ideas, he argues, are always numerically distinct, and they are also different in kind. Ideas of sight, then, are both numerically and qualitatively different from ideas of touch. However, at one point he brings up abstract ideas as something that would function as a threat to this heterogeneity thesis. That is, he tells us that if there were abstract ideas of a certain sort, then the heterogeneity thesis would be false. Hence, it becomes quite important to attack abstract ideas, lest his theory of visual perception be undermined by falsification of a conclusion which follows from that theory. That is, as Berkeley sees it, the main project in the *New Theory* requires, and so is intimately related to, rejection of the abstract ideas thesis. Yet this fact has no relationship to the issues of nominalism and language use and learning which are actually broached in the introduction to the *Principles*.

No one would be similarly tempted to think that the issue of perception and its objects is of marginal importance in Berkeley. But even on this topic, I think, the nature of perception for Berkeley has been misunderstood. Specifically, all too often one finds it said that for Berkeley ideas make up the *only* objects of perception. This view, in turn, makes it difficult to see Berkeley as consistently defending common sense since, most would agree, it is a matter of common sense that physical objects are perceived, indeed, perceived immediately. Thus, one might be tempted to hold that Berkeley's defense of common sense is a kind of ruse, something he does only when he is speaking with the vulgar. His *real* view, one might claim, is not at all a commonsensical view. His real view, expressed when he is speaking with the learned, is that physical objects are at best mediately perceived, and that this mediate perception is wholly dependent on the immediate perception of ideas. Moreover, this latter result has implications for other elements of common sense.

Another common sense view, many philosophers have said, is that we gain knowledge of objects by means of perception, and that the knowledge so gained is both immediate and certain. Yet this piece of common sense also seems excluded if we interpret Berkeley as holding that the only objects of immediate perception are ideas, and never physical objects. For it seems to follow from such a view that if we acquire knowledge of objects as a result of perception, it is only by uncertain inferences we make from beliefs about objects which are immediately perceived. Any such knowledge, if dependent on inference in this way, would not qualify as immediate, and neither would it be certain, since the inferences in question would nearly always be inductive.

These apparent conflicts with common sense are avoided if we understand Berkeley's account of perception and its objects in a different way. That is, if we take seriously Berkeley's occasional claims that physical objects and (some of) their qualities are immediately perceived, then there would be no clash with common sense in regard to perception. Neither, in Berkeley's view, would there be epistemological clashes with common sense. For, he would say, immediate perception of physical objects is often sufficient for our gaining immediate and certain knowledge of such objects. It is true that if we interpret Berkeley in this way, as some of his comments suggest we should, then we must understand his concept of perception in a certain way, namely as essentially *not* itself an epistemological concept. That is, perceiving an object for Berkeley would not be the same as, or essentially include, gaining some knowledge of the object, even if in many cases, when one immediately perceives an object one thereby acquires some knowledge of the object. Knowledge acquisition by means of immediate perception would be an accompanyment of such perception, but would not itself be included in what it is to immediately perceive. Such an interpretation of Berkeley's concept of perception and of its objects, developed more fully in later chapters, is suggested by this passage from the *Three Dialogues:*

> Wood, stones, fire, water, flesh, iron, and the like things which I name and discourse of are things that I know. And, I should not have known them but that I perceived them by my senses; and the things perceived by the senses are immediately perceived.[1]

Some evidence that Berkeley's notion of immediate perception is not an epistemic concept is given by a distinction he makes between perceiving and judging:

> To perceive is one thing; to judge is another. So likewise to be suggested is one thing, and to be inferred is another. Things are suggested and per-

1. George Berkeley, *Three Dialogues between Hylas and Philonous*, ed. A. A. Luce and T. E. Jessop, vol. 2, *The Works of George Berkeley* (London: Thomas Nelson and Sons, 1948–57), p. 230. See Bibliography and Cited Works for full references to author–date text citations in main text and footnote apparatus.

ceived by sense. We make judgments and inferences by the understanding. (Berkeley 1948–57, 1:265)

This passage is not decisive, but it is instructive nonetheless, since it suggests that for Berkeley perceiving is not a conceptual activity in something like the Kantian sense, that is, not an activity in which concepts are applied. Concept application occurs paradigmatically when one makes a judgment or inference of some sort. If Berkeleyan perception is not and does not include concept application, then it is reasonable to infer that perception for him is not itself an event of knowledge acquisition. For certainly in acquiring knowledge one is thereby making use of some concepts.[2]

Berkeley's attempt to align his philosophical views with common sense, however, is not without its problems, for it is natural to ask, why should common sense make a difference? If the common sense view is that the sun rises every morning and goes down or sets every evening, we know that this view is false. This was something known in Berkeley's time as well. Other examples can be readily adduced in which the common sense belief on some matter falls short of truth. So, why should according with the views of common sense have any special weight when common sense may be shot through with falsity?

There is, further, another problem. Berkeley's philosophy actually diverges from common sense in fairly dramatic ways. Perhaps the most obvious departure from common sense comes in Berkeley's acceptance of the *esse is percipi* thesis, the thesis that physical objects and their several qualities exist if and only if they are perceived by some mind. However, there are other less well known breaks with common sense, such as Berkeley's denial that there is genuine causation between physical events. In his view, real causation is always agent causation, so that a baseball flying through the air is not caused by its collision with a wooden bat.

The second of these two problems is essentially that of the consistency of Berkeley's philosophy with common sense. Berkeley himself was well aware of this problem, and attempted to resolve it. Regarding the *esse is percipi* principle, Berkeley asks what an ordinary person would say if asked why that person believes that some object exists. He tells us that this person will reply that he so believes because he perceives the object. However, this ploy only goes part of the way towards resolving the conflict, for it deals with only one consequence of the *esse is percipi* principle and leaves other elements untouched. That is, asking the ordinary person

2. These remarks do not suffice to rule out interpreting Berkeley's notion of immediate perception as something akin to Russell's notion of acquaintance. So interpreted, immediate perception would be epistemic and essentially incorporate knowledge acquisition, but would also not include elements of either judgment or inference. For further discussion of this possibility, see chapter 6.

only relates to whether objects exist *if* they are perceived, and on this we would likely side with the ordinary person. The existence principle (the *esse is percipi* principle), however, also says that objects exist *only if* they are perceived, and Berkeley's strategy of consulting the ordinary person does not address this aspect of the principle. Hence, we are apt to find his attempt to reconcile this part of his philosophy with common sense less than satisfactory.[3]

However, this is not the end of the story, because there are many other components of Berkeley's philosophy that have to be examined in relation to common sense. As noted earlier, it is a matter of common sense that, typically physical objects are immediately perceived, and some evidence has already been adduced that Berkeley wants to go along with this point. Moreover, as we have noted, it is a common sense truism that we gain immediate and certain knowledge of physical objects by means of perception, another point that Berkeley says he accepts. Questions of consistency intrude here, too, for we need to ask whether these two common sensical beliefs are consistent with Berkeley's metaphysical views. If they are not, then though Berkeley may signal his intent to accept these beliefs, he would not actually be entitled to that acceptance.

On these two beliefs of common sense, I think Berkeley's position can be vindicated; the consistency questions can be resolved in his favor. But not all consistency questions can be, as we have seen. Hence, Berkeley's wonderfully sweeping claim that "I side in all things with the Mob" has to be called into question.[4] This leads us directly to another question: to what degree or extent do Berkeley's metaphysical views comport with common sense? It may be that Berkeley is in no position to accept every dictum of common sense, but that he is better off on this score than is any alternative metaphysical theory, especially those proposed by philosophers he considers rivals, notably Descartes and Locke.

Without actually mentioning Locke and Descartes, this is exactly the story Berkeley tells in the *Three Dialogues*. That is, he contends that his philosophical theory agrees more with the dictates of common sense than does any of its extant rivals, and this he takes as a mark in favor of his theory. However, such a conclusion on Berkeley's part immediately returns us to the first problem concerning common sense noted earlier: since so many beliefs of common sense are false, why should agreement with com-

3. Putting a hypothetical question to the ordinary person occurs when Philonous invites Hylas to ask the gardener why he thinks that the cherry tree in the garden exists, and the presumed answer is that he so believes because he sees and feels it. The exchange is in the third *Dialogue*, Berkeley 1948–57, 2:234.

4. On siding in all things with the Mob, see *Philosophical Commentaries*, 405, Berkeley 1948–57, 1:51.

mon sense count in favor of one theory and against another? Indeed, should not the very opposite be the case? The theory most in line with common sense should be counted as false, or at least less plausible than its competitors, all else between the theories being equal.

Berkeley's answer to this question has two parts: first, all else may not be equal because his philosophical theory has a great many "advantages" which do not accrue to alternative theories; and second, the weight that he places on agreement with common sense is actually minimal. Common sense is just one mark of evidence which is set in a context of many other marks of evidence to be considered in evaluating a philosophical theory. Moreover, in the specific context of the *Dialogues*, Berkeley seems to think that all else other than common sense is equal between his theory and that of his "materialist" opponent, and in that particular context degree of agreement with common sense serves only as a tie-breaker. When the competing theories are unequal, and one theory is superior to the others on theoretical grounds, then agreement with common sense need not have any special weight. Berkeley may tout agreement between his theory and common sense, but if his theory is superior to its rivals on other grounds, then agreement with common sense plays no special role in supporting his theory.

One of the supposed advantages which Berkeley claims for his theory is that it avoids scepticism regarding ordinary physical objects and their perceivable qualities, while competing theories, he argues, either entail or strongly support scepticism. Berkeley certainly takes this as a mark in favor of his theory and as a strike against the competition. It thus becomes important to investigate both sides of the scepticism issue. What is it about the competing theories that leads to scepticism? On this point, Berkeley thinks that a number of his competitor's contentions have sceptical consequences: acceptance of abstract ideas, countenancing material substance, holding that ordinary physical objects exist unperceived, and acceptance of what we would call the representative realist theory of perception—each of these claims, individually, he seems to say, leads to scepticism. Alternatively, Berkeley seems to say that it is his existence principle, *esse is percipi*, that serves to vanquish scepticism.

None of the first three items singled out by Berkeley, I argue, leads to scepticism. It is only the representative realist theory of perception that tends to support scepticism, and this theory of perception is not itself entailed by these three items, taken singly or jointly. It is only when these three items are conjoined with the thesis that in every perceptual experience at least one idea is immediately perceived that some connection to representative realism is made; but this conjoined thesis is a non-trivial addition.

The other side of the scepticism issue, namely Berkeley's claim to have vanquished scepticism, can be taken in two quite different ways which he does not distinguish. Vanquishing scepticism may amount to undermining some important arguments that lead to scepticism. Such a result would of course be important, but it would leave untouched the truth or falsity of scepticism. A stronger notion of vanquishing scepticism, then, would be one in which the doctrine itself is refuted. Berkeley sometimes writes as if he has the latter in mind, and not just the former. Further, as already noted, he makes it seem that it is the existence principle which allows him to reach this important conclusion. However, if this is Berkeley's position, I believe it is a mistaken one. Establishing the existence principle serves only to vanquish scepticism in the weak sense, that of undermining it by demolishing arguments that lead to scepticism. What really serves to show that scepticism is false is something else, namely, the thesis that physical objects are often and indeed typically immediately perceived. It is on this point more than anything else that the crucial epistemic difference between Berkeley and his opponents actually depends.

Overview of the Chapters

Berkeley's concern with abstract ideas seems to be *local,* both textually and philosophically. That is, the main source in his texts for discussion of abstract ideas is the introduction to the *Principles*, and there is but scant and scattered reference to abstract ideas in other texts, and even in the body of the *Principles*. Also, abstract ideas, for him, seem to be philosophically local in that they connect only to issues of nominalism and language which, though themselves of some importance, do not ramify into other elements of Berkeley's philosophy. In chapter 2, after explaining these points about locality, it is noted at some length that Berkeley himself rejects philosophical locality of the abstract ideas issue. In his account of the matter, on the contrary, nearly every other important aspect of his philosophy is connected to abstract ideas, though the exact connections will differ from case to case.

The main burden of this chapter is to delineate the connections Berkeley finds between abstract ideas, or their rejection, and other elements of his philosophy. Three such connections are probed in some detail to help shed light on how Berkeley thought on these matters. Abstract ideas are related to the heterogeneity thesis that Berkeley defends in the *New Theory of Vision*, so the exact relation between these themes is examined. Similarly, Berkeley holds that abstract ideas are related to the existence principle, both in the sense that if there are abstract ideas, then the existence principle is false; and in the sense that if there are no abstract ideas, then the existence principle is true. Finally, Berkeley holds that the existence of abstract ideas has some implications for scepticism about the external world. This issue is discussed in a preliminary way in this chapter; more detailed treatment of the connection to scepticism is given in chapter 9.

What Berkeley means by abstract ideas, and by the process of abstraction, together with his main arguments against each, forms the main topic of chapter 3. Loosely following Craig,[5] I distinguish four different types of abstract ideas that Berkeley identifies, and I also consider in some detail the various arguments he gives against abstract ideas of one or more type. I contend his arguments do not require that abstract ideas be images, as some commentators on Locke have maintained. Instead, the arguments require that each idea have determinate content in the sense that no idea has just determinable features. This, I argue, is enough to insure the success of Berkeley's arguments against Locke, for Locke does seem to have held that some abstract ideas have merely determinable features.

It is also important to ask whether Berkeley's arguments, if successful, establish that abstract ideas are impossible. I argue, contrary to what I think is the prevailing view, that the arguments do not establish impossibility in full generality, i.e., as applying to all abstract ideas, and that for at least one sort of abstract idea, Berkeley seems to have been aware of this fact. He seems to see, that is, that the abstract idea of existence—what for me is an abstract idea of type 4—is not shown to be impossible by any of his arguments.

Berkeley also gives, or seems to give, a simplicity argument against abstract ideas. He argues that such entities are not needed for purposes of explaining pertinent facts about language use and learning, but that a much simpler explanation of these phenomena is more than adequate. He seems to infer from this that there is reason to suppose that abstract ideas do not exist. However, I think the simplicity argument actually has a different purpose, and is restricted just to criticizing the arguments, concerning language learning and communication, that Locke had given in favor of abstract ideas

Berkeley regards the abstract idea of existence as the most incomprehensible of all abstract ideas. Yet this very sort of idea is one that Locke expressly allows for, and so Berkeley is on safe ground in wondering about it. The abstract idea of existence is related by Berkeley directly to the *esse is percipi* principle. Suppose one can have an abstract idea of a tree, and an

5. Edward Craig 1968.

abstract idea of existence. Then on the plausible assumption that conceiving an abstract idea is not perceiving, one can conceive a tree existing unperceived. Hence, since Berkeley himself allows that such conceiving is sufficient for the falsity of his existence principle, it would follow that the *esse is percipi* principle is false. As this would be a devastating result for Berkeley, naturally he has to take steps to fend off this argument, something, I argue, he sees perfectly well. Hence the attack on abstract ideas in the introduction to the *Principles*.

It might be wondered just what is wrong with the abstract idea of existence, and in particular just which of Berkeley's several arguments against abstract ideas applies to it. In chapter 4 I argue that the argument he has against this abstract idea is never explicitly presented, though he provides us with hints. My reconstruction of his argument on this crucial point is briefly this: Berkeley notices that existence is not a property, or what he would have called a quality. Hence, even if one can acquire the abstract idea of a tree, one cannot by the same means acquire the abstract idea of existence. Since we never have a sensible idea of existence to start with, there is nothing to abstract from. So, even granting that we have some abstract ideas, we lack the abstract idea of existence, and so a threat to the existence principle is removed. Thus, if I am right in this interpretation of Berkeley's worries about existence, we find that he is aware that existence is not a property well in advance of this point being uncovered and put to great use by Hume and Kant.

In fact, it seems that Berkeley believes the *non*-existence of abstract ideas implies the *truth* of the existence principle. I take this possibility seriously, though ultimately I conclude that there is just not enough evidence for us to attribute this view to Berkeley. There are, however, interepretations of Berkeley that may secure the existence principle, provided that certain additional points were accepted by Berkeley. I have called one such interpretation the *inherence account*, because it interprets Berkeley as holding that ideas actually inhere in the minds that are said to immediately perceive them. According to this account, Berkeley has an unsure grasp of the concept of inherence that has come down from Aristotle, and he perhaps unwittingly adopts inherence as the correct account of the relation between ideas and minds. If this is right, it may explain why Berkeley thought the existence principle is an obvious truth, maybe even a necessary truth. An alternative account, also discussed in chapter 5, interprets Berkeleyan ideas of sense as events of sensing rather than as objects of which we are aware. In this view, a Berkeleyan idea of red is really an event of sensing red-ly. If this "adverbial" account of Berkeleyan ideas of sense is correct, then it is clear that the existence principle will hold for all sensible ideas, since an event of sensing cannot exist apart from a mind.

I take both of these interpretations very seriously, because each in its own way makes sense of much of what is central in Berkeley's philosophy. In the end, though, these two interpretations are rejected. The inherence account is rejected because there are too many texts with which it cannot be squared; and the adverbial interpretation is rejected on the grounds that there is nearly decisive textual evidence that Berkeley regarded his sensible ideas as objects of which we are aware rather than as events of sensing. With these accounts out of the way, an alternative account of Berkeley's case for the existence principle is proposed and defended. I argue that the existence principle is underwritten by the fact that the sort of conceiving involved in conceiving an object existing unperceived is impossible, though not in the sense that conceiving a sensible object existing unperceived is a contradiction. Instead, the act of so conceiving is a self-defeating action, an action which, when attempted, guarantees that it will fail to be performed. The impossible performance aspect of Berkeley's main argument for the existence principle has the result that the existence principle is not a necessary truth, which may seem to be opposed to Berkeley's view of the matter. However, I argue that Berkeley was actually aware of this consequence of his argument for the existence principle, and that he embraced it.

However, Berkeley *does* talk of the *esse is percipi* principle as a necessary truth, for he says that its denial is a contradiction. I explain why Berkeley makes such comments, and also why he sometimes says that the denial of the principle is meaningless, by distinguishing two concepts of existence which concern Berkeley. In one concept of existence, found in Locke, the principle is a necessary truth, while with the other, Berkeleyan, concept of existence the principle is contingently true.

The next two chapters investigate Berkeley's complex of views about perception and about its objects. The key concept here is that of immediate perception which is best understood by studying how Berkeley deploys the concept in the *New Theory of Vision*. The term 'immediately perceives' is non-propositional in that it takes a grammatical direct object rather than a propositional clause. Further, for Berkeley immediate perception occurs when one's perception is not dependent on perception of an intermediary object, and when one's perception is not dependent on an element of suggestion. Also, immediately perceiving something is not an act which includes making a judgment of any sort, and so does not include making a judgment about the object then perceived. What is unclear is what Berkeley takes the objects of immediate perception to be.

Certainly Berkeley thinks that ideas of sense are immediately perceived. Moreover, he sometimes writes as though he holds that ideas are the only things immediately perceived. However, as indicated in the preceding section, Berkeley also sometimes writes as though he thinks that physical objects are immediately perceived, though perhaps not to the exclusion of ideas being so perceived. I think this is Berkeley's considered view on perception and its objects, and that he realizes that he needs to defend this position in order to be able to claim that his account accords with common sense. To be in a position to defend such an account, however, Berkeley has to understand the concept of immediate perception to be extensional in the sense that it licenses certain inferences, among them these:

Person S immediately perceives object O.	Person S immediately perceives object O.
O is identical to R	O is a part or group of parts of object R.
Hence, S immediately perceives R.	Hence, S immediately perceives R.

Examples from ordinary ways of speaking fit these patterns easily. Thus, if S sees the man in the corner, and the man in the corner is (identical to) the dean of the college, then S sees the dean of the college. And, if S sees the parts which make up the facing side of College Hall, then S also sees College Hall. Familiar inferences such as these need to be valid when Berkeley's term 'immediately perceives' or one of its close kin such as 'immediately sees' is the operative verb.

Inferences of both of these kinds are related to the question of whether physical objects are immediately perceived. For instance, if person S immediately perceives a "collection" of ideas O, and this collection of ideas is identical to a physical object R, then S will immediately perceive R. And if S immediately perceives a cluster of ideas O, and the ideas in the cluster are constituents of the physical object R, then S will also immediately perceive R.[6] Securing these inferences for certain substituends of 'O' and 'R,' then, depends not just on how the term 'immediately perceives' is understood, but also on Berkeley's phenomenalist account of physical objects.

Establishing by way of this phenomenalist route that physical objects are immediately perceived, however, requires Berkeley to give up the claim that he defends every important claim of common sense. The com-

---

6. Here we have to say 'constituent' rather than 'part,' because in Berkeley's account of objects, ideas are not parts of objects.

mon sense view of physical objects, after all, does not take them to be "collections" of ideas. Hence, Berkeley's defense of common sense has to be somewhat mitigated. The main task of chapter 8 is to explain to what degree Berkeley's central doctrines are consistent with common sense, and to examine the role that Berkeley assigns to agreement with common sense. I argue that this role is actually very minimal, amounting to just one small bit of evidence invoked and relied on, in a context of a number of other evidential factors. Thus, when Berkeley through Philonous tells us that his theory is more in line with common sense than the "materialist" theory described by Hylas, this fact (assuming it to be one) does only a little to count in favor of Berkeley's theory as against that of Hylas. The superiority of Berkeley's theory over that of the materialist, if it is to be found at all, will also depend on the fact that Berkeley's theory enjoys a greater range of theoretical virtues than the materialist theory. On this point I argue that Berkeley is surprisingly modern. He holds that there are a number of "virtuous" features of theories, including explaining certain things in need of explanation, and solving certain problems and avoiding others, and that his theory scores better than the materialist competition on these grounds alone. Alignment with common sense, though invoked by Berkeley, actually plays a reduced role in this argument against his competition.[7]

One other aspect of the issue of common sense in Berkeley is whether he is best construed as a common sense realist. This interpretation, defended at various points by T. E. Jessop and A. A. Luce, includes a number of components, and full examination of this topic requires that all of these components be investigated. One component, already mentioned above, is that physical objects are immediately perceived, a claim that Berkeley consistently defends. Another is an epistemic component, namely, that we often acquire non-inferential and certain knowledge of physical objects by perceiving them. Berkeley strives to incorporate these epistemic components into his overall theory, something that is thought to be problematic, because doing so requires that we have non-inferential and certain knowledge of complex subjunctive conditionals, a condition that is not plausible.[8] But even if these epistemic points can be successfully incorporated, Berkeley cannot be plausibly construed as a common sense realist, since, as already indicated, he does not accept that objects exist independently of perception, a claim crucial to common sense realism.

---

7. I elaborate this argument more fully in "Adversary Metaphysics" (1983), though in that paper I claimed that agreement with common sense functioned solely as a tie-breaker, a view I modify in chapter 8.

8. Berkeley's phenomenalist account of physical objects seems to require that if one has non-inferential and certain knowledge that there is a tree in the yard, then one non-infer-

Hence, the Jessop and Luce interpretation of Berkeley, though correct on Berkeley's theory of perception, and possibly correct on his epistemic theory, is ultimately not fully correct. Berkeley is not a commonsense realist for the most obvious reason that he is not a realist at all. This is so despite the fact that he may consistently accept some of the elements that make up commonsense realism.[9]

Excursus on Methodology

In the succeeding chapters an interpretation of many of Berkeley's central ideas will be presented. Also, some alternative interpretations of these same ideas will be considered. Further, some evaluation of Berkeley's doctrines and his arguments will be presented, issuing in a number of cases in conclusions that are critical of Berkeley. So it will be helpful at the outset to say a few words about the notions of interpretation and evaluation as they figure in writing about the history of philosophy. I take what I say here to be general, going beyond the special case of Berkeley's philosophy but of course applying to it, as well.

The first task in setting out an interpretation of a philosopher is that of determining what the philosopher said. I understand this point literally and mean by it a determination of just what the philosopher in question asserted on relevant philosophical topics. In some cases this is relatively easy, amounting merely to consulting pertinent texts authored by the philosopher. Many other cases, however, present greater difficulties. Beyond texts, typically published ones, there are other documents to consider, including correspondence, diaries and other notebooks of the philosopher, unpublished drafts of papers and books, and unpublished papers presented at conferences, colloquia, and the like. All of these items contain assertions made by the philosopher, and all count as things the philosopher said. Two examples will bring out potential difficulties with texts such as these.

Imagine that an early draft of a philosopher's published text exists, and there is a discrepancy in that the draft contains the assertion A while the

---

entially and certainly knows that if one were to experience certain ideas, then most likely one would experience certain other ideas. In other words, the phenomenalist position seems to require that we have non-inferential certain knowledge of complex subjunctive conditionals. It is this last claim that seems problematic, a point discussed in chapter 7.

9. These points are discussed more fully in my "Berkeley and Common Sense Realism" (1991), and below, chapter 9.

published text contains a claim incompatible with A. Should we then say that the philosopher has asserted, or has said, both A and not-A? It is not immediately clear how to answer this question. Or consider a case in which the philosopher has a correspondence with a person not fully versed in philosophical intricacies, and so the philosopher has to over-simplify his explanation of his doctrine in the letter sent to the correspondent. If the overly-simplified sentences in the letter distort the same ideas expressed in the published texts, would we nonetheless say that the philosopher has asserted or said these overly-simplified sentences, in addition to those in the published texts, even when the former distorts the latter? Again, it is not easy to know what to say.

If we distinguish between what a philosopher said and what that philosopher held, then we can reasonably say that in the cases mentioned above, the philosopher said all of the things in the unpublished essays and in the correspondence, but he may not have held what was asserted in those places. Determining what the philosopher held is not the same as determining what he said, though probably doing the former presupposes that one has done the latter.

So, I think we can be liberal in taking what the philosopher said to include assertions made in a wide variety of texts beyond the published ones. Doubtless we will want to restrict our attention, even thus liberalized, to *philosophical* texts, insofar as one is aiming to give an interpretation of that philosopher's philosophy. Thus, in determining what the philosopher said, we will not pay attention to what he may have said or written on non-philosophical topics.

Probably we should also include, as things asserted or said, comments made in conversation or in interviews by the philosopher under interpretation, insofar as these are available. Difficulties in these cases concern reliability, except in situations where the philosopher's comments were taped or otherwise recorded. Usually one has only some person's testimony, or worse, some third party's testimony, concerning what the philosopher may have said in conversation or interview. In such cases one needs to make a decision as to whether these other people can be relied upon, and there will doubtless be circumstances when we will see that we cannot rely on them. We may have independent evidence concerning the testimony of such individuals and this evidence may move us to disregard what they report as having been asserted by the philosopher. Yet in some cases we may have corroborative evidence which will lead us to exactly the opposite conclusion. These same points will hold, I think, for notes that students may have taken at the philosopher's lectures. Points contained in the notes will count as things asserted by the philosopher only when we have independent corroborative evidence regarding the trustworthiness of this note-taker on such topics.[10]

As we have seen, I take the matter of what a philosopher said to be distinct from what he held, what doctrines he actually accepted. It is in these latter cases that serious issues of interpretation arise after one has concluded one's determination of what the philosopher said. A critical factor in this regard comes when one tries to determine what the philosopher means by certain words or phrases. I take this to have two distinct but often interrelated parts. What is the meaning of what the philosopher said? And what did the philosopher intend to convey by what he said? In the simplest case, perhaps, these have but a single answer. But there are other possibilities as well.

With respect to the question about the meanings of a philospher's sentences, I aim to focus on the meanings of the words in those sentences. In many cases this issue can be readily resolved in cases where the meanings of the words are quite clear and uncontroversial. Often enough, however, the word meanings are unclear, even when the philosopher wrote in the idiom of the commentator. The philosopher's words may have been familiar, even if for us their meanings may have shifted over time. Or the philosopher's use of familiar words may be unusual, either because of the chosen syntax or other contextual factors, so that the meaning of those familiar words is difficult to grasp. Two other cases arise when the philosopher uses words from the philosopher's lexicon. The word may be familiar enough, but used with a special twist, as in the case of the word 'idea' in the philosophies of the seventeenth and eighteenth centuries. Or the term may be coined just for philosophical purposes with no evident relation to familiar usage. Modern examples abound: the terms 'trope' and 'bare particular' are but two of many. There are historical examples, too, such as Kant's term the 'transcendental aesthetic.'

In these historical situations we strive to recover the historical meaning of the word. Often this will require collateral study of additional texts, including but not limited to other philosophical texts of the same period. Even with such aids, though, in some circumstances we may have but limited success.

---

10. Typically such independent evidence will consist in the degree to which the comments in the notes accord with what we know the philosopher to have asserted elsewhere. This point is of epistemological interest, because it shows that we rely on general coherence to make this determination. But we should not assume that *only* factors of this sort will count as independent corroborative evidence. Thus, we rely on the notes of Alice Ambrose and G. E. Moore as guides to what Ludwig Wittgenstein said in lectures, partly because we have a high regard for Ambrose and Moore as philosophers, and thus as people whom we can count on to accurately transcribe what Wittgenstein asserted in the lectures.

A related issue pertains to when a philosopher uses a term, either familiar or invented, that he takes over from other philosophers, but the meaning of the term is changed by the new use to which it is put. The familiar term 'idea' can serve here again. This term as used by Arnauld is different in meaning from the same term as used by Malebranche, and both of these uses differ, in turn, from those found in Locke and Berkeley.[11] An example of a philosophical term for which the same thing holds would be the term 'sense impression,' there being no agreed upon use of this term in twentieth century writings on perception.

Another query concerning meaning concerns what the philosopher intended to convey by certain words. The default position here, so to speak, is one where the word meaning and the intended meaning coincide. However, sometimes there is no coincidence, for the philosopher's intended meaning differs from the familiar or from the meaning of the term as used by other philosophers. In such cases we may be aided by the philosopher's declarations of how he intends the words to be understood. But there are contexts where no such aids are available, and the intended meaning must be reconstructed with varying degrees of success.

Determining what the philosopher meant and what he intended to convey (or intended to mean) is thus preliminary to ascertaining what the philosopher held. It might be further supposed that knowledge of what the philosopher said and meant is sufficient for us to infer what he held. This reasoning would be straightforward: the philosopher said or asserted p, in the extended sense of 'said' earlier discussed; the assertion that p means q, or perhaps the philosopher intended to mean q by asserting p; hence, the philosopher held q. Repeated use of this pattern of reasoning would then give us the overall interpretation of the philosopher.

I agree that this sort of reasoning suffices in many contexts; however, it does not work in all cases. Perhaps the most obvious example where this reasoning fails is one in which the philosopher says things in different texts that are inconsistent with one another. For example, Locke explicitly tells us that ideas of sensation are not to be confused with qualities of bodies, but he also occasionally uses the term 'idea' to refer to qualities of objects and not to mental entities. Hence, the simple reasoning given above would have us conclude that for Locke ideas are wholly distinct from qualities of bodies and ideas just are qualities of bodies. This is an interpretive position one should accept only if no other alternative is available.

A related example is one in which, in introductory comments, the philosopher tells the reader what is to be covered in the body of some text and then in later chapters has altogether forgotten these earlier promises.

11. On this point see Robert Macrae 1965, 175–84.

Some find this problem, for example, in Hume's *Treatise of Human Nature*. In prefatory comments, Hume says that he aims to provide a science of the human mind and of its operations, thus betokening a committment to a broadly naturalistic philosophic position. However, in the actual text, Hume seems to reach a generally sceptical conclusion with regard to nearly everything. So, an interpretive problem for the Hume scholar is to decide whether Hume is sceptical regarding various matters, or whether he really has a non-sceptical, naturalist account of those same things. Reliance on the simple reasoning above will not help solve this question. So, in determining what a philosopher held, it is sometimes not enough merely to know what he said and what he meant by what he said.

Still, it is tempting to think that once one has ascertained what the philosopher held, however one has finally arrived at this determination, one has thereby fixed an interpretation of that philosopher. Going beyond what the philosopher held, we may think, would stray over into evaluation of that philosopher's doctrines, and this would strictly speaking exceed the bounds of interpretation. I think we should resist this line of thought, because we often need to pay attention to what the philosopher was committed to holding, over and above what he actually may have held. These two items may coincide in many contexts, but they need not. For instance, philosophers such as Locke and Berkeley held the view that in every case of perception some idea is immediately perceived. Such a view implies, and so commits them to holding, that direct realism is a false account of perception. However, neither Locke nor Berkeley actually held that direct realism is false, for neither even so much as considered the theory. Yet in giving an interpretation of Locke or Berkeley, if we do not take into account that they are committed to holding the falsity of direct realism, we may run the risk of not fully understanding their overall position. A reasonable interpretation, then, does not end merely with what the philosopher held, though of course that has to be included.

Besides interpretation we are often interested in evaluation of the work of a philosopher. Having established that the philosopher held that P, and perhaps having unearthed as well the reasons R on the basis of which he holds that P, we may want to ask whether he was right to hold P for reason R and, indeed, whether he was right to hold R. However, this interest in whether the philosopher was right really subsumes a number of different questions,

Suppose the philosopher holds that P for reason R, and R is a statement which everyone at the time finds true, something for which no argument need be given. Imagine, too, that everyone then would have found the inference from R to P quite acceptable. Then, of course, it was right for the philosopher to hold P based upon R, that is, it was right given criteria of appraisal operative at that time. As an example of this type, think of the first cause argument which Aquinas gives in the *Summa Theologica* (the second of the famous five ways), and let P be the statement that an infinite causal series is not possible. Aquinas concludes P in part because he also held the principle of sufficient reason, which we will here suppose is R. If P were false and the causal series were infinite, then R would be violated. But R, the principle of sufficient reason, in Aquinas' philosophical climate, is a principle which nobody would reject; indeed, all would have found it to be obviously true. So he is not to be faulted for holding R. Neither is he to be faulted for inferring P from R, for this inference, too, would generally have been regarded as acceptable at that time.

The philosopher may hold P based upon R, but R may not be an obvious truth relative to that philosophic time, but instead a statement which is itself based upon something else, perhaps Q. In that case our attention will focus on Q. If it is a widely shared assumption, then the foregoing reasoning will likely apply and we will probably find the philosopher right to have accepted P. However, statement Q may be held because it is based upon yet something else. We will be fortunate if we can divine that upon which Q is based, and more fortunate still if that additional statement is or would be regarded as an obvious truth. However, what about a case in which Q is not a statement which would have been widely accepted at the time, but instead would have been taken as quite dubious? In that situation, in the absence of novel arguments supporting Q, we will have to say that the philosopher was wrong to have held P, that it was unreasonable for him to have held P as it was based ultimately upon having held Q. Here again, I would stress, there is a time and philosophic millieu-based relativity in this judgment. Relative to how matters stood vis-a-vis Q at that time, it was then implausible or wrong for the philosopher to have held that P. Exactly the same applies to our judgments that he was right to have held that P.

There may also be situations in which the philosopher held that P was based upon R and we cannot discover whether R would have been taken as plausible at that time. There are also instances in which a philosopher held that P, but we cannot determine the basis upon which he accepted that P. In these instances, we just cannot make a plausibility determination vis-à-vis the philosopher's acceptance of P. One hopes that such cases are rare, but there is no telling in advance of an investigation. It is, though, one sort of genuine advance in studies in the history of philosophy when a number of commentators have acquiesced in the sort of indeterminacy just noted, and a new investigation uncovers both the reasons on which the philosopher held that P and also the general acceptability, then, of those reasons.

An altogether different sort of evaluation is one in which we ask whether the philosopher under study was right, *simpliciter,* to have held that P, or right *simpliciter* to have held P based upon R. If we are being especially candid, we will want to understand this to mean whether the philosopher was right to have held P, given *our* present standards of appraisal, and given *our* set of assumptions. We sometimes do ask these evaulative questions, and it seems to me both appropriate and important to do so. We may call this *evaluation by our lights.* It is an activity which differs from the previous evaluation, since it is not relative to what was taken to be plausible in the historical period under study. The results of this difference are often marked. The example of Aquinas will serve again. The first cause argument he gave, at least up to the conclusion that there was a first cause, is eminently plausible when judged relative to his assumptions and criteria for argument construction in place at his time. This same argument, however, when evaluated by our lights, is apt to be regarded as quite implausible. There is no incompatibility in these two plausibility assessments, for they are of a different order and based upon different considerations.

It is particularly exciting, though, when we judge some doctrine of a past philosopher to be plausible, or even right, when assessed by both of these types of appraisal. We are then apt to regard that philosopher as especially relevant to today's philosophical worries and theories, a person from whom we can still learn a great deal. There are points in Berkeley which, I shall argue later, are precisely of this sort.[12]

We can now better locate the treatment of Berkeley which is to follow on these methodological fronts. It will be relatively easy to determine what Berkeley said. He nearly always wrote in English (the exception is *De Motu,* which he wrote in Latin), and his style is particularly clear. Two areas which cause some difficulty arise, however, when one considers the early notebooks and the *Three Dialogues.* In the former, problems arise when an entry is incomplete, or when, though complete, we cannot tell exactly what the context is in which that entry is asserted. Incompleteness often arises in questions which Berkeley puts to himself, but which he

---

12. I think some commentators on historical figures take the position that *only* the first sort of evaluative task is appropriate, and that evaluation by our lights is a procedure to be avoided, perhaps on the grounds that it is unfair to the philosopher that is being studied. I do not side with this position, but it is instructive to see the real truth behind it, which I take to be that unfairness to the historical figure arises when we engage *only* in evaluation by our lights. Not merely doing the latter, I believe, should assuage worries concerning unfairness.

does not answer. For example, Berkeley writes in *Philosophical Commentaries*,

> W' if succession of ideas were swifter, w' if slower?

Comments in which the immediate context is hard to determine include this:

> Powers Quaere whether more or one onely? (Berkeley 1948–57, 1:9, 15, entries 16 and 84.)

He may be talking about the powers with which Locke identifies qualities, or he may be talking more generally. Which we take him to be saying will depend on the context, which is not here nor in surrounding entries supplied.

The main difficulty with the *Three Dialogues* comes with the occasional passage in which Philonous gives an oratory on the beauty and organization and design of nature. While this is of great literary value, philosophically it causes difficulties, because it falls short of explicitly stating some thesis. Here is an example from the second *Dialogue:*

> Philonous: Look! are not the fields covered with a delightful verdure? Is there not something in the woods and groves, in the rivers and clear springs that soothes, that delights, that transports the soul? At the prospect of the wide and deep ocean, or some huge mountain whose top is lost in the clouds, or of an old gloomy forest, are not our minds filled with a pleasing horror? Even in rocks and deserts, is there not an agreeable wildness? How sincere a pleasure is it to behold the natural beauties of the earth! To preserve and renew our relish for them, is not the veil of night alternately drawn over her face, and doth she not change her dress with the seasons? (*Works*, Berkeley 1948–57, 2:210)

However, while determining what Berkeley said presents few problems, the same cannot always be said about what he held. These cases will come up as we proceed, but an illustration can already be given here. Most of the time Berkeley treats ideas of sense as *objects* of some sort, entities that are immediately perceived. This is certainly true of the *New Theory of Vision* and true, as well, of most of the *Three Dialogues*. However, on occasions he treats ideas differently, so that they seem not to be objects but rather events of sensing. Thus in the first *Dialogue,* Hylas says:

> One great oversight I take to be this: that I did not sufficiently distinguish the *object* from the *sensation*. Now though this latter may not exist without the mind, yet it will not thence follow that the former cannot.

Philonous eventually says:

> Besides, since you distinguish the *active* and *passive* in every perception, you must do it in that of pain. But how is it possible that pain, be it as little active as you please, should exist in an unperceiving substance? In short, do but consider the point, and then confess ingenuously, whether light and colours, tastes, sounds, etc are not all equally passions or sensations in the soul. You may indeed call them *external objects* and give them in words what subsistence you please. But examine your own thoughts, and then tell me whether it be not as I say. (Berkeley 1948–57, 2:194, 197)

Philonous' point seems to be that he wants to collapse the distinction between the act or event of immediately perceiving and the idea or ideas which are immediately perceived. There is just one event without an object, he seems to say: ideas are just events of sensing, not objects.

On this important matter, we cannot infer directly from what Berkeley says to what he held, because he says more than one thing, and the things he says are quite different. Hence, on this point as on some others, considerable interpretive work is called for, and any conclusion reached will go considerably beyond merely citing what Berkeley may have said.

As for the evaluative enterprise, it will come as no surprise that Berkeley does best when he is assessed relative to the assumptions he makes which would have been widely accepted, and relative to criteria for appraisal current in his time. However, there are points on which he scores favorably even when evaluated *by our lights*. For example, Berkeley backs away from strong Cartesian notions of certainty, notions that require the impossibility of mistaken belief. For Berkeley, by contrast, a belief counts as certain provided one actually has no grounds for doubting the believed proposition. This account of certainty is much more in line with accounts given recently, and it is his use of this notion which allows for the plausibility in Berkeley's claim that he is certain of the existence and nature of physical objects.

CHAPTER 2

The Importance of Abstraction

In this and the next two chapters the topic of abstract ideas will be discussed in depth. My view is that this topic is not marginal in Berkeley's thought, related merely to questions concerning language learning and use, and to the question of whether a certain form of nominalism is correct. Not that these two matters are unimportant to Berkeley. Indeed; I will stress that these issues are of great importance on both counts. However, the doctrine of abstract ideas, as Berkeley calls it, and the companion issue of the process of abstraction, ripples much farther and deeper into Berkeley's positive philosophy than has commonly been appreciated. The question of how the doctrine of abstract ideas is related to other important themes in Berkeley's thought will be taken up in this chapter as well as in chapter 4. Chapter 3 will consider what Berkeley takes abstract ideas and abstraction to be, his arguments against each, and the relationship his arguments have to his targets. On the latter issue, of course, due attention has to be paid to Locke and to whether Berkeley correctly interpreted Locke. But I will also maintain that Berkeley had a wider group of targets in mind and that consideration of this wider group and of their relevant doctrines is important to understanding Berkeley's overall message about abstract ideas and to finally seeing whether he was fair to Locke.

Locality

Berkeley devotes a considerable bit of energy and space in the introduction to the *Principles* to a discussion of abstract ideas. This includes, of course, his well-known attack on such entities and on the process of abstraction. However, in the body of the *Principles* following the introduction, there is comparatively little mention of abstract ideas and even less mention of the process of abstraction. This suggests that the attack on abstraction and abstract ideas plays a comparatively small role in Berkeley's overall philosophy.

This general point is reinforced when we notice that a concern with abstract ideas has no prominent place in the *Three Dialogues*. There is, for example, nothing in that work corresponding to the extended discussion in the introduction to the *Principles*. Moreover, there is virtually no discussion of abstract ideas in the *New Theory of Vision*, published just one year before the *Principles*, and there is but scant mention of abstract ideas in *De Motu, Alciphron*, and the *Theory of Vision Vindicated and Explained*.

Further, a close examination of the introduction to the *Principles* leads one to believe that Berkeley's concern with abstract ideas is wholly connected to Locke, and so is a *local* issue in the following double sense: first, Berkeley seems to confine the issue to Locke's thoughts on abstract ideas as expressed in the *Essay*; Berkeley's target is not widened to include other philosophers. Also, and more importantly, the issue of abstract ideas seems local in the further sense that whether there are abstract ideas or not is apparently connected only to whether a sort of nominalism is correct, and with whether specific kinds of ideas are needed to help explain language learning and language use. But the matters of nominalism and language do not themselves ripple farther out and relate to other more central topics in Berkeley's metaphysics or epistemology, either in supporting those more central topics or by helping to cast light on how they are to be best understood.

So, the locality I have in mind might be thought of first as *textual*—Berkeley's concern with abstract ideas is largely confined to just a part of one of his major texts; and as *philosophical*—what Berkeley has to say about abstract ideas has little or no bearing on either the truth of his main metaphysical and epistemological doctrines, nor on how those doctrines are to be understood.

Now the textual locality of abstract ideas is something that may be readily conceded, though we will see that there are a fair number of passages outside of the introduction where Berkeley alludes to abstract ideas.

However, the philosophical locality of the abstract ideas issue is one which seems to me to be in error, and this in two inter-related ways: first, Berkeley himself does not think of his philosophy in this way. Indeed, for him, as we will see below, the question of whether there are abstract ideas plays an absolutely pivotal role, ramifying and touching on nearly every other substantive point in his mature philosophy. Second, there is reason to think that Berkeley is right about the connections between abstract ideas and other elements of his philosophy. I will not argue that he is right in all cases where he sees a connection. But he is right, or at least has strong arguments, enough of the time that we have additional reason to reject the philosophical locality of the abstract ideas issue.

Locke

Besides the matter of locality, another important issue concerns whether and to what degree Berkeley has correctly represented Locke's views on abstract ideas. Here, I think, there are three important aspects to be considered. First, does Berkeley properly understand Locke's arguments in favor of abstract ideas? This part of the question is fairly easy to resolve, requiring only close attention to relevant texts. Second, does Berkeley correctly represent what Lockean abstract ideas are supposed to be? This question directs us to query just what Lockean ideas are and what it is that makes some of them abstract and invites us to consider whether Berkeley's notion of an idea is the same as Locke's. Third, what does Berkeley understand the process of abstraction to be, and is his account of this process the same as what we find in Locke? On the latter two aspects, there is serious disagreement among commentators, some favoring the view that Berkeley misunderstands Locke, so that his several criticisms of abstract ideas or of abstraction simply miss the mark. That is, they fail to make contact with any actual doctrine of Locke's and in that sense fail to count as effective criticisms of Locke's philosophy. Others have viewed the debate in a manner more favorable to Berkeley and are thus more inclined to agree that Locke's views of abstract ideas and of abstraction have been shown to be implausible.

In this chapter, the question of the locality of abstract ideas in Berkeley is examined more closely. The question of Berkeley's relationship to Locke is actually quite complex and will be taken up in the next chapter after we have had a look at most of Berkeley's argument and of his conception of abstract ideas.

Berkeley's View of the Importance of Abstract Ideas

We have noted two senses of locality, textual and philosophical. On the former, we may grant straightaway that the issue of abstract ideas occupies a prominent place in Berkeley's texts only in the introduction to the *Principles*. Of course, there is the draft introduction as well, Berkeley's first draft of the latter material, but that is just a version of the same text. Through the rest of Berkeley's writings, there is but scattered reference to abstract ideas, and nowhere does he dwell on and develop the issues very much.

However, while granting this sort of textual locality, we should also take note of the various places, outside the introduction to the *Principles*, where Berkeley does discuss abstract ideas. Doing so will not only give us a better view of the degree of textual locality, but will also enable us to begin the examination of philosophical locality more fully.

In Berkeley's notebooks, composed before he began his publishing career, there are some twenty-six numbered entries that deal with abstract ideas. In fact, there are five additional entries that concern the idea of existence and, as we will see later, Berkeley takes this to be an especially important abstract idea. Adding these gives us thirty-one entries in the *Philosophical Commentaries* that consider abstract ideas. Although Berkeley is not focusing mainly on abstract ideas in the notebooks, his comments also do not amount to a spotty treatment. There are sufficient numbers to indicate how important Berkeley took the topic to be. Moreover, in some of the entries, he connects abstract ideas to other themes, an endeavor at which he takes some pains in the body of the *Principles*. Thus at section 401 abstract ideas are said to lead to mistakes in mathematics, and at 564 unspecified evils in the sciences are held to flow from the doctrine of abstraction. However, a more common complaint in the notebooks is that the vulgar make no use of and have no need for abstract ideas. Abstract ideas are used only by the learned and, indeed, he suggests that they are *invented by* the learned (sections 552, 703, 725, and 867).

In the body of the *Principles* the topic of abstract ideas comes up some fifteen times and is related by Berkeley to many different issues, including the absolute existence of physical objects, general ideas of sensible qualities, existence, scepticism, time, motion, absolute space, geometry, arithmetic, and moral knowledge.[1] So, while Berkeley does not dwell on abstract ideas in the main text, he certainly does not ignore them either. Moreover, as we can see from just this list of topics, he thinks they are con-

---

1. The concept of the absolute existence of physical objects is discussed below in chapter 5.

nected to some of the most important conepts in his philosophy. A look at a few passages will give a better idea of these connections.

At *Principles* 100, moral properties are briefly mentioned:

> What is it for a man to be happy, or an object good, every one may think he knows. But to frame an abstract idea of *happiness*, prescinded from all particular pleasure, or of *goodness*, from every thing that is good, this is what few can pretend to. So likewise, a man may be just and virtuous, without having precise ideas of *justice* and *virtue*. The opinion that those and the like words stand for general notions abstracted from all particular persons and actions, seems to have rendered morality difficult, and the study thereof of less use to mankind. And in effect, the doctrine of *abstraction* has not a little contributed towards spoiling the most useful parts of knowledge.(Berkeley 1948–57, 2:84)[2]

Here it is instructive to notice that Berkeley complains about abstract ideas; the thesis that there are such entities and that moral properties are among them he reckons an impediment in moral philosophy, indeed, one which leads philosophers astray. This is a theme that he repeats in other contexts. For example, consider *Principles* 143.

> It will not be amiss to add, that the doctrine of *abstract ideas* hath had no small share in rendering those sciences intricate and obscure, which are particularly conversant about spiritual things. Men have imagined they could frame abstract notions of the powers and acts of the mind, and consider them prescinded, as well from the mind or spirit it self, as from their respective objects and effects. Hence a great number of dark and ambiguous terms presumed to stand for abstract notions, have been introduced into metaphysics and morality, and from these have grown infinite distractions and disputes amongst the learned. (Berkeley 1948–57, 2:106–7)

The same sort of double theme that abstract ideas create needless obscurities and that they lead philosophers into errors is repeated regarding the infinite divisibility of space in *Principles* 125; and time, space, and motion in *Principles* 97.

Berkeley finds another connection between abstract ideas and the denial of his famous principle of *esse is percipi*, that is, the principle that for all non-perceiving things, to be is to be perceived. Berkeley thinks that the thesis that there are abstract ideas helps to support what we would call metaphysical realism: the thesis that there are objects existing independently of all perception. This, of course, is just the denial of Berkeley's *esse is percipi* principle. Notice what Berkeley says at *Principles* 5:

2. Hereafter reference is made in the text to the relevant edition of Berkeley's texts followed, where needed, by volume number and page. See the bibliographic listing.

> If we thoroughly examine this tenet, it will, perhaps, be found at bottom to depend on the doctrine of *abstract ideas*. For can there be a nicer strain of abstraction than to distinguish the existence of sensible objects from their being perceived, so as to conceive them existing unperceived? (Berkeley 1948–57, 2:42)

Berkeley is alluding to the tenet that sensible objects exist independently of perception. This was made clear in *Principles* 4.

> It is indeed an opinion strangely prevailing among men that houses, mountains, rivers, and in a word all sensible objects, have an existence, natural or real, distinct from their being perceived by the understanding. But, with how great an assurance and acquiescence soever this Principle may be entertained . . . whoever shall find in his heart to call it in question may . . . perceive it to involve a manifest contradiction. For, what are the forementioned objects but the things we perceive by sense? and what do we perceive besides our own ideas or sensations? and is it not plainly repugnant that any one of these, or any combination of them, should exist unperceived. (Berkeley 1948–57, 2:42)

Now the *esse is percipi* principle is probably the most central point within Berkeley's philosophy, and in these passages we find him saying that this most central principle is called into question by the doctrine of abstract ideas. There could be no greater importance, then, to Berkeley's philosophy than the refutation of the doctrine of abstract ideas. Without that refutation, the *esse is percipi* principle would be in danger of collapse, and with it would go much of the rest of Berkeley's philosophy.

Another connection Berkeley finds is between abstract ideas and scepticism. In the introduction to the *Principles*, Berkeley says that the ordinary person, that is,

> . . . the illiterate bulk of mankind that walk the high road of plain, common sense, and are governed by the dictates of nature, for the most part easy and undisturbed. To them nothing that's familiar appears unaccountable or difficult to comprehend. They complain not of any want of evidence in their senses, and are out of all danger of becoming *sceptics*. (Berkeley 1948–57, 2:25)[3]

Some would say that the cause of this scepticism would be tied to the general obscurity of things which makes them difficult to understand, while others might note that the human intellect is too feeble to comprehend

---

3. Berkeley added the first sentence of this passage to the published version of the introduction; it does not appear in the draft introduction.

many intricate matters it tries to investigate. But Berkeley has a different diagnosis in *Principles* 3 and 4.

> Upon the whole, I am inclined to think that the far greater part, if not all, of those difficulties which have hitherto amused philosophers, and blocked up the way to knowledge, are entirely owing to ourselves. That we have first raised a dust, and then complain, we cannot see. . . . My purpose, therefore is, to try if I can discover what those principles are, which have introduced all that doubtfulness and uncertainty, those absurdities and contradictions into the several sects of philosophy. (Berkeley 1948–57, 2:26)

Among the principles that have this effect of leading to scepticism is the principle that there are abstract ideas. As Berkeley says,

> . . . what seems to have had a chief part in rendering speculation intricate and perplexed, and to have occasioned innumerable errors and difficulties in almost all parts of knowledge . . . is the opinion that the mind hath the power of framing *abstract ideas* or notions of things. (Berkeley 1948–57, 2:27)

Now the primary message of the *Three Dialogues* is that Berkeley aims to refute scepticism and to defend common sense. In these passages, however, we find that the doctrine of abstract ideas stands in the way of that refutation and defense, just as that same doctrine blocks establishment of the *esse est percipi* principle. The doctrine of abstract ideas, then, *as Berkeley himself sees it,* is directly related to the deepest and most important elements in his philosophy.

Interestingly, though the issue of abstract ideas surfaces a few times in the *Three Dialogues,* Berkeley never asserts in that book that the doctrine of abstract ideas leads to difficulties, perplexities, scepticism, or the denial of the *esse is percipi* thesis. Instead, his focus throughout that work is on how some other doctrines lead to scepticism, doctrines such as metaphysical realism, the thesis that physical objects are partially constituted by material substance, and the representative causal account of perception.[4] However, he does not ignore abstract ideas entirely in the *Three Dialogues.* He argues against the abstract ideas of extension in general and motion in general, much as he argued against such abstract ideas in the introduction

---

4. Berkeley's claims that these doctrines lead to scepticism are examined in chapter 9.

to the *Principles*. He also mentions the abstract general ideas of being and identity, and points out that he finds such ideas incomprehensible.[5]

Abstract ideas are also mentioned in other works, though infrequently, specifically in the *Essay Towards a New Theory of Vision*, and in *De Motu*. However, we should not think that infrequency of mention signals philosophical unimportance. Consider these passages in the *Essay Towards a New Theory of Vision* which come up in Berkeley's discussion of those ideas (allegedly) common to more than one sense.

> I find it proper to take into my thoughts extension in abstract:[. . .] I am apt to think that when men speak of extension as being an idea common to two senses, it is with a secret supposition that we can single out extension from all other tangible and visible qualities, and form thereof an abstract idea, which idea they will have common to sight and touch.[6]

He continues in the next section:

> . . . I do not find that I can perceive, imagine, or anywise frame in my mind such an abstract idea as is here spoken of. A line or surface which is neither black, nor white, nor blue, nor yellow, nor square, nor round, etc., is perfectly incomprehensible. (Berkeley 1948–57, 1:220)

One of the main points of the *New Theory of Vision* is the heterogeneity thesis according to which each sensible idea is specific to a given sense. Hence, the statement that some ideas are common to two senses is in direct conflict with the heterogeneity thesis. Thus, if Berkeley is right in thinking that the doctrine of abstract ideas implies that some ideas are common to more than one sense, then the abstract ideas doctrine implies the falsity of the heterogeneity thesis. Once again the doctrine of abstract ideas proves pivotal to a cardinal point in Berkeley's thought.[7]

So far we have noticed that from Berkeley's own perspective, the doctrine of abstract ideas is closely connected with many of his philosophy's central themes, and not merely with issues of nominalism and language

5. The argument against abstract ideas of motion and extension is given in the first interlocation of *Dialogue*, Berkeley 1948–57, 2:192–93. The abstract general idea of being and the abstract general idea of identity are discussed in Berkeley 1948–57, 2:247–48. As I argue below, the claim that some abstract ideas are incomprehensible is important and helps serve as a way to demarcate types of abstract ideas in Berkeley's account.

6. In the third and fourth editions of the *Essay on Vision*, Berkeley dropped the phrase 'take into my thoughts' and replaced it with 'consider.'

7. The influence of the abstract ideas doctrine is actually deeper than I bring out here, because Berkeley seems to think that the doctrine of ideas common to two senses is closely tied to the distinction between primary and secondary qualities. This connection is discussed further below in chapter 4.

as discussed in the introduction to the *Principles*. So, in one of the senses noted earlier, the abstract ideas doctrine is not philosophically localized. But consider another sense of philosophical locality that I referred to, namely, one that concerns not doctrines but philosophers. Is it true that when he discusses abstract ideas Berkeley's sole target is Locke, or can we identify additional philosophers he might have had in mind?

The introduction to the *Principles* certainly makes it seem as though Locke is Berkeley's only opponent on the matter of abstract ideas. However, there is some evidence that Berkeley thought of things less locally. For example, in a letter to Samuel Johnson of 1730, Berkeley writes:

> Abstract general ideas was a notion that Mr. Locke held in common with the Schoolmen, and I think all other philosophers. (Berkeley 1948–57, 1:293)

Elsewhere in his Introduction to the *Principles* Berkeley makes a similar though more expansive point.

> He who is not a perfect stranger to the writings and disputes of philosophers, must needs acknowledge that no small part of them are spent about abstract ideas. These are in a more especial manner, thought to be the object of those sciences which go by the name of Logic and Metaphysics, and all of that which passes under the notion of the most abstracted and sublime learning. . . . (Berkeley 1948–57, 2:27)

Berkeley attributes acceptance of abstract ideas to a wide group of philosophers, both contemporary with himself and of his immediate past, and not just Locke and the Schoolmen. Presumably, though he gives no names, he is including great philosophers such as Malebranche, Leibniz, Spinoza, and Descartes, though doubtless he had others in mind as well. Indeed, there is independent evidence that he had Malebranche in mind, since he singles him out in the *Three Dialogues*.

> I shall not therefore be surprised, if some men imagine that I run into the enthusiasm of Malebranche, though in truth I am very remote from it. He builds on the most abstract general ideas, which I entirely disclaim. (Berkeley 1948–57, 2:214)

In the draft introduction Berkeley mentions the Schoolmen, as well as unnamed ancient and modern logicians and metaphysicians, as friends of abstract ideas. However, he also names Aristotle as a " . . . great admirer and promoter of the doctrine of abstraction," though he also notes that Aristotle himself points out how difficult it is to understand abstract notions.[8] In *De Motu* Berkeley mentions Torricelli and Leibniz as great thinkers who have commitments to abstract ideas and concludes:

> Thus even the greatest men when they give way to abstractions are bound to pursue terms which have no certain significance and are mere shadows of scholastic things. Other passages in plenty from the writings of younger men could be produced which give abundant proof that metaphysical abstractions have not in all quarters given place to mechanical science and experiment, but still make useless trouble for philosophers. (Berkeley 1975, 212)

It is clear, then, that Berkeley thinks he has many opponents on the issue of abstract ideas. Although Locke is one of these opponents, and indeed the focus of Berkeley's criticisms, Berkeley thought the doctrine of abstract ideas was very widespread. So in neither sense, as to doctrines or as to philosophers, is the issue of abstract ideas philosophically local.[9]

A Closer Look at the Connections

We have seen that, according to Berkeley, the abstract ideas doctrine is closely connected to other important issues in his philosophy. In this section I look more fully at three of these further issues and their connections to abstract ideas. I begin with the heterogeneity thesis from the *Essay*.

The thesis that some ideas are perceivable by more than one sense and so are common to more than one sense was defended in Locke. Regarding ideas of sensation, Locke said:

> There are some, which come into our minds *by one Sense only*. . . . There are others, that convey themselves into the mind *by more Senses than one*.[10]

---

8. Berkeley refers to a passage in Aristotle's *Metaphysics* 982a. 23–25. See "Draft Introduction," Berkeley 1948–57, 2:130.

9. Abstract ideas are also taken up in *Alciphron*; indeed, the matter makes up a fair portion of chapter 7 of that book. I discuss those arguments from *Alciphron,* along with those from *De Motu* in connection with what I call *wide* abstract ideas, in chapter 3. The importance of Berkeley's attack on abstract ideas has not been missed by some recent commentators. Margaret Atherton notes the general importance of the abstract ideas thesis for other elements of Berkeley's philosophy in Atherton 1987. Douglas Jesseph (1993) gives a penetrating detailed account of the relation of abstract ideas to Berkeley's views on mathematics. Berkeley's targets in the attack on abstraction are discussed in Jesseph, and in Bolton 1987, and Winkler 1989.

10. John Locke, *An Essay concerning Human Understanding,* ed. P. Nidditch (Oxford: Clarendon Press, 1975), bk. 2, chapter 3, section 1. Hereafter, references to this work are made in the text, with book, chapter, and section listed in that order.

Subsequently, Locke enumerates the ideas he thinks are common to different senses.

> The *Ideas* we get by more than one Sense, are of *Space*, or *Extension, Figure, Rest*, and *Motion*: For these make perceivable impressions, both on the Eyes and Touch; and we can receive and convey into our Minds the *Ideas* of the Extension, Figure, Motion, and Rest of Bodies, both by seeing and feeling. (Locke 1975, 2:5, 1)

To the contrary, Berkeley holds to the heterogeneity thesis—each idea is proper to a given sense. Nobody thinks, for example, that sounds can be seen or touched (or felt). Sounds, we would suppose, can only be heard. Sundry tastes are proper to gustatory sense perception, and smells (odors) can only be experienced by means of one's sense of smell. Everyone would agree with this much, Locke included. It is the sense of sight and touch that seem to admit of ideas that are common. The round figure of a dish, for example, can be both seen and touched or felt. Locke's way of putting this point is that at least in some cases the idea of sight we get when we see the round dish is identical to the idea of touch we experience when we also touch the dish. The most obvious case where this might occur would be when one simultaneously sees and touches the round dish.

So understood, Locke's point would be that the visual idea is *numerically identical* to the tangible idea in a case of simultaneous visual and tactile perception of the round dish. In contrast Berkeley thinks that the visual and tangible idea are numerically distinct. He takes this numerical distinctness claim, which is *one* of the ways that he understands the heterogeneity thesis, to follow from the theory of visual distance perception that he elaborates in the first part of the *Essay*. According to that theory, whose details I will not examine here, visual distance perception is accomplished by correlating visual ideas and tangible ideas, something each person has to learn to do, since ideas of these two sorts have no necessary connections to one another.[11] If some ideas were common to sight and touch, however, one would presumably not need to learn to make this correlation. So Berkeley's theory, which requires learning to make these correlations, implies the (first) heterogeneity thesis, that is, that each idea of sight is numerically distinct from each idea of touch.

A second heterogeneity thesis is more narrow, requiring not merely numerical distinctness but difference *in kind*. Thus in section 121 of the *Essay* Berkeley writes:

---

11. The details of the theory are very insightfully explicated by Atherton 1991.

... the question is not now concerning the same numerical ideas, but whether there be any one and the same sort or species of ideas equally perceivable to both senses; or, in other words, whether extension, figure, and motion perceived by sight are not specifically distinct from extension, figure and motion perceived by touch.

In the following section Berkeley raises the question of abstract ideas and connects them to common ideas. He says,

> But before I come more particularly to discuss this matter, I find it proper to consider extension in abstract:[. . .] I am apt to think that when men speak of extension as being an idea common to two senses, it is with a secret supposition that we can single out extension from all other tangible and visible qualities, and form thereof an abstract idea, which idea they will have common both to sight and touch. (Berkeley 1948–57, 1:220)

He then goes on to argue that we do not have any abstract ideas of extension.

In interpreting these pasaages, two questions arise immediately. First, which of the two notions of heterogeneity does Berkeley think is connected with the claim that some ideas are common to two senses? Second, exactly what is this connection supposed to be? I believe Berkeley intends the second notion of heterogeneity, for he says in the passage quoted above that the issue is not now (in section 121) about the numerical identity of ideas of sight and touch, but rather whether such ideas are the same in kind. As for the second question, we have to ask what Berkeley means by the term "secret supposition." Is he saying that abstract ideas are sufficient for common ideas of sight and touch, necessary for common ideas, or perhaps both? I think the answer is that abstract ideas supply just a sufficient condition. For, following his arguments against abstract ideas, Berkeley does *not* draw the conclusion that the thesis of common ideas is false. But this would be an obvious conclusion to draw had he been claiming that there are ideas that are common *only if* there are abstract ideas. With these points in place, we can say that the argument of sections 122–23 of the *Essay* is the following:

(1) If there are abstract ideas of extension, then there are ideas common to two or more senses.
(2) If there are ideas common to two or more senses, then the (second) heterogeneity thesis is false.
(3) There are abstract ideas of extension.
(4) Hence, the (second) heterogeneity thesis is false.

Now just as there are two notions of heterogeneity, so there are two notions of common ideas, the latter notion being a direct correlative of the former. So we can think of common ideas, first, as numerically one idea perceived by both sight and touch; or, we can think of common ideas, second, as the same kind of idea perceived by both sight and touch. In the example we have used, sameness in kind would be signaled by the fact that the ideas of sight and touch are both ideas of round shape. Which notion of common ideas is being used in premises (1) and (2)? The argument works best (indeed only) if the second notion of common ideas is used, which we can see by focusing on (2). It is clear that if the second notion of common ideas is used there, the premise comes out true. The second notion of common ideas is simply the denial of the second notion of heterogeneity, so premise (2) would be a truism. But I doubt the premise would be true at all if the first notion of common ideas were used. For the first notion of common ideas is, in effect, a limited form of token identity. It says that some instances or tokens of visual ideas are numerically identical to some instances or tokens of tangible ideas. However, token identity does not imply type identity, or identity in kind. Hence, (2) would turn out to be false on this reading. To do the argument most justice, then, we need to read premises (1) and (2) as using the second notion of common ideas.

Moreover, premise (1) seems clearly true if the second notion of common ideas is intended. Consider again the round dish perceived by both sight and touch. What would make the visual idea of round shape the same in kind as the tangible idea of round shape would be that the quality is (numerically) the same in each. That is what makes them kind or type identical. Now how does one acquire an abstract idea of round shape? One perceives many instances of round shape, of different diameters, and separates out the idea of round ingredient in all of the instances. So as far as the acquisition of the abstract of round shape is concerned, it does not matter if all of the perceived instances of round shape have been visual, or all tactile, or a mixture of the two. The same quality, round shape, would be present in each, there to be abstracted. Hence, an abstract idea of round shape would imply that there is just one quality of round shape, variously instanced or tokened. Premise (1) would thus turn out true.[12]

Of course, this is not an argument Berkeley would give and endorse; after all, we know he is diametrically opposed to its conclusion. Rather, what he is doing with this argument is pointing out that armed with the doctrine of abstract ideas, his *opponent* (e.g., Locke) would be in a position to refute the (second) heterogeneity thesis. This, in turn, is of considerable importance to Berkeley since the second heterogeneity thesis is supposed to follow from his theory of visual perception of distance, magnitude, and

12. Notice that the second notion of common ideas has to mean that ideas perceivable by sight are the same in kind as ideas perceivable by touch. Ideas of sight and touch are the same in kind even for the person who is blind and has never experienced ideas of sight.

situation. It is an argument Berkeley is prepared to regard as sound if step (3) is correct. Step (2), for him, is plainly true, and on the sufficient condition interpretation, lately endorsed, as the connection Berkeley sees between abstract and common ideas, he would likely accept (1) as well. So, he has to argue against (3), as he certainly does in sections 123–126 of the *Essay*, in order to block the refutation of the second heterogeneity thesis, and thus to block the refutation of his entire theory of visual perception. Thus, the rejection of abstract ideas is of fundamental importance to the theory of vision that Berkeley propounds, and not because rejection of abstract ideas establishes the theory of vision. Rather, the rejection is necessary to stave off elimination of the theory. Berkeley, thus, cannot afford to ignore the question of abstract ideas, even if he has no concern with nominalism or language learning and use.

Berkeley also thinks that his famous principle of *esse est percipi* is related to the abstract ideas doctrine. Recall what he says at *Principles* 5:

> If we thoroughly examine this tenet, it will, perhaps, be found at bottom to depend on the doctrine of *abstract ideas*. For can there be a nicer strain of abstraction than to distinguish the existence of sensible objects from their being perceived, so as to conceive them existing unperceived? (Berkeley 1948–57, 2:42)

The tenet is metaphysical realism, the thesis that objects exist independently of perception. Of course, this tenet is the denial of the *esse est percipi* principle. Thus, the denial of the latter principle depends on the abstract ideas doctrine. If we understand Berkeley's use of the term 'depend on' in terms of a sufficient condition, which is a natural reading of the term, then he is claiming that if there are abstract ideas, the *esse est percipi* thesis is false. If this claim is true, it can readily be used by Berkeley's opponents as part of a simple argument:

(1) If there are abstract ideas, then the *esse is percipi* principle is false.
(2) There are abstract ideas.
(3) Therefore, the *esse is percipi* principle is false.

This is not Berkeley's argument, naturally, what with its second premise. It is an argument that, as he sees it, is available to defenders of metaphysical realism, i.e., those who reject the *esse is percipi* principle.

Moreover, if this argument were to succeed, it would not just do minor damage to Berkeley's philosophy, because the very core of that philosophy would be swept aside. Thus, it is critical that Berkeley attack and neutralize the abstract ideas doctrine. By denying abstract ideas, he is rejecting a key premise in an argument which, if sound, would defeat his entire philosophy. This attack is especially important in this context since Berkeley seemingly accepts the first premise.[13] Small wonder, then, that Berkeley attacked abstract ideas. Without the success of that attack, he would maintain, very little else in his philosophy could be sustained.

Berkeley writes as though the denial of the *esse is percipi* thesis leads to scepticism, as in *Philosophical Commentaries*, 304 and 411 respectively.

> The Reverse of ye Principle introduc'd Scepticism.

And, more emphatically:

> The Reverse of the Principle I take to have been the chief source of all that scepticism & folly all those contradictions & inextricable puzzling absurdities, that have in all ages been a reproach to Human Reason, as well as that Idolatry whether of Images or of Gold etc that blinds the Greatest part of the World, as well as of that shameful immorality that turns us into beasts. (Berkeley 1948–57, 1:52.)

Further, as we have seen, Berkeley holds that the abstract ideas doctrine implies the denial of the *esse is percipi* principle. He is therefore committed to holding that the abstract ideas doctrine leads to or implies scepticism. And this is just what he says in passages from *Principles* quoted earlier but worth repeating.

> The illiterate bulk of mankind . . . walk the high road of plain, common sense, and are governed by the dictates of Nature, for the most part easy and undisturbed[. . .] They complain not of any want of evidence in their senses, and are out of all danger of becoming *sceptics*.

He then points out that his aim in the *Principles* is to determine which principles lead to results such as scepticism. To this end he says that he will take notice of,

> . . . what seems to have had a chief part in rendering speculation intricate and perplexed, and to have occasioned innumerable errors and difficulties in almost all parts of knowledge. And that is the opinion that the mind hath a power of framing *abstract ideas* or notions of things. (Berkeley 1948–57, 2:25, 27.)

---

13. One might puzzle over why Berkeley finds premise (1) acceptable, and whether it would be reckoned acceptable by philosophers such as Locke. I examine these questions in chapter 4.

On the plausible asumption that Berkeley would include scepticism among the innumerable errors and difficulties in the parts of knowledge, then what these passages indicate is that Berkeley thinks that the abstract ideas doctrine leads to scepticism. Of course one might question the accuracy of this contention. I consider this issue in chapter 9 where I contend that Berkeley is in error on the point. Neither the abstract ideas doctrine, nor the denial of the *esse is percipi* thesis, leads to scepticism, nor does their conjunction. Nevertheless, as we will see, it was not implausible for Berkeley to have held that scepticism results from each of these doctrines. Here we can at least preview some of that discussion by asking what is the exact connection, as Berkeley sees it, between abstract ideas and scepticism.

His reasoning on this point, I think, is straightforward. The abstract ideas doctrine implies the denial of the *esse is percipi* thesis. He thus holds that the abstract ideas doctrine implies metaphysical realism, the thesis that objects exist independently of perception. The latter thesis, in turn, commits one to an indirect, causal theory of perception, at least as long as one assumes the thesis that in every perceptual experience, some ideas are immediately perceived. Berkeley claims that this theory of perception, leads to scepticism. Thus the abstract ideas thesis is connected to scepticism, too. The connection is not immediate; instead, it is mediated by these several additional doctrines. Still, in Berkeley's view, there is a genuine connection. And since he regards scepticism as a disastrous result, he is naturally drawn to an attempt to refute what he thinks leads to it, including, *inter alia*, the doctrine of abstract ideas.

This chapter has shown that despite its relative textual locality, the doctrine of abstract ideas is certainly not philosophically local by Berkeley's lights. Rather, it is closely connected to many of the central themes in his positive philosophy. As will become clear, perhaps the deepest connection is to be found between the abstract ideas doctrine and the concept of existence. To unravel that connection, we first need to examine what Berkeley thinks abstract ideas and the process or activity of abstracting are.

CHAPTER 3

Abstract Ideas

Berkeley attacked the doctrine of abstract ideas in the introduction to the *Principles*, and also in the draft introduction, which was probably the penultimate draft of the published introduction. These function as the primary texts. However, these are not the only texts, for there are many other places where Berkeley mentions abstract ideas. In some of these places he even presents new arguments that serve to highlight the connections he observes between abstract ideas and additional important aspects of his philosophy. Hence, these additional passages take on special significance. We looked at a few of these additional passages in the preceding chapter and considered some of the connections Berkeley noted between abstract ideas and other doctrines. In this chapter, as well as in the next, we will consider a few more lines of connection between abstract ideas and other parts of Berkeley's philosophy.

As an aid in this regard, it will be important first to get clear on just what Berkeley took abstract ideas to be and how he understood the process of abstraction to operate. His arguments against abstract ideas and abstraction are also important, both in themselves and for matters that will be taken up later.

Kinds of Abstract Ideas

Berkeley considers four different kinds of abstract ideas.[1] The first is suggested by comments he makes in Introduction 7, and in a companion passage in the *Three Dialogues*. The former passage is this:

> It is agreed on all hands, that the qualities or modes of things do never exist each of them apart by itself, and separated from all others, but are mixed, as it were, and blended together, several in the same object. But, we are told, the mind being able to consider each quality singly, or abstracted from those other qualities with which it is united, does by that means frame to itself abstract ideas. For example, there is perceived by sight an object extended, colored and moved; this mixed or compound idea the mind resolving into its simple constituent parts, and viewing each by itself, exclusive of the rest, does frame the abstract idea of extension, color and motion. Not that it is possible for color or motion to exist without extension: but only that the mind can frame to itself by *abstraction* the idea of color exclusive of extension, and of motion exclusive of both color and extension. (Berkeley 1948–57, 2:27–28)

Focusing just on color, we can read this passage in either of two ways. Berkeley might have had in mind some specific color shade, separated from the specific extension with which it is, in reality, joined. Or, he might be thinking of the idea of color in general. But since he talks about the latter sort of idea in a later passage, as though he were remarking on something new, it is reasonable to opt for the former reading. In the *Three Dialogues* a similar problem of interpretation arises. For at one point Philonous says:

> I acknowledge, Hylas, it is not difficult to form general propositions and reasonings about those qualities, without mentioning any other; and in this sense to consider or treat of them abstractedly. But how does it follow that because I can pronounce the word *motion* by itself, I can form the idea of it in my mind exclusive of body?

These comments indicate a specific idea of motion as Berkeley's target. One sees a body in motion and so comes to have an idea of a moving body. Of course, *this* idea is of specific motion and of a specific body. The idea Berkeley refers to is formed just by separating the idea of motion from that of body (or figure); thus, the abstract idea he is talking about is the idea of a specific motion. Yet in the very next sentence, Berkeley's apparent interest shifts. He says, with Philonous still speaking:

---

1. For the first three types of abstract ideas, I loosely follow E. Craig (1968).

Or because theorems may be made of extension and figures, without any mention of *great* or *small*, or any other sensible mode or quality; that therefore it is possible such an abstract idea of extension, without any particular size, or figure, or sensible quality, should be distinctly formed and apprehended by the mind? (Berkeley 1948–57, 2:193)

Here it is clear that Berkeley is talking of extension in general, rather than some specific extension. And, since he has different arguments against these two different sorts of ideas, we ought to treat them separately.

Ideas of this specific sort, as in the cases of specific color (e.g., red) and specific motion (e.g., perfectly circular motion), I will call *Type I abstract ideas*. They are ideas of single sensible qualities, rather than of combinations of qualities. They are also specific ideas in the sense that they are ideas of specific, determinate color shades or degrees of motion. It is this that makes these ideas *not general*; being ideas of specific color shades or instances of motion, these ideas are wholly determinate particulars.[2]

Just as the sorts of ideas cited in the above passages are distinct, so Berkeley suggests two different ways one might come to have such ideas. On the one hand, he mentions merely *considering*, "each quality singly, or abstracted from those other qualities with which it is united," which suggests that all one does in the process of abstracting is *attend to* a single quality (in this case, color), knowing all along that this single quality cannot be separated from the others with which it is combined. But the same passage of Introduction 7 ends with lines that seem to express something different:

Not that it is possible for color or motion to exist without extension: but only that the mind can frame to itself by *abstraction* the idea of color exclusive of extension, and of motion exclusive of both color and extension. (Berkeley 1948–57, 2:28)

Here the use of the word 'exclusive' suggests that one *separates* the idea of color from the ideas of motion and extension. Berkeley uses the same term in the *Three Dialogues* discussion of abstract ideas, and then, in summing up and simultaneously shifting to another point, Philonous says:

Since therefore it is impossible even for the mind to disunite the ideas of extension and motion from all other sensible qualities, does it not follow, that where the one exist, there necessarily the other exist likewise? (Berkeley 1948–57, 2:194)

---

2. Here 'general' does not mean 'universal' as that term is typically used in discussions of the problem of universals. That is, it contrasts with 'determinable' and not with 'multiply exemplifiable.'

Here the use of the word 'disunite' makes it clear that Berkeley is speaking of some method of separation as the process of abstraction.

Following Mackie's discussion of Locke on the same point, I will refer to the former notion of the process of abstraction, in which one merely considers one quality apart from another, as the *selective attention model*, and the latter as the *separation model*.[3] Which of these Berkeley considers most appropriate to ascribe to the friends of abstract ideas I set aside for later discussion. For now, I simply note that Type I abstract ideas are formed by a process of abstraction that is to be thought of along one or the other of the two lines indicated by these respective models. The foregoing quoted passages suggest that Berkeley is well aware of both ways of understanding the process of abstraction.

Type II abstract ideas were also suggested by the passages lately quoted. They are ideas of such qualities as motion or color or extension *in general*, but not any specific color, or degree of motion, or particular shape or dimension. We can say that Type II abstract ideas are ideas of sensible qualities, but that they are *general* ideas, in the sense that they are ideas not of particular sensible qualities, but rather of sensible quality categories. That is, they are ideas of *determinables*, rather than ideas of determinate sensible qualities. But Type II abstract ideas are also general in another sense, namely, such ideas are *intrinsically general*. To illustrate, consider the Type II abstract idea of color. This is intrinsically general because, as Berkeley construes it, this idea has the general quality of color, but no specific color. That is, this idea is not general merely because it is generally *of* color. An idea *of* the general quality of color could be intrinsically determinate in all manner of ways, even as to color. Thus, an idea of a particular shade of green is an idea *of* color in general. Intrinsic generality as applied to ideas of the Type II sort means that the ideas themselves are merely colored.

To see that this is how Berkeley conceived of Type II abstract ideas we need only note how he speaks about them. Addressing the abstract general idea of motion, he says in Introduction 10 that,

> It is . . . impossible for me to form the abstract idea of motion distinct from the body moving, and which is neither swift nor slow, curvilinear nor rectilinear. (Berkeley 1948–57, 2:29)

3. J. L. Mackie 1976, 112–116. Mackie holds that interpreting Locke, in terms of making use of selective attention, effectively disarms Berkeley's criticisms of abstract ideas, a point considered later in this chapter. It should be noted, too, that the two models of abstraction do not quite line up with the different sorts of abstract ideas Berkeley examines, as in selective attention applying just to Type I abstract ideas and separation applying to the others. Berkeley is willing to think of Type I abstract ideas as formed by *either* of these two processes of abstraction, a point taken up below in connection with the No Separation Principle. However, it does seem to be true for Berkeley that some other sorts of abstract ideas, what I term Types II and III, *are* supposed to be formed by a process of separation.

Berkeley's point is that there are many different sorts of motion, both as to velocity and as to direction. Any actual motion will be of some velocity and in some direction. Hence, an idea of motion has to be an idea of some specific velocity and direction; it cannot be an idea of just motion per se.

And consider the *Three Dialogues:*

> How doth it follow . . . that . . . it is possible such an abstract idea of exten-sion, without any particular size or figure, or sensible quality, should be distinctly formed, and apprehended by the mind? (Berkeley 1948–57, 2:193)

In the first and second edition of the *Three Dialogues*, the phrase 'size or figure, or sensible quality' reads somewhat differently, namely, just as 'size, color, etc.' Thus, the point Berkeley is making is to hold for ideas of each of the several sensible qualities, not just for motion or extension. Any actual extension is of some degree and has some shape; and any actual color is some specific shade of one of the colors. So, he infers that any idea of extension must be an idea of some specific degree of extension and of some shape. Similarly, any idea of color must be an idea of a specific color shade. In all of these cases, the contrast is with ideas that are intrinsically general: the idea of motion in general, extension in general, and color in general. These are the ideas Berkeley is denying when he rejects Type II abstract ideas.

Type III abstract ideas are also general, but different from the foregoing because they are ideas of bodies rather than of qualities.[4] Berkeley writes in Introduction 9,

> The mind having observed that Peter, James, and John, resemble each oth-er in certain common agreements of shape and other qualities, leaves out of the complex or compounded idea it has of Peter, James, and any other particular man, that which is peculiar to each, retaining only what is com-mon to all; and so makes an abstract idea wherein all the particulars equal-ly partake, abstracting entirely from and cutting off all those circum-stances and differences, which might determine it to any particular existence. And after this manner it is said we come by the abstract idea of *man* or, if you please, humanity or human nature. (Berkeley 1948–57, 2:28)

In a similar manner, one is said to attain the abstract general idea of ani-mal, or of body. In all cases, Type III abstract ideas are (1) general and (2) ideas of objects or bodies of some sort. Thus, one might have the abstract

---

4. Alternatively we could think of these as abstract ideas of complexes or combinations of qualities, since any body has many qualities. Note that in doing so one is not identifying the body with the complex of qualities.

idea of man, but of no particular man; or woman, but of no particular woman; or of building, but not a particular building.

There is, however, a type of abstract idea of a still higher level of generality that Berkeley sometimes mentions, though he does not do so in the introduction to the *Principles* nor in the draft introduction. These are the abstract ideas of *being*, or of *entia*, or of *existence*. For instance, *Principles* 81 speaks of the abstract ideas of quiddity, entity, or existence, and in section 17 Berkeley mentions the abstract idea of being. In both passages Berkeley says that these are the most general and incomprehensible of all. There is also a notebook entry (*Philosophical Commentaries* 552) where such highly general ideas are mentioned:

> The abstract Idea of Being or Existence is never thought of by the Vulgar, they never use those words standing for abstract ideas. (Berkeley 1948–57, 1:69)

In the correspondence with Samuel Johnson, Berkeley writes:

> Abstract general ideas was a notion that Mr. Locke held in common with the Schoolmen, and I think all other philosophers; it runs through his whole book *Of Human Understanding*. He holds an abstract idea of existence exclusive of perceiving and being perceived. I cannot find that I have any such idea, and that is my reason against it. (Berkeley 1948–57, 2:293)

Abstract ideas of being or entity, as well as that of existence, are not merely more general than those already considered, they are category-transcendent in the sense that they do not fit into the categories of quality or object or body, whatever level of generality we move to within those categories. The most general level of the category of quality is that of attribute or feature; and within the category of object, the most general level is that of object, unspecified as to type. The concept of being fits within neither of these categories, but instead straddles them both. The same may be said of the concept or abstract idea of existence. So we will treat these abstract ideas of being and existence in a separate class, what I will refer to as Type IV abstract ideas. These are abstract ideas of the highest level of generality, even to the point of being category-transcendent.

Wide Abstract Ideas

In *De Motu* Berkeley speaks of abstract *terms*, such as 'force,' 'solicitation of gravity,' and 'dead forces.' He is not talking there of abstract *ideas*, at least not explicitly. Moreover, what he says about such abstract terms is not at all like what he says about abstract ideas of Types I, II, or III. Instead, abstract terms are more like highly theoretical terms in some science, terms that we apply to postulated entities. Here is what Berkeley writes in *De Motu*:

> While we support heavy bodies we feel in ourselves effort, fatigue, and discomfort. We perceive also in heavy bodies falling an accelerated motion towards the centre of the earth; and that is all the senses tell us. By reason, however, we infer that there is some cause or principle of these phenomena, and that is popularly called *gravity*. But since the cause of the fall of heavy bodies is unseen and unknown, gravity in that usage cannot properly be styled a sensible quality. It is, therefore, an occult quality. But what an occult quality is, or how any quality can act or do anything, we can scarcely conceive—indeed we cannot conceive. And so men would do better to let the occult quality go, and attend only to the sensible effects. Abstract terms (however useful they may be in argument) should be discarded in meditation, and the mind should be fixed on the particular and concrete, that is, on the things themselves. (Berkeley 1975, 211–12)

If we think of our having concepts connected to these obscure terms, these concepts would not be similar to abstract ideas of the first three types. The concept of force or gravity, for instance, would lack all qualitative content. This seems to be what Berkeley means by saying that these qualities of force or gravity would be occult. Thus, such concepts would not be Type I abstract ideas. Nor would the concept of force be a Type II abstract idea since it is not a determinable relative to some determinates, as the abstract idea of color is supposed to be. We cannot say it is a determinable because it is an unknown and occult quality. These physical concepts would also not be Type III abstract ideas, as they are not concepts of bodies or of objects. Finally, the concepts of force or gravity would not be Type IV category-transcendent abstract ideas because such scientific concepts lack the requisite degree of generality. The obscure concept of force, for instance, is in the category that contains the sensible qualities of exertion and resistance, and so the concept of force, though very general, is not category-transcendent.

Wide abstract ideas—as I am calling these obscure concepts which would be connected to general terms such as 'force' and 'gravity'—are far removed from sense; i.e., they are not the same as the familiar concepts of resistance or exertion, and neither are they definable by means of the latter concepts. Being far removed from sense, they lack qualitative content altogether. Further, they are not formed by abstraction either in the sense of separation from instances or in the sense of selective attention. Finally, their content is obscure to the point of being unknown, because the quality they purport to represent is occult.

Such is the characterization of the concepts of force and gravity in *De Motu*. However, in the seventh dialogue of *Alciphron*, composed about a decade later than *De Motu*, the concept of force is discussed again and is regarded as an abstract idea similar to those made familiar from the introduction to the *Principles*. Speaking through Euphranor, Berkeley says,

> . . . let us examine what idea we can frame of force abstracted from body, motion and outward sensible effects. For myself I do not find that I have or can have any such idea. (Berkeley 1948–57, 3:293)

Here the term 'abstracted from' most likely means 'separated from' in which case the abstract idea of force would be most like a Type I abstract idea. From the sensible qualities of the motion of some object, its collision with another object and the perceived effects of the collision, one separates or abstracts away just the force inherent in the impact, leaving the motion, the body and the effects alone and unabstracted. This is how Berkeley is telling us the abstract idea of force would be formed. However, here Berkeley does not go on to argue that the force, motion of the body, and subsequent perceivable effects cannot exist separately in reality. In this respect, the abstract idea of force is not fully analogous to Type I abstract ideas.

Returning to the wide abstract ideas of *De Motu*, we can ask two important questions: first, does Berkeley regard the terms for these ideas as altogether without meaning, as some of his comments make it seem? And, second, what does he mean when he says that we would do better to "let the occult quality go"? The importance of the first question is two-fold: in the first instance one must comprehend a main point in *De Motu*, and in the second instance one must determine whether that point conflicts with and thereby threatens Berkeley's remarks about notions in the *Principles*.

Abstract terms, or wide abstract ideas, seem to be meaningless for Berkeley, because he says we do not have ideas for these terms; indeed, he says that such ideas are *inconceivable*. If this is his thought, we will need to reconsider what he says about notions. In the case of terms such as 'self' and 'soul' or 'mind,' Berkeley agrees that we have no ideas for entities presumably denoted by these terms, though he does not conclude that the terms lack meaning. On the contrary, he is at pains to say that these terms are meaningful, although their meaning is not carried by their signifying ideas, since they do not do that. On this latter point he diverges from Locke, who held that all meaningful terms immediately signify ideas.[5]

---

5. At *Philosophical Commentaries* 312 and 378, however, Berkeley seems to endorse the Lockean view about signification and meaning.

I think the key to understanding Berkeley's argument in *De Motu* is to focus attention on the second question, where Berkeley says it is better to let the occult quality go. Notice that he does not say that such qualities are impossible, something we might think he would infer from the inconceivability of the idea. Instead, his point is much weaker, admitting of three different readings:

a) There are no occult qualities.
b) We have no reason to suppose that there are occult qualities.
c) It is advisable to assume that there are no occult qualities.

These statements are ordered in strength, with (c), a practical recommendation, being the weakest.

I believe that (b) is most in line with the sense of Berkeley's argument in *De Motu*. It is clear that he is making at least an epistemic point. His claim is that our senses are limited, telling us only so much about heavy bodies falling with accelerated motion. Specifically, the senses fail to inform us of the causes of this motion, and reason only goes so far as to add that there is a cause of accelerated motion without further informing us of the nature of that cause. He then says that as a result the cause is unseen and unknown, and so that "It is therefore an occult quality." That the cause is occult is inferred directly from unknowability, and it is this that suggests his overall point is epistemic, just as we have it in statement (b). Hence he is relying on an epistemic principle such as,

> We have knowledge of X's only if either X's are given in sense, or propositions about X's are derivable either deductively or inductively from propositions about what is given in sense.

Armed with such a principle, Berkeley concludes that we have no knowledge of qualities like force of gravitation, and then concludes that we have no good reason to think that there is such a quality. From this, in turn, Berkeley can conclude that we have no reason to suppose that terms like 'force of gravitation' succeed in denoting.[6]

Although this explanation of Berkeley's argument avoids raising *semantic* problems with his doctrine of notions, it raises another, epistemic, problem. There are some entities for which we lack ideas and have only notions, about which we certainly have knowledge even if the knowledge fails to accord with the epistemic principle we have noted. For example, Berkeley says that we have knowledge of the self, one's own self or mind,

---

6. There is a good discussion of these semantical worries in Lisa Downing 1995.

and that this knowledge is neither sense-knowledge nor derivable from sense-knowledge. Instead, it is intuitive knowledge, not mediated by knowledge of ideas or by any other sense knowledge. As he puts it:

> I know what I mean by the terms *I* and *myself*; and I know this immediately, or intuitively, though I do not perceive it as I perceive a triangle, a colour, or a sound.

The epistemic principle of *De Motu* can be easily modified to accommodate intuitive self-knowledge. Berkeley introduces the term 'reflex act' to designate that procedure by which one is aware of one's self. He says:

> I say lastly, that I have a notion of spirit, though I have not, strictly speaking, an idea of it. I do not perceive it as an idea or by means of an idea, but know it by reflection. (Berkeley 1948–57, 2:231, 233)

Thus, a reflex act is a mode of awareness in which one cognizes or apprehends one's own mind or self, even though this awareness does not then consist in having ideas.[7] To accommodate intuitive knowledge gained by way of reflex acts, the epistemic principle should be revised:

> One has knowledge of X's only if either X's are given in sense, or X's are the objects of reflex acts, or propositions about X's are derivable either deductively or inductively from propositions which are known by means of sense or reflex acts.

Here we assume that propositions known because their objects are given in sense or are targets of reflex acts are intuitively known; hence, this principle really amounts to the claim that we have knowledge of X's only if the knowledge is intuitive or is properly derived from knowledge that is intuitive.

To see that this principle will support the argument of *De Motu*, we need only note that force of gravity and similar qualities are not known either by sense—as Berkeley explicitly tells us—or by reflex acts, since the latter yields only knowledge of the self. But neither are propositions describing forces of gravity derivable from propositions known by sense— again as Berkeley explicitly and rightly claims—or from propositions

---

7. I discuss this mode of knowledge acquisition in both Locke and Berkeley in "Epistemology in the Empiricists" (1998). Knowledge of the self via a reflex act, I there argue, should not be thought of as knowledge by reflection, because it is not mediated by knowledge of ideas; but neither is it inferential knowledge, because both Locke and Berkeley regard knowledge of the self as immediate.

known by reflex acts, since this last instance would derive force of gravity propositions from propositions about the self.

These arguments concerning wide abstract ideas, or abstract terms, and the qualities they putatively denote, are quite different from those Berkeley deploys against abstract ideas in the introduction to the *Principles*. The latter are generally not epistemic, and generally result in much stronger conclusions.

Arguments against Abstract Ideas

We now concentrate on abstract ideas proper and leave aside wide abstract ideas. Berkeley initially writes as though his main complaint against abstract ideas is that *he* does not have them, or that *he* finds it difficult to acquire them. He writes in Introduction 10:

> Whether others have this wonderful faculty of *abstracting their ideas*, they best can tell; for my self I find indeed I have a faculty of imagining or representing to my self the ideas of those particular things I have perceived and of variously compounding and dividing them.

And in the draft introduction he writes:

> I cannot by any effort of imagination frame to my self an idea of man prescinding from all particulars that shall have nothing in it. For my life I cannot comprehend abstract ideas. (Berkeley 1948–57, 2:29, 125)

The fact that Berkeley cannot acquire these abstract ideas, however, would hardly be a decisive or even especially forceful objection to them.

However, it is no part of Berkeley's case against abstract ideas to decry them based just on his own inability to frame them. His arguments are intended to strike much deeper than this. In fact, he has two main arguments against abstract ideas. These arguments are *a priori*, depending on what Berkeley takes to be conceptual truths. A third argument is strongly suggested by remarks Berkeley makes about the evidence Locke had proposed in favor of abstract ideas. This third argument is empirical, and appeals to the fact that there is no need to assume or postulate abstract ideas. However, these three arguments apply just to abstract ideas of Types I, II, and III. A much different argument is reserved for the abstract idea of existence.

One *a priori* argument is aimed squarely at Type I abstract ideas. In Introduction 10 Berkeley writes,

> I own my self able to abstract in one sense, as when I consider some par-
> ticular parts or qualities separated from others, with which though they
> are united in some object, yet, it is possible they may really exist without
> them. But I deny that I can abstract one from another, or conceive sepa-
> rately, those qualities which it is impossible should exist so separated.
> (Berkeley 1948–57, 2:30)

Assuming that Berkeley is talking about anyone's conceiving and not
merely his own, the last quoted sentence gives expression to a general
principle whose first part coincides with the two models of the procedure
of abstracting noted earlier—the separation model and the selective attention model. Thus, the phrase 'abstract from one another' indicates
abstracting in the sense of separating, and the phrase 'conceive separately'
indicates selectively attending. So, the principle Berkeley is using is the
No Separation Principle:

> One cannot separate in thought (in idea) or conceive separately sensible
> qualities which cannot exist separately in reality.[8]

But which qualities cannot exist separately in reality? We know what
Berkeley has in mind. Color cannot exist separately from shape or figure;
nor can figure or shape exist separately from color. But even so, we can
think of colors and shapes in either of two ways: as tokens or instances, on
the one hand, or as types.

Suppose we consider a specific triangle which has been colored some
shade of red. If we are thinking of tokens, or what some call property-in-
stances, then we would be thinking of that very instance of red shade, that
exists in one particular triangle on that one instance of a triangular shape.
Or we might be thinking of quality-types. In that case, we would be thinking of the repeatable items—red of that shade, and triangle of that sort,
say isosceles. So, Berkeley might be alleging that some quality-tokens (or
instances) cannot exist separately; or, rather, that some quality-types cannot exist separately, or perhaps both.

Notice that we cannot determine which of these he has in mind simply
by examining Type I abstract ideas more finely. To qualify as Type I
something need only be an idea of a single quality, such as red and be
wholly determinate, as in being an idea of a particular shade of red. Both
of these conditions are met if an abstract Type I idea is abstracted from either a red-token in the triangle or a red-type in the triangle, so long as we
think of the red in the triangle as being a very specific shade. Hence, focusing on the nature of Type I abstract ideas will not help us understand

8. A principle like this one is very helpfully discussed in D. Flage 1986.

which version of the principle referring to quality-tokens or quality-types, Berkeley is relying on in his argument against such ideas.

Suppose that he is thinking of quality-*tokens*. He is thereby committed to holding that the token of some shade of red painted or otherwise imposed on the triangle cannot exist apart from that triangular shape. This claim seems to me to be true. For one individuates the color-token in part by specification of the spatial configuration which it suffuses, as opposed to other color-tokens, even others of the same shade of red. If one then thinks of ideas one has of such a red triangular shape as visual images, as most probably Berkeley did, then it seems clear that one can neither separate the idea of the red shade from the idea of the triangular shape, nor even attend to one apart from attending to the other. The image of the red triangle will itself be red and triangular, and in conceiving or attending to the color one is *eo ipso* attending to or conceiving the shape.[9]

Let us suppose Berkeley is talking about quality-tokens. Then, using the example from above, his claim would be that the quality-token red, of this shade, cannot exist apart from the quality-token that is a triangular shape. This claim is clearly true. For, as already noted, we individuate the quality-token red of the shade in question by specification of its shape. Moreover, the claim is true in reverse; the quality-token isoceles triangular shape cannot exist apart from the quality-token red of this shade. The reason is the same: the former is individuated by specification of the red expanse whose border it constitutes. So, one part of Berkeley's No Separation Principle would be true, namely, the part dealing with what is separable in reality.

The second part of Berkeley's principle has two sub-elements, corresponding to the separation and selective attention models. In the first, he claims that one cannot separate in thought or idea what cannot be separated in reality, where the latter are items restricted to sensible qualities. So, his point would be that the idea of the quality-token of red of a particular shade cannot be separated from the idea of the quality-token of traingular shape with which it is combined. Now there is one sense, surely, in which Berkeley is wrong about this. Imagine that one looks at the red triangular shape but that it then looks orange and trapezoidal. Then one acquires an idea of an orange, trapezoidal shape, and thus one has separated in idea what cannot be separated in reality. However, I think this is not the sort of situation Berkeley has in mind, because he assumes that one's visual experience is veridical.

9. Strictly speaking, this claim is true only if one is speaking of what is called below *de re conceiving*, i.e., roughly, a conceiving which takes objects, properties, and events as its "targets," rather than propositions. This concept is clarified below and also in chapter 5, where it surfaces in connection with the master argument for the *esse is percipi* principle.

But suppose this is so; why cannot one separate the idea of the red from the idea of the triangular shape? The answer is that according to Berkeley one has only *one* idea, and it is both red *and* triangular. Every visual idea in his account has both a color and a shape, and removal of the color would mean that one no longer had an idea. This view differs from the account Locke seems to support, for he seems to think that the idea of red is distinct from the idea of the triangular shape. Such simple ideas, he tells us, can enter the mind singly or one at a time. His view seems to be that when one looks at the red triangular shape one receives *two* simple ideas of sensation: a simple idea of red and a simple idea of triangular shape. Such a view encourages the thought, perhaps, that these are separable. For Berkeley, however, there is just one idea present to the mind in such a circumstance, so that in a sense there is nothing to separate. Berkeley does not subscribe to Locke's account of simple ideas.[10]

Thus, according to the separation model, Berkeley's principle would be correct, where the principle is understood throughout to apply to tokens both in reality and in idea. We pass, then, to quality-types. Then the red color of some shade in the triangular shape under consideration is a repeatable item, the very same red shade that occurs in other shapes and surfaces. And, of course, the same would be true of the tiangular shape. So understood, it is *not true* that the quality-type red of this shade cannot exist apart from the quality-type isoceles triangular shape. What is true, instead, is that the quality-type red of this shade cannot exist apart from *some shape-type or other*. It is this which holds true for qualities.[11]

Now consider matters at the level of ideas, and again imagine one has an idea of a red, triangular shape. If we think of the red in the idea as a repeatable item, then of course *it* is separable from the triangular shape. One might, after all, have an idea of a rectangular shape. The same is true of the triangular shape. If it is a repeatable item, then it is separable at the level of ideas from the red color: just think of having an idea of an orange triangular shape. Thus, what Berkeley must mean at the idea level in this case of types is that one cannot have an idea of red of some shade which itself is wholly lacking in *some shape or other*. What is to hold at the idea level would then be a strict analog of what holds at the level of qualities.

The plausibility of Berkeley's argument here will depend heavily on what Berkeleyan ideas are supposed to be. I noted above that when one

10. Locke discusses simples ideas of sensation and reflection in Book II of the *Essay*, beginning in chapter I and often thereafter. Berkeley, however, rejected simple ideas. On this, see K. Winkler 1989, chap. 3.

11. This claim is true only if we assume an ontology of individuals taking properties. It will fail in a process ontology of the sort described in Wilfrid Sellars' Carus Lectures. See Sellars 1981.

looks at a red triangular shape and one's perception is veridical, then one acquires a visual idea which itself is red and has a triangular shape. Such an assumption, then, takes Berkeleyan visual ideas either to be images of some sort, or at least to be entities with determinate phenomenal content. Given either of these assumptions, Berkeley is on safe ground; for surely visual images must have both a color and a shape. If ideas are not strictly images, but still must have determinate content, something similar will hold; visual ideas would have to have both color and shape determinate content.

It is worth stressing the differences in Berkeley's principle depending on whether it is taken to range over quality-tokens or types. In the case of tokens, a specific instance (token) of red is not separable from a particular instance of shape at the idea level. In the case of types, however, the red color of the idea is separable from the triangular shape, in the sense that the red color could exist in some other shape. What it cannot do is exist without some shape or other. Here we assume that Berkeley's principle is not equivocal: if it is referring to tokens at the quality level, it is also talking of tokens at the idea level, and the same carry–over holds for types.

Berkeley's principle, however, mentions both separation and separate conceiving, and we have yet to consider the latter. Consider again quality-tokens and assume veridical perception of the red, triangular shape, so that one receives a visual idea that is itself red and triangular. Can one conceive or attend to the shape without thereby conceiving or attending to the color, or conversely? Here the answer depends on what Berkeley means by the terms 'conceives' and 'attends to.' Nearly always when Berkeley uses the term 'conceives,' what is conceived is an object, or a property, rather than a proposition. Thus he speaks of conceiving a red triangle, rather than conceiving that something which is red is also triangular. In this way, Berkeley's use of 'conceives' is akin to non-propositional uses of perception verbs.[12] The paradigm here is in the perception of objects, where the perception verb takes a grammatical direct object as complement, as in "Mary hears the bells chiming." Such a construction is quite different, both grammatically and in sense, from constructions that are propositional, i.e., those in which the perception verb takes a clause that is expressive of a proposition as complement, as in "Mary hears that the bells are chiming."[13]

12. The term 'non-propositional perception' comes from Roderick Chisholm (1957).

13. There are passages where Berkeley seems to use 'conceives' in a propositional way, e.g., in *Principles* 22, where he talks of conceiving it to be possible for something to exist outside the mind. See the discussion of the master argument and impossible performances in chapter 5.

The issue then becomes whether one can conceive the red color of one's idea, in this non-propositional sense of 'conceives,' separately from one's idea of the triangular shape? It should be clear that the answer is no, provided that we are talking of tokens of red and triangular shape at the idea level. So construed, there is but one idea to attend to or conceive, and it is both red and triangular. *By* conceiving the former, one is thereby conceiving the latter. Compare seeing George Bush. He happens to be the former president. Hence, it is not possible to see George Bush without seeing the former president. Of course, this is not true if 'sees' means 'sees that' or 'sees as.' One can easily enough see that George Bush is playing golf without thereby seeing that the former president is playing golf, so long as one fails to know that George Bush is the former president. So, too, one can conceive that some presently had visual idea is red without thereby conceiving that it is triangular in shape, provided one lacks the concept of triangular shape. What one cannot do is non-propositionally conceive the color itself without at the same moment and in the same act conceive the shape. The reason is simple: there is just one idea there to be conceived and it, as it happens, is both red and triangular.

If ideas are thought of as taking quality-types as properties, matters are somewhat different, but quite parallel to what was said above about the separation model. Imagine that one has the idea of a red, triangular shape, so that one's idea is both red and triangular. It is possible to conceive the red color, construed as a repeatable item, apart from the triangular shape, even in the non-propositional sense of "conceives." The reason is that one might conceive that color red in some idea of a different shape. What one cannot do is conceive an idea that is red but that has no shape whatever. One cannot do this because, according to Berkeley's conception of visual ideas, every such idea has both a color and a shape. There is no visual idea, he would maintain, which is merely red, or merely shaped.[14]

Thus, Berkeley's principle that what cannot be separated in reality cannot be separated in thought or idea, or conceived separately in thought, is quite plausible and well underwrites the argument he gives against Type I abstract ideas. However, the argument requires some substantive assumptions that should also be noted. Among them are that the sensible ideas he is thinking of are acquired in veridical perception of an object's sensible qualities; that these sensible ideas either are images that themselves have (phenomenal) qualities, or at the least entities with determi-

---

14. A. J. Ayer once suggested that when one sees a many-speckled chicken, the sense-datum one experiences might have an indeterminate number of speckles. To this Chisholm responded (writing in 1942) that this is like saying that peace will come in 1943, but not in January, nor in February, nor in . . . December. Chisholm's argument is structurally the same as Berkeley's. See R. Chisholm 1942.

nate phenomenal content; that there are no ideas that are simple in the sense that Locke accepts; and that the conceiving at issue is non-propositional conceiving. Without all of these assumptions his argument would break down.

It also is important to see that Berkeley's argument against Type I abstract ideas is one that questions the *method* by which such ideas are to be acquired. Overall, the problem he finds with such ideas is that this method cannot be carried out. And, if this is the *only* method by which such ideas might be acquired, then it would be fair to say that one cannot have Type I abstract ideas. The criticisms he aims at Type II and III abstract ideas are quite different and do not concern the method by which such ideas are to be acquired or attended to. These ideas, Berkeley says, cannot be had because *they* are defective in some important way.

Consider the Type II abstract idea of color. This is not an idea of some specific color, say red, nor an idea of some specific shade of a color, but rather of color itself, what Berkeley calls "color in general." Again on the assumption that an abstract idea of color is an idea that has some color, there cannot be an abstract idea of mere color. For this would be an idea that has some color, but no specific color or color shade, a state of affairs that is obviously impossible. Moreover, it is clear that an exactly similar argument will apply in the case of extension or shape. Nothing, including an idea, can be merely extended (without any actual dimension) or merely shaped (without any actual shape). Berkeley forwards this argument first by regarding abstract ideas of bodies (Type III), and then by extending this to abstract ideas of qualities in general (Type II). Notice what Berkeley writes in Introduction 10.

> I can imagine a man with two heads or the upper parts of a man joined to the body of a horse. I can consider the hand, the eye, the nose, each by it self abstracted or separated from the rest of the body. But then whatever hand or eye I imagine, it must have some particular shape and colour. Likewise the idea of man that I frame to my self, must be either of a white, or a black, or a tawny, a straight, or a crooked, a tall, or a low, or a middle-sized man. I cannot by any effort of thought conceive the abstract idea above described. And it is equally impossible for me to form the abstract idea of motion distinct from the body moving, and which is neither swift nor slow, curvilinear nor rectilinear; and the like may be said of all other abstract general ideas whatsoever. (Berkeley 1948–57, 2:29)

The abstract ideas of motion in general is actually a little more difficult than Berkeley indicates, but ultimately susceptible of the same sort of argument as given above for color. To see the problem, consider the sensible idea of circular motion: one looks at some object that is undergoing circular motion, and receives an idea of circular motion. Is this visual sensible idea itself in motion, analogously to a visual color idea having some specific color? If we say yes, we have to conceive of things as a single visual idea moving in a circular path in one's phenomenal visual space. However, it might be that one experiences a succession of visual ideas, each occupying a different spot on a circumference, so that what we call a visual idea of circular motion is really a succession of visual ideas, each located at a different spot in one's phenomenal visual space. There is no way to settle this question, because there is no principled way to individuate ideas. The answer is indeterminate; there is no fact of the matter here.[15]

So we should consider the idea of motion in both ways. If one's abstract idea of motion is formed from single ideas that themselves have some motion, such as the circular case given here, or some other sort of motion (elliptical, rectilinear, and so on), then the abstract idea itself will undergo some motion, but none of these specific motions. This case is just like the color example, and falls to the same argument. The abstract idea cannot undergo mere motion that is not motion of some specific sort. What if the entity we call a visual idea of motion is really a succession of visual ideas? Then I imagine we would have to say that the abstract idea is itself a succession of ideas, occupying a series of spots but no specific spots. This, too, is incoherent; however, this is not exactly what Berkeley says about abstract ideas of motion because he does not consider a succession. He says, instead, in Introduction 8,

> By considering motion abstractedly not only from the body moved, but likewise from the figure it describes, and all particular directions and velocities, the abstract idea of motion is framed; which equally corresponds to all particular motions whatsoever that may be perceived by sense. (Berkeley 1948–57, 2:28)

This passage suggests that Berkeley has the first way of conceiving of visual ideas of motion in mind, and if so his argument will carry over as an analog to the color and figure arguments. But he is also tacitly choosing a method of individuating visual ideas.[16]

15. Suppose one has a very complex visual idea, as when one looks in one glance at a multifaceted scene. How many visual ideas does one then experience? We could say ONE, taking the complex visual idea as one entity, with a lot of variety. Or, we could say that each proper part of this complex is itself an idea. So, the complex visual idea of the facing side of a large building might contain an idea of a door, and another idea of a window, and so on. There is no determinately correct answer as to whether one has one or many visual ideas in this case. One can choose to individuate these visual ideas in one of these ways; what should be clear is that one is making a choice, not settling for what one discovers in the ideas.

16. Perhaps Berkeley is aware of the difference here, however, for at one point he has Hylas say in *Three Dialogues*: "So likewise as to motion, *swift* and *slow* are altogether relative to the succession of ideas in our own minds" Berkeley 1948–57, 2:192. This passage suggests the second way of construing the abstract idea of motion.

Once again we see that Berkeley's argument is driven in part by an assumption he makes about ideas. The argument is not carried solely by the conceptual point that something cannot have mere color without some specific color, or mere shape without some specific shape. That conceptual point needs to be bolstered with the assumption that sensible ideas have determinate qualities, which would have to carry over in some fashion to abstract ideas. Why must abstract ideas of Type II have determinate qualitative content? The answer is because they are either formed by separation from sensible ideas which have determinate content, or because they are "formed" by selective attention to parts or aspects of sensible ideas with determinate qualitative content. But why are sensible ideas entities with such determinate content? One answer here is that they are images which are objects of immediate perception, and certainly images cannot have merely determinable content. Or, if Berkeleyan sensible ideas are not strictly images, they are at least iconic in some way, and so must have determinate phenomenal qualities. Either of these last two assumptions about sensible ideas, and its carry–over to abstract ideas of Type II, is needed in the argument along with the conceptual point that nothing is merely colored or shaped.

A related assumption is operative in the argument against Type III abstract ideas. One's abstract idea of a woman is not itself a woman, of course, but if it is an image then it must be an image of a specific woman, or at least an idea with determinate features. The alternative would be an idea of a woman with a mouth of indefinite shape, a nose of indefinite shape and size, hair of no specific color or length, and so on, and it is clear that there can be no image of this sort. If these ideas are not strictly images, but at a minimum iconic to some degree (think of a stick figure of a person, which is not an image but is iconic), they will then have some determinate features even though not exactly those that would be possessed by an image. A similar argument will apply to other Type III abstract ideas, always dependent on the assumption that either these ideas are images or they are iconic entities which must have determinate features.

While Berkeley's arguments against the three types of abstract ideas considered so far are different, the conclusion is the same. Against Type I abstract ideas, he argues that the method of acquiring them or attending to them cannot be engaged in, and he concludes that there cannot be Type I abstract ideas. Abstract ideas of Types II and III, however, are ideas which are themselves impossible objects in the sense that their respective descriptions are inconsistent. An abstract idea of mere color, for example, is such an object, because (using "I" for "idea") "I has some color" implies "There is a specific color I has." Hence, the statement expressed by "I has some color and it is false that I has color a, and it is false that I has color b . . . and it is false that I has color n," where the number of different colors there are equals n, is a contradiction. Thus, there cannot be Type II abstract ideas, since this sort of argument generalizes across all of them. And the same sort of argument applies, as we saw, to Type III abstract ideas. Hence, it would seem, for all three types, we reach Berkeley's conclusion that such ideas are impossible; they cannot exist.

What the Arguments Show

We have noted a number of assumptions that Berkeley's arguments require. We know that the argument against Type I abstract ideas squarely rests on the No Separation Principle. This principle, in turn, holds only when certain assumptions are made: (1) that the sensible ideas spoken of are acquired in veridical perception, (2) that no sensible ideas are simple in the Lockean sense, (3) that the conceiving spoken of in the principle is non-propositional, and (4) that sensible ideas are either images or entities taking determinate content. The first assumption governs the scope of the principle, or the context in which it is held to apply. The third assumption concerns how we are to understand the principle itself and in that sense may be thought of as part of the principle. Assumptions (2) and (4), however, are independent; neither entails nor is entailed by the No Separation Principle.

We can now represent the modal status of the conclusion of Berkeley's argument against Type I abstract ideas. The argument does not establish that, the statement "there are abstract ideas of (just) single qualities" entails a contradiction, and so it does not show that it is impossible that there should be such abstract ideas. It establishes something a bit more modest, namely, that the statement "There are abstract ideas of (just) single qualities, and assumption (2) is correct, and assumption (4) is correct, and the No Separation Principle is correct." entails a contradiction. Berkeley's argument shows that Type I abstract ideas are impossible *given* the assumptions above, not that such ideas are impossible *simpliciter*.

I think this is not *Berkeley's* position regarding Type I abstract ideas; he holds that these abstract ideas *are* impossible *simpliciter*. He thinks that the two assumptions (2) and (4) are a part of, or entailed by, the claim that there are abstract ideas of single qualities. These assumptions govern how he thinks of ideas, and so govern how he thinks of abstract ideas, as well. Hence, we should consider Berkeley to be saying that, the statement "There are abstract ideas of (just) single qualities and the No Separation Principle" entails a contradiction. From this it will follow that it is absolutely impossible that there are Type I abstract ideas, provided we grant that the No Separation Principle is a necessary truth, a point on which we may expect Berkeley to insist.

The argument against Type II and III abstract ideas is different, principally because it makes no use of the No Separation Principle. We can illustrate it by focusing on Type II abstract ideas, specifically that of the general idea of color. Berkeley's contention is that, the statement "There are abstract ideas of (just) color, and all ideas are entities with fully determinate content" entails a contradiction. As above, Berkeley takes the claim about determinate content to be one that is true of all ideas, and so true of abstract ones. Hence, his point is that, the statement "There are abstract ideas of (just) color" by itself entails a contradiction. For, nothing that has color has mere color; necessarily, if something has color, then there is some specific color that it has. Hence, such ideas are absolutely impossible. This argument generalizes across all Type II abstract ideas, and a similar argument applies to those of Type III. All three types of abstract ideas are impossible *simpliciter*, or absolutely impossible.

An Alternative Account

The foregoing treatment of Berkeley's arguments against abstract ideas of Types I, II, and III, contains the result that there are two such arguments. The first proceeds by way of the No Separation principle, and is aimed only at Type I abstract ideas. The second finds abstract ideas of Types II and III to be intrinsically logically incoherent or inconsistent, and thus concludes that neither sort of abstract idea can exist. The logical incoherence of the abstract ideas of Types II and III is held to derive from the fact that these ideas are themselves supposed to be just generic objects, entities with merely determinable features. For convenience we can call this the Generic Natures account, applicable just to abstract ideas of Types II and III. There is, however, an alternative reading of Berkeley's discussion of abstract ideas that finds just one argument against abstract ideas of all three types. In this account, once proposed by Julius Weinberg and more recently discussed at some length by Douglas Jesseph and especially Kenneth Winkler, Berkeley's argument always proceeds from what is impossible in reality to what is impossible in idea.[17] Here is how Winkler summarizes Berkeley's argument against abstract ideas.

> What an abstract idea purports to represent is impossible. But what is impossible is inconsistent, and what is inconsistent cannot be conceived. It follows that there can be no abstract ideas. (Winkler, 33)

17. J. Weinberg 1965, 5–32. D. Jesseph 1993, chap. 1. K. Winkler 1989, chap. 2.

To illustrate, an abstract idea of color purports to represent an object that has color but no specific color, that is, an object with merely generic color. It is impossible for there to be an object with just generic color but no specific color. Such an object is inconsistent, and so cannot be conceived. Hence, there cannot be an abstract idea of color that represents this inconsistent object. Such an idea cannot be conceived.

The same argument would apply to Type I and III abstract ideas. For instance, a determinate color of some object cannot be separated from the object's shape. An object with these two properties separated is an impossible object, and so is inconsistent and cannot be conceived. And a merely generic person, with no specific height, color and so on, is also an impossible object, and cannot be conceived any more than generic color can. Thus, one argument applies across the board to all abstract ideas, and shows that none of them can exist.

Adapting Jesseph, I will refer to this argument as the Impossibility Argument.[18] A good passage in its support is found in the first and second editions of *Alciphron*:

> EUPHRANOR. Pray, Alciphron, which are those things you would call absolutely impossible?
>
> ALCIPHRON. Such as include a contradiction.
>
> EUPHRANOR. Can you frame an idea of what includes a contradiction?
>
> ALCIPHRON. I cannot.
>
> EUPHRANOR. Consequently, whatever is absolutely impossible you cannot form an idea of.
>
> ALCIPHRON. This I grant.
>
> EUPHRANOR. But can a colour or triangle, such as you describe their abstract general ideas, really exist?
>
> ALCIPHRON. It is absolutely impossible such things should exist in Nature.
>
> EUPHRANOR. Should it not follow, then, that they cannot exist in your mind, or in other words, that you cannot conceive or frame an idea of them? (Berkeley 1948–57, 3:333–34)

This is not the only passage supporting the Impossibility Argument, but it is an especially clear and compelling one. Also relevant is a passage from the *Defense of Freethinking in Mathematics*:

18. Jesseph refers to the Argument from Impossibility. Jesseph 1993, 21.

I desire to know whether it is possible for anything to exist which doth not include a contradiction: And if it is, whether we may infer that what cannot possibly exist, the same doth include a contradiction: I further desire to know, whether the reader can frame a distinct idea of anything which includes a contradiction? For my part, I cannot, nor consequently of the above-mentioned triangle; though you (who it seems know better than myself what I can do) are pleased to assure me of the contrary. (Berkeley 1948–57, 4:134)

Berkeley is referring to the famous triangle discussed by Locke.

For example, Does it not require some pains and skill to form the *general Idea* of a *Triangle* (which is yet none of the most abstract, comprehensive, and difficult,) for it must be neither Oblique, nor Rectangle, neither Equilateral, Equicrural, nor Scalenon; but all and none of these at once. (Locke 1975, *IV, VII* 9, 596)

This is the same example from Locke that Berkeley had discussed years earlier in the published Introduction, so it is clear that he had not changed his mind on this issue over the passage of more than twenty years.

It is especially noteworthy that the Impossibility Argument does not require, though it allows, that ideas be images or even that ideas have determinate content. For example, it does not require that an idea of the man across the room be an image of the man, nor even that the idea have color and shape. Neither does it require that the idea one gets when seeing some determinate shade of red should itself be determinately red. Indeed, it seems to by-pass completely any specification of the nature of the abstract idea one would have to have in order to represent what is common to all triangles, or what is common to all things having some color. The Impossibility Argument does not deny that abstract ideas of this sort have some nature or other, nor deny that they have some specific nature. It simply need make no mention of that nature in its premises.

The foregoing specifies a difference between the Impossibility Argument and the account proposed in the previous section as Berkeley's argument against Type II and III abstract ideas. For the latter account does specify the nature of the abstract ideas in question, and this specification is the crucial element in that account's elaboration of Berkeley's case against such ideas. In the account I have proposed, it is the generic, general nature of these ideas that Berkeley objects to, and it is this generic, merely determinable nature that shows that there cannot be any ideas of that sort. In contrast, the Impossibility Argument, staying silent on the exact nature of the ideas which would be abstract, derives the impossibility of these ideas from certain principles which are accepted by Berkeley and which function as premises in the Impossibility Argument itself, namely, that what is impossible is inconsistent, and what is inconsistent is inconceivable.

Certainly we might ask whether one of these accounts is supported by relevant texts to the exclusion of the other We have already seen that there are ample texts supporting the Impossibility Argument. However, the Generic Natures account proposed earlier is also found in the texts. In the *Defense*, Berkeley writes:

> It is Mr. Locke's opinion that every general name stands for a general *abstract* idea, which prescinds from the species or individuals comprehended under it. Thus, for example, the general name *colour* stands for an idea which is neither blue, red, green, nor any other particular colour, but somewhat distinct and abstracted from them all. (Berkeley 1948–57, 4:135)

Here it is clear that Berkeley attributes generic color to the abstract idea itself. He is not talking about generic color existing in nature. Indeed, he recognizes that Locke agrees that nothing in nature is merely generic, but instead everything in nature is particular and completely determinate. At Introduction 11, for example, he even quotes Locke on this point. (Berkeley 1948–57, 2:31)

In *Alciphron* Berkeley also alludes to the triangle example:

> After the same manner, you may observe particular triangles to differ one from another, as their sides are equal or unequal, and their angles greater or lesser; whence they are denominated equilateral, equicrural or scalenum, obtusangular, actuangular or rectangular. But the mind, excluding out of its idea all these peculiar properties and distinctions, frameth the general abstract idea of a triangle, which is neither equilateral, equicrural nor scalenum, neither obtusangular, actuangular nor rectangular, but all and none of these at once.

Here the phrase "all and none of these at once" can be read either as saying that the general idea of triangle has inconsistent properties, or that it has just the general property of triangular shape.

To see that in this passage Berkeley is attributing generic triangular shape *to* the abstract idea of a triangle, we may notice how he continues:

> The same may be said of the general abstract idea of colour, which is something distinct from and exclusive of blue, red, green, yellow and every other particular colour, including only that general essence in which they all agree. (Berkeley 1948–57, 3:332)

Here the phrase "the same may be said" is important, for Berkeley is clearly referring back to the immediately preceding discussion of the abstract idea of a triangle, while in this color case he is clearly attributing generic color to the abstract idea.

In the *Draft Introduction* where he is talking of the abstract idea of man, Berkeley speaks of omitting from one's ideas whatever is peculiar to each patricular man and keeping what is common to all the men. He continues:

> And so it makes one general complex idea, wherein all the particulars do partake, abstracting entirely from and cutting off all those circumstances & differences, which might determine it to any particular existence. & after this manner you come by a clear, precise, abstract idea of a man. In which idea it is true there is included colour, because there is no man but hath some colour, but then it can be neither, white colour nor black colour nor any particular colour, but colour in general, because there is no one particular colour wherein all men do partake.

Here again we see Berkeley attributing generic color to the abstract idea. But he sees that this is not enough to have the abstract idea of man.

> In the like manner, you will tell me there is included stature, but it is neither tall stature, nor low stature, nor yet middling stature, but stature in general. And so of the rest.

Here Berkeley is attributing generic shape to the abstract idea of man to go along with generic color.

Consider, next, how Berkeley argues against these abstract ideas in the *Draft Introduction:*

> I can imagine a man with two heads, or the upper parts of a man joyn'd to the body of a horse. I can consider the hand, the eye, the nose each by itself singled out & separated from, the rest of the body. But then whatever eye or nose I imagine they must have some particular shape & colour. The idea of man that I frame to my self must be either of a white, or a black, or a tawny, a straight or a crooked, a tall or a low or a middling sized man. I cannot by any effort of imagination frame to my self an idea of man prescinding from all particulars that shall have nothing particular in it. For my life I cannot comprehend abstract ideas.

In this passage, and in the parallel passage in section 10 of the published Introduction, Berkeley argues that abstract ideas with merely generic properties are not conceivable. This is because any idea one could have, for example of color, has to be an idea of some particular color. Necessarily, if something has a color, there is some particular color it has; and, similarly, for shape. One cannot conceive ideas of this abstract sort because there cannot be ideas of this sort; and, the latter is true because, being ideas which are general, having merely generic properties, they are logically defective.

To see that this is how Berkeley thought of his argument against abstract general ideas (i.e., abstract ideas of Types II and III), notice how he begins a passage from the *Draft Introduction*:

> For besides the incomprehensibility of abstract ideas (which may pass for an argument, since those gentlemen do not pretend to any new facultys, distinct from those of ordinary men) there are not wanting *other proofs* against them. (Emphasis mine.)

Berkeley then gives one of these other proofs and, interestingly enough, it is a species of the Impossibility Argument:

> It is, I think, a receiv'd axiom that an impossibility cannot be conceiv'd. For what created intelligence will pretend to conceive, that which God cannot cause to be? Now it is on all hands agreed, that nothing abstract or general can be made really to exist, whence it should seem to follow, that it cannot have so much as an ideal existence in the understanding. (Berkeley 1948–1957, 2:123, 125)

What I think these comments show, as far as Berkeley conceived of his own work, is that both the Generic Natures argument and the Impossibility Argument were deployed against abstract general ideas. The former is limited in scope, insofar as it applies just to abstract ideas of Types II and III, while the latter is quite general and applies across the board. Still, since Berkeley makes it clear that he has more than one argument, we should think of these arguments as supplementary to one another rather than as competitors for the one, correct Berkeleyan account.

Proponents of the Impossibility Argument do not distinguish between Berkeley's arguments against abstract ideas of Types I, II, and III, and the abstract idea of existence. In that respect, it is probably fair to say that they regard the Impossibility Argument as applicable to abstract ideas of all types. I think that would be an error. Berkeley singles out the abstract idea of existence as special in a certain way, and has what I think is a different, and special argument against it.

The Abstract Idea of Existence

Earlier I discussed Type IV abstract ideas that were category-transcendant ideas of being or existence. Have I will focus on the abstract idea of existence. Berkeley hints at an argument against this sort of abstract idea in *Principles* 5 when he writes:

If we thoroughly examine this tenet, it will, perhaps, be found at bottom to depend on the doctrine of *abstract ideas.* For can there be a nicer strain of abstraction than to distinguish the existence of sensible objects from their being perceived, so as to conceive of them existing unperceived?

He goes on to argue that this separation is impossible:

> For my part I might as easily divide a thing from it self. . . . So far I will not deny I can abstract, if that may properly be called *abstraction*, which extends only to the conceiving separately such objects, as it is possible may exist or be actually perceived asunder. (Berkeley 1948–57, 2:42, 43)

Here he seems to be appealing to the same principle he utilized in his argument against Type I abstract ideas. One cannot separate in thought (in idea) or conceive separately those qualities which cannot exist separately in reality. However, this principle cannot be quite what he is appealing to, because neither existence nor perceiving are *qualities.* In these passages he seems to be relying on a somewhat more general principle of which the foregoing is an instance, such as, One cannot separate in thought (in idea) or conceive separately those things which cannot exist separately in reality.

If we think of this principle as stating that impossibility is a sufficient condition for inconceivability, it is equivalent to the following statment: If it is impossible for two things to exist separately in reality, then one cannot separate those things in thought (in idea) or conceive those things separately. This seems to be what Berkeley is saying in the second passage, quoted above. What is suggested by the first-quotation is this: If there were an abstract idea of existence, then one could conceive sensible objects existing distinct from being perceived. An additional premise is needed, one stating that sensible objects cannot exist distinct from being perceived, which we know Berkeley accepts (it is a version of the *esse is percipi* thesis) and, more importantly, something he hints at earlier in this same passage:

> Light and colours, heat and cold, extension and figures, in a word the things we see and feel, what are they but so many sensations, notions, ideas or impressions on the sense; and is it possible to separate, even in thought, any of these from perception. (Berkeley 1948–57, 2:42–43)

If we put all of these elements together, we can form an argument that he may be driving at in *Principles* 5:

(1) If there were an abstract idea of existence, then one could conceive of sensible objects existing distinct from being perceived.

(2) But, it is not possible for sensible objects to exist distinct from their being perceived. (This is the *esse is percipi* principle).

(3) If it is not possible for two things to exist separately in reality, then one cannot separate those things in thought (in idea) or conceive them separately. (the general principle)

(4) Therefore, one cannot separate in thought (in idea) sensible objects from their being perceived, or conceive sensible objects separately from their being perceived. (from 2 and 3)

(5) Therefore, there could be no abstract idea of existence. (from 1 and 4)

This is admittedly a reconstructed argument. Only some of its elements are clearly in the text of *Principles* 5 (steps 2, 3 and 4), while the first premise is just barely suggested by Berkeley's comments. He does not actually talk of an abstract idea of existence in this passage; instead, he speaks of distinguishing the existence of sensible objects from being perceived and achieving this *by abstraction*. What is *unstated* is that in making this distinction one would be entertaining an abstract idea of existence. Still, it is not unreasonable to read the passage this way, i.e., as committing Berkeley to premise (1).

However, there are two good reasons to believe that this is not Berkeley's argument against the abstract idea of existence. The first is that premise (1) will not suffice as it stands, because its antecedent is incomplete. To accomplish the relevant conception, one would need both the abstract idea of existence and the abstract idea of some sensible object, e.g., a chair. This means that the premise needs to be understood as, (1a) If there were an abstract idea of existence and abstract ideas of sensible objects, then one could conceive of sensible objects existing unperceived.

However, with this change in the first premise, the conclusion of the argument must likewise change to, (5a) There could not be both an abstract idea of existence and abstract ideas of sensible objects. Of course, this conclusion only allows us to infer that either there are no abstract ideas of sensible objects, or there is no abstract idea of existence. It does not tell us which we are entitled to reject.

Another independent reason to think we have not uncovered the argument against the abstract idea of existence is that it would come close to yielding straightforward circularity when coupled with what Berkeley tells us in the so-called master argument. We can see the point here by just noting one crucial element of the master argument, reserving a fuller discussion until chapter 5. Berkeley presents the master argument in the form of a challenge. In the *Principles* it is put this way:

> . . . I am content to put the whole upon this issue; if you can but conceive it possible for one extended moveable substance, or in general, for any one idea or any thing like an idea, to exist otherwise than in a mind perceiving it, I shall readily give up the cause.

He goes on to note that one cannot succeed in meeting this challenge. In trying to do this one has some ideas of objects, but Berkeley notes, in *Principles* 22–23,

> it only shows you have the power of imagining or forming ideas in your mind; but it doth not show that you can conceive it possible, the objects of your thought may exist without the mind: to make out this, it is necessary that you conceive them existing unconceived or unthought of, which is a manifest repugnancy. (Berkeley 1948–57, 2:50)

A similar challenge is put in the *Three Dialogues*:

> But (to pass by all that hath been hitherto said, and reckon it for nothing, if you will have it so) I am content to put the whole upon this issue. If you can conceive it possible for any mixture or combination of qualities, or any sensible object whatever, to exist without the mind, then I will grant it actually to be so.

Hylas rises to this challenge and tries to engage in this very conceiving, to which Philonous responds,

> Is it not . . . a contradiction to talk of *conceiving* a thing which is *unconceived?* (Berkeley 1948–57, 2:200)

In both of these passages, Berkeley is saying that if one can conceive sensible objects existing without the mind, then he is willing to concede that the *esse is percipi* thesis is false. It is this action that he says one cannot perform.

The important point is this: if there were abstract ideas of sensible objects, and also an abstract idea of existence, then one *could* successfully carry out this conceiving. This is precisely what premise (1a) asserts. Hence, in the master argument itself, Berkeley must be assuming that there are no abstract ideas of either existence or of sensible objects. If in the master argument he were assuming that there is no abstract idea of existence, then circularity would be patent when the master argument is put along side the supposed argument against the abstract idea of existence we have located in *Principles* 5.

Now the absence of either the abstract idea of existence, or abstract ideas of sensible objects, would be enough to block being able to conceive a sensible object existing unperceived. So, in the master argument Berkeley does not need to assume that neither sort of abstract idea exists, only that one or the other does not. We cannot decide which he is assuming not to exist when he gives the master argument, because he does not tell us. What we can say is that if Berkeley assumes, in the master argument, that there is no abstract idea of existence, as he well might be doing, then circularity will arise if he also argues against such an abstract idea by using the *esse is percipi* thesis as an assumed premise.

It is possible, of course, that Berkeley has no argument against the abstract idea of existence at all. Perhaps he simply takes it for granted that an idea like that does not exist, and maybe he supposes this is obvious. This would be atypical of Berkeley, since on important points he generally has one or more arguments that he provides in favor of his position. I think Berkeley has an argument against this abstract idea, but one he does not highlight. This argument, to be discussed more fully in the next chapter, can be briefly indicated here. It takes its start from *Philosophical Commentaries* 670 and 671:

> Strange it is that Men should be at a loss to find their Idea of Existence since that (if such there be distinct from Perception) it is brought into the mind by all the Ways of Sensation & Reflection; methinks it should be most familiar to us & we best acquainted with it. This I am sure I have no such idea of Existence or annext to the Word Existence. & if others have that's nothing to me. They can Never make me sensible of it, simple ideas being uncommunicable by Language. (Berkeley 1948–57, 1:82)

In saying there is no idea of existence, Berkeley is directly opposing Locke's view, according to which the idea of existence is simple and original and we acquire it along with every other idea of sensation or reflection which we experience. Here is Locke in the *Essay*.

> *Existence* and *Unity*, are two other *ideas*, that are suggested to the Understanding, by every Object without, and every *Idea* within. When *Ideas* are in our Minds, we consider them as being actually there, as well as we consider things to be actually without us; which is, that they exist, or have *Existence*. (Locke 1975, II, VII, 7, 131)

Now whatever the abstract idea of existence is, it is derived from the non-abstract idea of existence, or at least it requires that there be non-abstract ideas of existence. So, Berkeley's argument against the abstract idea of existence is remarkably simple:

(1) There are abstract ideas of existence only if there are (non-abstract) ideas of existence.
(2) There are no (non-abstract) ideas of existence.
(3) Hence, there are no abstract ideas of existence.

I do not claim that Berkeley presents this argument anywhere in his published work; instead, it is one we can reconstruct from what he says about the idea of existence, together with some relevant thoughts of Locke's. For Locke, an abstract idea of existence would have to be what we have called a Type I abstract idea. This is because for him the idea of existence is itself simple and original, one which corresponds somehow either with a simple quality or with a power. So, for Locke the abstract idea of existence, like the abstract idea associated with any simple quality, would just be the non-abstract idea of existence taken by itself, unconnected to any other simple idea. Berkeley is denying, at premise (2), that there are any non-abstract ideas of existence of just this sort.

It is intriguing to speculate on what Berkeley's reason would be for denying non-abstract ideas of existence. One reason would be that he denies all simple ideas. I believe that he has another deeper reason, namely, that there is no simple quality or power of existence of which we might have an idea of existence. This is why I argue in chapter 4 that we lack the idea of existence. We would have such an idea only if existence were a simple quality, and whatever existence is, it is not that. This is not because it is a complex quality, but rather because it is not a quality at all. Thus ultimately, if I am right, Berkeley thinks we lack the abstract idea of existence because existence itself is not a quality.

Further details on this matter await the next chapter's discussion, but even with the little that has here been said we may notice the following important point. Berkeley's argument against the abstract idea of existence does not issue in the conclusion that such an idea is impossible. For the claim that there are no ideas of existence is a contingent truth, if it is true at all. With respect to this abstract idea, Berkeley holds only that there are none, not that there cannot be any. In this respect, the abstract idea of existence is quite different from all the others which he attacks.

The Simplicity Argument

Berkeley seems to give one other argument against abstract ideas which is of some importance. This argument, which I think we can take as fully general, applying to all sorts of abstract ideas, does not even purport to establish that abstract ideas are not possible. It shows, if it is successful, only that there are no such entities. His argument is an "explanationist" one: abstract ideas are not needed to explain either language learning or language use, contrary to what Locke had maintained. Hence, assuming that what is not needed for explanatory purposes should be dispensed with provided there is no other compelling reason to accept such entities, Berkeley seems to conclude that we have no reason to believe that there are abstract ideas, and so that there are none.

This explanationist argument is presented over many sections of the Introduction. Beginning in section 11, Berkeley surveys some of Locke's reasons for thinking that abstract general ideas are needed if we are to adequately explain how people communicate in or by the use of language, and how words are made general. Then in section 15 he writes,

> Nor do I think them a whit more useful for the *enlargement of knowledge* than for *communication*.

Thus he signals that he considers the preceding few sections to have shown that abstract ideas are not needed for communication. They are not needed, in essence, because there is a better, simpler explanation of success in communication, and of how words become general, than that offered by abstract ideas. The better, simpler explanation is that,

> A word becomes general by being made the sign, not of an abstract general idea but, of several particular ideas, any one of which it indifferently suggests to the mind.

His point is spelled out a little more fully in section 15 which merits a full statement:

> It is I know a point, much insisted on, that all knowledge and demonstration are about universal notions, to which I fully agree: but then it doth not appear to me that those notions are formed by *abstraction* in the manner premised; *universality,* so far as I can comprehend not consisting in the absolute, positive nature or conception of any thing, but in the relation it bears to the particulars signified or represented by it: by virtue whereof it is that things, names, or notions, being in their own nature *particular*, are rendered *universal.* Thus when I demonstrate any proposition concerning triangles, it is to be supposed that I have in view the universal idea of a triangle; which ought not to be understood as if I could frame an idea of a triangle which was neither equilateral nor scalenon nor equicrural. But only that the particular triangle I consider, whether of this or that sort it matters not, doth equally stand for and represent all rectilinear triangles whatsoever, and is in that sense *universal.*

Here the point is that notions, or ideas, as well as words, are general in use or function because they signify or are made to signify many different particulars; they are not universal in nature but rather in function. This latter idea about function, Berkeley insists, can account for how our knowledge increases by means of demonstration of new propositions, and it is simpler because this functional hypothesis does not lead to

all the manifold inextricable labyrinths of error and dispute, which their [the Schoolmen] doctrine of abstract natures and notions seems to have led them into. (Berkeley 1948–57, 2:31–35)

So, the explanationist argument overall amounts to this: explanations of sundry phenomena, having to do with language learning and use, are given in terms of abstract general ideas. These explanations are not needed, because there are alternative explanations of the same phenomena which are simpler in positing fewer kinds of entities, and in the sense that the alternative explanation does not lead to puzzles and problems, whereas the explanation in terms of abstract ideas does. Hence, we are justified both in rejecting the doctrine of abstract ideas, and in accepting the alternative, simpler explanatory hypothesis.[19]

A related broadly explanationist argument that Berkeley discusses, most fully in the Draft introduction, involves the point that earlier philosophers likely assumed that every common noun had to have a precise signification consisting of ideas.

That which seems to me principally to have drove men into the conceit of general ideas, is the opinion, that every name has, or ought to have, one only precise and settl'd signification. Which inclines them to think there are certain abstract, determinate, general ideas that make the true and only immediate signification of each general name. (Berkeley 1948–57, 2:134–35)

Berkeley's reply is that the premise is false: it is not true that every general noun has a settled signification of specific ideas. Moreover, one would only be led into thinking that every general noun signifies specific ideas if one further supposed that the chief end and function of language was for communication of one's thoughts to others. This, too, Berkeley says is false.

In truth, there is no such thing as one precise and definite signification annexed to any general name, they all signifying indifferently a great number of particular ideas. (Berkeley 1948–57, 2:36)

19. Jesseph has a full discussion of this functionalist account. Jesseph 1993, 33–38.

While regarding the claim that the main function of language is communication, he writes,

> Besides, the communicating of ideas marked by words is not the chief and only end of language, as is commonly supposed. There are other ends, as the raising of some passion, the exciting to, or deterring from an action, the putting the mind in some particular disposition; to which the former is in many cases barely subservient, and sometimes entirely omitted, when these can be obtained without it, as I think doth not infrequently happen in the familiar use of language.

The general argument suggested by these passages is this: one explanation of the general working of language is that words are used typically for communicating ideas, and this provides support for thinking that general names must signify specific ideas. However, a better explanation of the working and uses of language is that words, including general names, have many more functions other than signifying specific ideas. Once this is noticed, the ground for positing abstract general ideas to be the signification of general names has been swept aside.

As arguments against abstract general ideas, these explanationist arguments would be strengthened if Berkeley were to add that the points he has raised about language use and communication are the *only* reasons that have been proposed for positing abstract ideas. However, Berkeley does not make such a claim, and the fact that he does not makes one suspect that the overall point of these last two arguments is more modest. That is, his aim is not to provide an additional argument against abstract ideas, but rather merely to undermine the support that had been adduced in their favor. This suspicion is further motivated once we notice that immediately following these explanationist arguments, Berkeley says what he thinks he has accomplished vis-à-vis abstract ideas:

> We have, I think, shewn the impossibility of *abstract ideas*. We have considered what has been said for them by their ablest patrons; and endeavored to shew they are of no use for those ends, to which they are thought necessary. And lastly, we have traced them to the source from whence they flow, which appears to be language. (Berkeley 1948–57, 2:37, 38)

It would be decidedly odd to supply empirical arguments against abstract ideas, and then claim that one had shown such ideas, at least those of Types I, II, and III, to be impossible. Moreover, this passage seems to say that these considerations concerning language are supplementary to showing that abstract ideas are impossible. For these reasons, then, we can say that while Berkeley is in a position to claim that there are good explanationist arguments against abstract ideas, he is best interpreted as not advocating such arguments for that end. Instead, the explanationist arguments he actually gives have more limited aims and targets, functioning merely as criticism of arguments others had given in favor of abstract ideas.

Locke and Berkeley's Criticisms

Berkeley says that the doctrine of abstract ideas was accepted by a wide range of philosophers, including nearly everyone in his own time. He mentions the Schoolmen, though without naming any philosopher in particular, and also says that the doctrine may be traced back to and found in Aristotle. He also mentions Malebranche who, according to Berkeley, builds throughout his philosophy on abstract ideas. It is clear, however, that his main target in what he says against abstract ideas is Locke.[20]

The scholarly community with respect to Locke, however, has been divided. A fair number of acute commentators have pointed out that Berkeley simply misunderstood Locke on various key points, so that his criticisms largely miss the mark. It has also been suggested that Berkeley is unfair to Locke, in that he selectively quotes from Locke's *Essay*, and even that he gives uncharitable readings to passages that he actually cites from Locke.

One question on the matter of whether Berkeley misunderstood Locke has to do with the procedure of abstraction. Earlier in this chapter we noted that this procedure can be taken in either of two ways which, following John Mackie, we called the separation model and the selective attention model. The first important charge of misunderstanding levelled at Berkeley, then, is that he took Locke to be endorsing mental separation as the procedure by which abstraction is effected. However, this is a mistake, for Locke actually adopted the selective attention model. This is an exegetical, interpretive question. However, there is more to it, for the selective attention model would allow Locke's account of abstract ideas to avoid all or most of Berkeley's criticism. These are separate points which will be taken up in turn.

Certainly Locke does talk of selective consideration in the *Essay*. In his discussion of the idea of space, he writes:

> The Parts of pure Space are inseparable one from the other; so that the Continuity cannot be separated, neither really, nor mentally. For I demand

20. For discussion of these predecessors see Weinberg 1965, *op.* 5–13; Jesseph 1993, 9–20; and J. Urmson 1982.

of anyone, to remove any part of it from another, with which it is continued, even so much as in Thought. To divide and separate actually, is, I
think, by removing the parts one from another, to make two Superficies,
where before there was a Continuity: And to divide mentally, is to make in
the Mind two Superficies, where before there was a Continuity, and consider them as removed one from the other; which can only be done in
things considered by the Mind, as capable of being separated; . . . a Man
may consider so much of such a *Space*, as is answerable or commensurate
to a Foot, without considering the rest; which is indeed a partial Consideration, but not so much as mental Separation, or Division. . . . But a partial
consideration is not separating. A Man may consider Light in the Sun,
without its Heat; or Mobility in Body without its Extension, without thinking of their separation. One is only a partial Consideration, terminating in
one alone; and the other is a Consideration of both, as existing separately.
(Locke 1975, *II, XII*, 13, 172–73)

In this passage Locke clearly recognizes a distinction between mental separation and selective attention, or partial consideration. However, he is
not talking about abstraction here, and our concern is whether that is to be
understood as selective attention. In another passage he links the two:

the Mind makes the particular *Ideas*, received from particular Objects, to
become general; which is done by considering them as they are in the
Mind such Appearances, separate from all other Existences, and the circumstances of real Existence, as Time, Place, or any other concomitant
Ideas. This is called ABSTRACTION, whereby *Ideas* taken from particular
Beings, become general Representatives of all of the same kind. . . . Such
precise naked Appearances in the Mind, without considering, how,
whence, or with what others they came there, the Understanding lays
up . . . as the Standards to rank real Existences into sorts, as they agree
with these Patterns, and to *denominate* them accordingly. . . . the same
Colour being observed today in Chalk or Snow, which the Mind yesterday
receiv'd from Milk, it considers that Appearance alone, makes it a representative of all of that kind; and having given it the name *Whiteness*, it by
that sound signifies the same quality wheresoever to be imagin'd or met
with; and thus Universals, whether *Ideas* or Terms, are made. (Locke 1975,
II, XI, 9, 159)

In the first of these passages, which Winkler takes as decisive in showing that Locke adopted the selective attention model, Locke does note that
some things that are inseparable in reality are likewise inseparable in
thought.[21] However, his remark is not entirely general. Specifically, he
does not refer to qualities that are inseparable in reality, but rather parts of

---

21. Winkler 1983, 38.

space; these cannot be separated further in thought since they are insep-arable in reality. Hence, this passage does not carry with it the force of showing that Locke rejected mental separation of the sort relevant to the issue of abstract ideas.

However, the passage *does* indicate that Locke was aware of the selec-tive attention model as applied to qualities, since he explicitly brings this up at the end of the passage. Thus Locke is aware of selective attention in the context relevant to abstraction. This point is confirmed more strik-ingly in the second passage, one on which Mackie rests a lot of weight.[22] It is perhaps significant that in this second passage, where selective atten-tion and abstraction are explicitly connected, Locke makes no mention of the difference between separation and selective attention, nor does he deny that the former has any application in the matter of abstraction.

Citing these passages, however, does not settle the question, even though they are strongly suggestive and supportive of Locke as a selec-tive attention proponent. For there are other passages where Locke talks of mental separation and says that *it* is what one does in abstracting and forming abstract ideas. Here is an example:

> Words become general, by being made the signs of general *Ideas*: and *Ideas* become general, by separating from them the circumstances of Time, and Place, and any other *Ideas*, that may determine them to this or that particu-lar Existence. By this way of abstraction they are made capable of repre-senting more Individuals than one. (Locke 1975, *III, III*, 6, 410)

Moreover, this is not an isolated passage, as Locke repeats essentially the same point a bit later in Book III. Speaking of a child who has seen her mother and father and who then is learrning the term 'man,' Locke says:

> Afterwards, when time and a larger Acquaintance has made them observe, that there are a great many other Things in the World, that in some common agreements of Shape, and several other Qualities, resemble their Father and Mother, and those Persons they have been used to, they frame an *Idea*, which they find those many Particulars do partake in; and to that they give, with others, the name *Man*, for Example. And *thus they come to have a general Name*, and a general *Idea*. Wherein they make nothing new, but only leave out of the complex *Idea* they had of *Peter and James, Mary* and *Jane*, that which is peculiar to each, and retain only what is com-mon to all. (Locke 1975, *III, III*, 7, 411)

22. Mackie 1976, 109–10.

He gives just the same story for how one forms the abstract idea of *animal* in the following section, again stressing that one leaves out of many particular ideas what is perculiar to each and retains what is common. Further, speaking of the various ways in which the mind is not passive in its traffic with ideas, Locke talks of three methods of making complex ideas. Of these methods,

> The 3*d*. is separating them from all other *Ideas* that accompany them in their real existence; this is called *Abstraction*: And thus all its General *Ideas* are made. (Locke 1975, II, XII, 1, 163)

On the basis of texts, then, the separation model is much more prominent than the selective attention model. The former is widely mentioned in the different parts of the *Essay* and is always connected directly to abstraction and abstract ideas. Selective attention is seldom brought up, and even less often related by Locke to abstract ideas. However, as Winkler notes selective attention ought to be reckoned Locke's real position, as it is what is demanded by other metaphysical doctrines that Locke accepts. This point, presuming that Locke is consistent across the range of doctrines he accepts, should be laid along side the observation that mental separation was the sort of account one would find in the logic texts of Locke's time, including that of Port Royal, of which Locke may have had some knowledge. The fact that the separation model was the received view of abstraction in Locke's time provides some evidence that, when he directly brings up separation as an account of abstraction in his texts, we may take him at his word, even if doing so causes problems with his metaphysical presuppositions.

That the separation model was a widely shared account of abstraction endorsed in many passages in Locke, was surely known to Berkeley, and this made it reasonable for Berkeley to have interpreted Locke as holding a separation model. We should also recall that Berkeley claims to be attacking not just Locke, but a whole range of Schoolmen and moderns who accepted abstraction as Berkeley portrays it, namely, as separation. There is reason to believe that many of these medieval and modern philosophers endorsed separation as the account of abstraction.[23]

However, our claim that it was plausible of Berkeley to have interpreted Locke and other partisans of abstraction in this way needs to be tempered. After all, Berkeley was a close student of the *Essay*, and we therefore suppose that he, too, was aware of those passages cited above in which Locke talks of partial consideration and links it to the process of ab-

---

23. Weinberg 1965, 19–23, has a good discussion of this.

straction. Berkeley makes no attempt to even consider the question of whether partial consideration is Locke's official view and then adopts what is in effect that same position with a new name: 'selective attention' replaces Locke's term 'partial consideration' with no indication that he is indebted to Locke on this point. It is difficult to believe that Locke's comments were wholly without influence on Berkeley in this matter.[24]

Supposing that selective attention was Locke's official view of abstraction, what effect would this have on Berkeley's criticisms? Some scholars think that it would altogether vitiate those criticisms, and I believe that for some abstract ideas, those of Types II and III, they are right. To see this, it suffices to consider a Type II abstract idea of color. Any particular idea of color which one acquires in seeing an object with color will also be an idea of shape. In the selective attention model one does not make this idea abstract by leaving anything out, or separating, or creating any new idea with a generic color quality. Instead, this idea of sense is partially considered, to use Locke's phrase, in the sense that one attends to just the color, and pays no special attention to the figure. One also pays no special attention to the actual determinate color in the idea, but concentrates on its being colored, on the fact that it has color. Such a process does not require anything having the generic quality of mere color. The same sort of thing could be said if one selectively attended to the figure. One can also see how this account can be extended to abstract ideas of Type III. The abstract idea of *man*, for instance, would really be a particular idea or range of particular ideas of men, to which one selectively attends just to certain features held in common by all of these particular ideas. However none of these ideas would be a generic idea of *man*. Moreover, in this view there is no requirement that there be entities in nature which are merely colored, so the Impossibility Argument would have no starting point.

Nevertheless, selective attention avoids these difficulties only if the notion of *attending*, or *considering partially*, is understood in a certain manner. That is, it cannot be understood as what I earlier termed "de re conceiving," for such a cognitive act demands that every presented feature of an idea be actually conceived. Recall what was said about abstract ideas of Type I on this point. The reason that conceiving an idea of determinate red is also conceiving a determinate shape is because one is not then conceiving that something is red, but not conceiving that something is also shaped a certain way. Rather, when one *de re* conceives an idea of determinate red, one cannot fail to also *de re* conceive a shape, because the idea has both determinate color and shape.

---

24. Winkler suggests that Locke discovered selective attention, but that Berkeley treats the concept as his own philosophical discovery. Winkler 1983, 42.

The result is that if Locke means by the word 'consider' in his phrase 'partially consider,' something like 'notice that,' or 'conceive that,' then the selective attention model will effectively neutralize the arguments against abstract ideas, even those of Type I. For attending, when one selectively attends, would be a species of noticing that something is the case, or conceiving that some property is there instantiated, and one can engage in that activity even when there are other properties there instantiated that one fails to notice.

It is also sometimes said that Locke's position emerges unscathed by Berkeley's criticisms because the latter assume that Lockean ideas are images, or at least objects with determinate features and, the argument goes, this is simply a mistake. Because Lockean ideas are altogether different, Berkeley's critical comments miss the mark.[25]

I think debate on the question of images is apt to prove fruitless in at least one respect, despite the fact that Locke sometimes says that his ideas of sensation are images.[26] The reason is that the concept of an image is not sufficiently sharp for us to be able to decide whether Lockean ideas are images, even if we know a great deal about what those ideas are supposed to be. The problem arises when we ask how closely an image must resemble that which it images. We certainly cannot require a perfect match, a so-called mirror image, for we can think of cases we would be inclined to say are images which do not meet that criterion. So, the resemblance between image and imaged item can be less than perfect; the difficulty comes when in a non-arbitrary way, we try to determine, how much something less than a perfect match will still qualify as an image. Neither Locke nor Berkeley say anything about their conception of ideas or about images which will help us settle how they would have thought it best to specify the less than perfect point up to which something still qualifies as an image.

We can ask, however, whether Lockean ideas are *objects* with determinate phenomenal features such as color and figure. Berkeley's criticisms assume that abstract ideas are entities of just this sort, as we have seen; and Locke, it is argued, will be largely immune to those criticisms if his ideas are not objects of this kind. But there is good evidence to support a reading of Lockean ideas as objects. First, Locke does sometimes say that ideas are images, whatever he means exactly, and surely images are objects with determinate features. At one point he uses an example of a look-

---

25. R. Aaron denies that Lockean ideas are images. R. Aaron 1955, 199.

26. Locke speaks of ideas as images at *Essay*, 2.1.15. Treating Lockean ideas as images has lately been defended by M. Ayers (1993), 45ff. For critical discussion see V. Chappell 1994, 44ff.

ing glass, "which constantly receives variety of Images or *Ideas*, but retains none", and then later he writes,

> *The Understanding can* no more refuse to have, nor alter, when they are
> imprinted, nor blot them out, and make new ones in it self, than a mirror
> can refuse, alter, or obliterate the Images or *Ideas*, which, the Objects set
> before it, do therein produce. (Locke 1975, II, I, 15, 25, 112, 118)

Locke also tells us that ideas of sensation are immediately perceived entities, and that some of them resemble actual qualities in bodies. To say that
ideas are immediately perceived is to say that they are objects of perceptual awareness; and ideas resemble qualities in bodies only if ideas themselves have resembling features such as shape. Further, in connection
with a discussion of cognitive penetration, i.e., the extent to which one's
judgment may affect and alter an appearance or idea, Locke says,

> ... the Judgement presently, ... alters the Appearance into their Causes;
> So that from that, which truly is variety of shadow or colour, collecting the
> Figure, it makes it pass for a mark of Figure, and an uniform Colour; when
> the *Idea* we receive from thence, is only a Plain variously colour'd, as is evi-
> dent in Painting. (Locke 1975, *II, IX, 8, 145*)

In this passage Locke not only treats ideas as objects, but as objects that
have color and figure or shape. There is, then, good reason to take Locke's
ideas in just the way Berkeley did, namely, as objects which themselves
have determinate features such as color and shape. Locke seems further to
have supposed that these ideas, at least in some cases, are images, though
exactly what he means by an image is left unclear.

CHAPTER 4

Existence, Abstraction, and Heterogeneity

A mong abstract ideas, Berkeley singles out that of existence as special in some way. He also presents very little, in the way of an argument against this abstract idea, despite his critique of the other types of abstract ideas we have examined. So, it will be important to investigate the special status Berkeley accords the abstract idea of existence, and to try to uncover the reasons he might have for thinking there are no such ideas. Also important is the connection Berkeley finds between this sort of abstract idea and the *esse is percipi* principle. He thinks that were one to have this sort of abstract idea, then the opponent of immaterialism would be in a good position to establish metaphysical realism, and thereby secure the absolute, real existence of physical objects. This would strike at the very heart of Berkeley's metaphysics, and so it is vital that the abstract idea of existence be countered. The abstract ideas thesis, if true, would also threaten the core elements of Berkeley's theory of vision and so in that area, too, it is crucial to Berkeley's various theories that the theory of abstract ideas be removed.

The Idea of Existence

Certainly Locke held that there is an idea of existence. In fact he seems to hold that this idea accompanies all other ideas, whether of sensation or reflection.

Existence and *Unity* are two other *Ideas,* that are suggested to the Understanding, by every Object without, and every *Idea* within. When *Ideas* are
in our Minds, we consider them as being actually there, as well as consider things to be actually without us; which is, that they exist, or have *Existence*: And whatever we can consider as one thing, whether a real Being, or
Idea, suggests to the Understanding the *Idea* of *Unity.* (Locke 1975, *II, VII, 7,*
131)

It is worth noticing that Locke is talking about simple ideas; this fact,
together with what Locke says about the *reality* of simple ideas, will be
important to Berkeley's argument against the abstract idea of existence.

The sentiment Locke expresses here concerning the idea of existence is
not isolated. He repeats the point in the chapter on retention:

But concerning the *Ideas* themselves, it is easie to remark, That those that
are *oftenest refreshed* (amongst which are those that are conveyed into the
Mind by more ways than one) by a frequent return of the Objects or
Actions that produce them, *fix themselves best in the Memory,* and remain
clearest and longest there; and therefore those, which are of the original
Qualities of Bodies, *viz., Solidity, Extension, Figure, Motion,* and *Rest,* and
those that almost constantly affect our bodies, as *Heat* and *Cold;* and those
which are the Affections of all kinds of Beings, as *Existence, Duration,* and
Number, which almost every Object that affects our Senses, every Thought
which imploys our Minds, bring along with them: These, I say, and the
like *Ideas,* are seldom quite lost. Whilst the Mind retains any *Ideas* at all.
(Locke 1975, *II, X* 6, 152)

In both of these passages, Locke makes the point that the idea of existence is brought into the mind whenever one has any other idea, of either
sensation or reflection. The idea of existence, then, is one we can scarcely
avoid having. Then in summing up his main message concerning ideas
later in Book II, Locke says,

And thus I have, in a short draught, given a view of our *original ideas,* from
whence all the others are derived, and of which they are made up; which if
I would consider, as a Philosopher, and examine on what Causes they
depend, and of what they are made, I believe they all might be reduced to
those very few primary, and original ones, viz.,
   Extension,
   Solidity,
   Mobility, or the Power of being moved; which by our Senses we
receive from Body;
   Perceptivity, or the Power of perception, or thinking;
   Motivity, or the Power of moving; which by reflection we receive
from our Minds. I crave leave to make use of these two new Words,

to avoid the danger of being mistaken in the use of those which are aequivocal. To which if we add

Existence,
Duration,
Number;

which belong both to the one, and the other, we have, perhaps, all the Original *Ideas* on which the rest depend. (Locke 1975, *II*, XXI, 73, 286–87)

Here we learn that the idea of existence is not just simple, but also one of the original ideas, that is, one of the ideas on which all other ideas depend in the sense that the originals serve to explain all the rest. In this respect, then, the idea of existence is on a par with the ideas of the primary qualities.

According to Berkeley, Locke thinks there are also *abstract* ideas of existence. In a letter to Samual Johnson, he writes:

Abstract general ideas was a notion that Mr. Locke held in common with the Schoolmen, and I think all other philosophers; it runs through his whole book of Human Understanding. He holds an abstract idea of existence; exclusive of perceiving and being perceived. I cannot find I have any such idea, and this is my reason against it. (Berkeley 1948–57, 2:293)

Berkeley may be right that Locke held to an abstract idea of existence, though Locke did not explicitly say so. For there is no point in the *Essay* where Locke actually claims this, though, as we have noted, he does talk often of the idea of existence. Moreover, matters are made worse by the fact that Berkeley does not tell us why he thinks Locke accepts abstract ideas of existence.

Still, we can speculate on why Locke would have been committed to, and in this sense held, an abstract idea of existence. We have seen that Locke thinks the idea of existence is both original and simple. Consider, then, another of these original and simple ideas, say, the simple idea of some specific shape such as a specific triangle. We may imagine that one sees an isoceles triangle and receives a visual idea of an isoceles triangle. Is there an abstract idea of this particular isoceles shape? It would be, of course, what we called in the preceding chapter a Type 1 abstract idea. There is reason to think that Locke accepts abstract ideas of this type, or at least that he was committed to them. In his discussion of real and nominal essences, Locke says,

Essences being thus distinguished into *Nominal* and *Real,* we may farther observe, that *in the Species of simple* Ideas *and Modes,* they *are always the same:* But *in Substances always quite different.* Thus a Figure including a space between three Lines, is the real, as well as nominal *Essence* of a Tri-angle; it being not only the abstract *Idea* to which the general Name is annexed, but the very *Essentia*, or Being, of the thing itself, that Foundation from which all its Properties flow, and to which they are all inseparably annexed. (Locke 1975, *III, III*, 18, 418)

What I find important about this passage is that Locke explicitly commits himself to there being abstract ideas for simple qualities, such as that of a specific shape. That is, he commits himself to there being Type I abstract ideas, an important fact because in his discussion of abstraction and abstract general ideas, his examples are all of bodies rather than of quali-ties, thus perhaps suggesting the thought that his abstract general ideas range only over complex ideas associated with bodies such as persons, or animals, and the like.

However, this passage suggests more, namely, that Locke thinks there is an abstract idea associated with each simple idea and simple mode. He says " . . . *in* the Species of *Simple* Ideas *and Modes*, they [the nominal and real essence] *are always the same:*" and further, this nominal essence is the abstract idea "to which the general Name is annexed." If this is right, he is not merely talking about simple ideas of qualities, but all simple ideas. For each of them, the nominal and real essence is the same, and is the abstract idea. Thus, on such an account, he would have to think there is an abstract idea of existence, as he certainly holds that there is a simple and original idea of existence. We cannot say if this is *Berkeley's* reason for thinking that Locke accepts an abstract idea of existence, for he merely makes the attribution, without telling us why he thinks Locke is so com-mitted. We can, though, make a plausible case for Berkeley's attribution, based on what Locke tells us about simple, original ideas, and what he says about nominal essences for simple ideas.

Fending Off Metaphysical Realism

Berkeley thinks the abstract idea of existence is important for more than one reason. For instance, at *Philosophical Commentaries* 552 he connects this sort of idea to what he elsewhere says about common sense:

The abstract Idea of Being or Existence is never thought of by the Vulgar, they never use those words standing for abstract ideas.

A similar point is made later in section 772:

Existence, Extension etc are abstract, i.e. no ideas. They are words unknown & useless to the Vulgar.

The vulgar, of course, are those of common sense. A related point is repeated elsewhere, though with respect to abstract ideas generally:

> Abstract ideas only to be had amongst the Learned. The Vulgar never think they have any such, nor truly do they find any want of them. Genera & Species & abstract Ideas are terms unknown to them.

In these same notebooks, Berkeley tells us that the abstract idea of existence was started in the Schools:

> N.B. That not common usage but the Schools coined the Word Existence supposed to stand for an abstract general Idea.

Somewhat later he connects this idea to the Cartesians:

> Locke is in yᵉ right in those things wherein He differs from yᵉ Cartesians & they cannot but allow of his opinions if they stick to their own principles or cause of Existence & other abstract Ideas. (Berkeley 1948–53, 1:69, 93, 86, 97)

Perhaps the most important comment Berkeley makes about the abstract idea of existence, however, comes in *Principles* 5, though to see his full point most clearly it helps to also see what he says in section 4:

> It is indeed an opinion strangely prevailing amongst men, that houses, mountains, rivers, and in a word all sensible objects have an existence natural or real, distinct from their being perceived by the understanding. But with how great an assurance and acquiescence soever this principle may be entertained in the world; yet whoever shall find in his heart to call it in question, may, if I mistake not, perceive it to involve a manifest contradiction. For what are the forementioned objects but the things we perceive by sense, and what do we perceive besides our own ideas or sensations; and is it not plainly repugnant that any one of these or any combination of them should exist unperceived?

In the opening lines of section 5, Berkeley is explicitly referring back to what was said in section 4.

> If we thoroughly examine this tenet, it will, perhaps, be found at bottom to depend on the doctrine of *abstract ideas*. For can there be a nicer strain of abstraction than to distinguish the existence of sensible objects from their being perceived, so as to conceive of them existing unperceived? (Berkeley 1947–58, 2:42)

The tenet Berkeley refers to in section 5, then, is the thesis that sensible objects have a natural or real existence, distinct from being perceived. This is one way to state metaphysical realism, viz., the view that ordinary physical objects and their parts exist wholly independently of perceivers and of events of perception. Metaphysical realism, in turn, is opposed to and entails the denial of Berkeley's thesis of *esse is percipi*, the view that sensible objects and their qualities exist when and only when they are perceived.

While it is clear what tenet Berkeley has in mind, it is not clear what he means by the claim that this tenet depends on the doctrine of abstract ideas. Typically, dependence of one thing X on another thing Y is thought of in terms of necessary conditions, so that X would exist or obtain only if Y were to exist or obtain. However, sometimes we think of dependence in terms of sufficient conditions: X depends on Y in that case just in case if Y exists or obtains, then X also exists or obtains. Of course, dependence can even involve both necessary and sufficient conditions. How are we to understand what Berkeley means in his talk of dependence?

Thinking of dependence as a necessary condition only, and identifying his tenet with metaphysical realism, his point would be that,

> Metaphysical realism is true only if there are abstract ideas.

We know, however, that metaphysical realism is the opposite of the *esse is percipi* thesis, so that this claim is equivalent to:

> The *esse is percipi* thesis is false only if there are abstract ideas.

By contra–position this becomes,

> If there are no abstract ideas, then the *esse is percipi* thesis is true.

If *this* last claim is what Berkeley is talking about, his view is very dramatic indeed. For he would then only need to add the additional premise that there are no abstract ideas, available from the arguments presented in the Introduction to the *Principles*, and he would directly have the truth of the *esse is percipi* thesis.

It is tempting to think that this is Berkeley's argument, and thus tempting to suppose further that we have uncovered a new argument for the *esse is percipi* thesis, one which is independent of those arguments given elsewhere in the *Principles* and the *Three Dialogues*. However, I believe this temptation should be resisted, for the denial of abstract ideas figures as a premise in the master argument.[1] So, Berkeley would not be giving a new argument for the *esse is percipi* thesis here, but just stating part of the master argument. Here is the gist of my reasoning. In the master argument, Berkeley presents a challenge to the effect that if one can conceive a sensible object existing unperceived, then he will be prepared to regard the *esse is percipi* thesis as false. This is on the negative side, so to speak. He is confident that this challenge cannot be met, and he is prepared to go the offensive and argue that if one cannot conceive a sensible object existing unperceived, then the thesis is true. Thus, in the master argument he uses the positive premise,

> If one cannot conceive a sensible object existing unperceived, then the *esse is percipi* thesis is true.

He affirms this antecedent, of course, and then concludes that the thesis is true. However, the affirmation of this antecedent in turn requires that there be no abstract ideas. That is, in Berkeley's argument for this antecedent, he uses the premise that there are no abstract ideas. As we will see in the next chapter, this premise is not explicit, but it is needed if the argument he gives for this antecedent is to be complete. Further, in this denial of abstract ideas the statement needs to be fully general, applying to all sorts of abstract ideas including that of existence.

To sum up: on one reading, *Principles* 5 is saying that metaphysical realism is true only if there are abstract ideas, and this statement is equivalent to the claim that if there are no abstract ideas then Berkeley's thesis is true. However, though I think Berkeley accepts this latter claim, the real work that the denial of abstract ideas does for him is to function as a premise in the master argument, albeit a premise he does not make explicit.

We here see again why *Principles* 5 is not to be taken as an argument against the abstract idea of existence. For, if it is so taken, one would be assuming the truth of the *esse is percipi* principle as a premise, just as was indicated in the previous chapter. But now we see that the denial of abstract ideas of existence is needed in the master argument *for* the *esse is percipi* thesis. Hence, taking *Principles* 5 as an argument against the abstract idea of existence results in circularity.

---

1. In earlier work on this point, I discussed this line of argument and more or less succumbed to the temptation. See my "Abstract Ideas and the '*esse is percipi*' Thesis" (1985). On the other hand, I believe Berkeley does affirm the statement "If there are no abstract ideas, then the *esse is percipi* thesis is true." Indeed, this thesis will come out as a necessary truth if there is no abstract idea of existence of the sort Berkeley takes Locke to be committed to. I discuss this point in the next chapter. The master argument is given in *Principles* 22–24.

We return to the topic of dependence, then, and consider it in the "other direction," so to speak, viz., as expressing a sufficient condition. In that case, what Berkeley is stating at *Principles* 5 is that metaphysical realism is true *if* there are abstract ideas. Once again, since metaphysical realism is the denial of Berkeley's thesis, what he would be asserting there is that,

> If there are abstract ideas then the *esse is percipi* thesis is false.

This is one alternative and quite natural way to read the dependence claim Berkeley makes in the passage under consideration.

This statement can be taken as a premise of an argument which, with the further premise asserting that there are abstract ideas, yields the conclusion that the *esse is percipi* thesis is false—or, alternatively, that metaphysical realism is true. So, the argument suggested by this reading of *Principles* 5 is this:

(1) If there are abstract ideas, then the *esse is percipi* thesis is false and metaphysical realism is true.
(2) There are abstract ideas.
(3) Hence, the *esse is percipi* thesis is false and metaphysical realism is true.

It is clear that Berkeley himself would not be giving this argument, since he is committed to the denial of its conclusion. His point would be, instead, that this is an argument that proponents of metaphysical realism would be in a position to give against his idealism.

This is a most interesting explanation of what is being discussed in *Principles* 5, because it gives us directly a powerful reason for Berkeley to have attacked abstract ideas so extensively in the published Introduction. That attack, understood in the light of this argument, is needed to fend off metaphysical realism, something he would be accomplishing by providing arguments against premise (2). In fact, if these remarks on how to understand what Berkeley is asserting at *Principles* 5 are on track, then we see that the rejection of abstract ideas is *doubly important* for Berkeley. That rejection is necessary to help fuel the master argument for Berkeley's most fundamental metaphysical principle. And it is needed to help fend off what would otherwise work as a decisive refutation of that same metaphysical principle. Seen in this way, nothing could be more important for Berkeley's overall metaphysical position than the rejection of abstract ideas. Moreover, in both of these connections to Berkeley's metaphysics, the abstract idea of existence is vital. The importance of this sort of abstract idea for the master argument has already been briefly indicated.

The other important role this idea plays in Berkeley's thinking emerges when we investigate this argument more fully for metaphysical realism which Berkeley says his opponents are in a position to give so long as they can make a good case for abstract ideas.

To fully bring this point to light, we need to consider the first premise. Imagine that there are abstract ideas of Types I, II, and III. Then if a person has an abstract idea of some sensible object, perhaps a tree, then the person certainly can conceive a tree without also perceiving the tree. She would need only to attend in the relevant way to her abstract idea of a tree. In so doing, however, she need not be conceiving of the existence of a tree, for she is neither perceiving an existing tree, we presume, nor attending to an idea of existence. Were she doing the latter, while also conceiving an abstract idea of a tree, then she would be simultaneously doing two things: (a) conceiving a tree without perceiving it; and, (b) conceiving of the existence of a tree. She would accomplish the latter by conceiving or attending to the abstract idea of existence at the same moment she conceives the abstract idea of a tree.

It is worth noticing that in conceiving the existence of a sensible object such as a tree, it does not follow that by conceiving the relevant abstract ideas one is conceiving an existing sensible object, one that exists at the moment one conceives it. One is simply conceiving the existence of the object, which may or may not in fact exist. Moreover, so conceiving the object is not itself an act of perceiving the object. Conceiving objects *by conceiving* abstract ideas of them is not perceiving those objects. It is only when one conceives objects in the *absence of abstract ideas* that, Berkeley feels, one is thereby perceiving them, a point he stresses in his statement of the master argument.

In his presentation of the master argument, as we have seen, Berkeley is prepared to let everything ride on a certain sort of conceivability. In particular, he says that if one *can* conseive a sensible object (e.g., a tree) existing unperceived, then he is willing to give up his thesis of *esse is percipi*, and regard it as false. Once we put this point together with the comments of the preceding paragraph, we see why Berkeley thinks that having abstract ideas of the relevant sorts suffices for refuting his thesis. That is, he would note that

1a) If there are abstract ideas of existence and of sensible objects, then one can conceive a sensible object existing unperceived.

From the master argument we have Berkeley's willing concession,

1b) If one can conceive a sensible object existing unperceived, then the *esse is percipi* thesis is false.

These two claims imply the first premise of the argument he belives is available to his opponent, namely,

1) If there are abstract ideas of existence and of sensible objects, then the *esse is percipi* thesis is false and metaphysical realism is true.

We can now restate the remaining steps, in order to have the entire argument before us in which metaphysical realism can be established by Berkeley's opponent.

2) There are abstract ideas of existence and of sensible objects.
3) Hence, the *esse is percipi* thesis is false (and metaphysical realism is true).

We can now clearly see why it is so important for Berkeley to reject abstract ideas. For by doing this and falsifying step (2) of this argument, he is undercutting what he believes to be the major reason anyone would have to accept metaphysical realism. Hence, he is sweeping aside perhaps the major threat to his idealist metaphysics.

Fending off metaphysical realism, then, is done by attacking premise (2), that is, by rejecting abstract ideas. However, to falsify premise (2) and thus undercut his opponent's argument, Berkeley does not need to show *both* (a) that there are no abstract ideas of objects, *and* (b) that there are no abstract ideas of existence. Premise (2) is a conjunction, and may be falsified by establishing the falsity of either conjunct. In the published Introduction and the Draft Introduction, Berkeley's target includes (a), as we saw in the last chapter, but he is silent about (b). But this is not a tactical blunder on Berkeley's part, at least not for purposes of fending off metaphysical realism. He does not need to establish that there are no abstract ideas of existence in order to accomplish this. Where Berkeley rejects the abstract idea of existence is in the master argument. There he cannot succeed simply by denying abstract ideas of Types I, II, and III.

Abstraction and Existence

Does Berkeley have an argument against the abstract idea of existence? In the preceding chapter, I suggested that his real argument against this sort of abstract idea depends on the fact that he rejects non-abstract ideas of existence. Unlike Locke, Berkeley holds that we do not have ideas of existence. On Locke's account, ideas of existence are simple and original, and so any abstract idea of existence would be a type I abstract idea.

Hence, an abstract idea of existence would be numerically identical with a simple idea of existence, just as the abstract idea of a determinate color shade would be numerically identical with a simple idea of that color shade.

This line of thought makes the rejection of abstract ideas of existence depend on the rejection of non-abstract ideas of existence. That Berkeley does the latter is clear from *Philosophical Commentaries* 670 and 671, which bear repeating:

> Strange it is that Men should be at a loss to find their Idea of Existence since that (if such there be distinct from Perception) it is brought into the mind by all the Ways of Sensation & Reflection; methinks it should be most familar to us & we best acquainted with it.

> This I am sure I have no such idea of Existence or annext to the Word Existence. & if others have that's nothing to me, they can Never make me sensible of it, simple ideas being uncommunicated by Language. (Berkeley 1948–57, 1:82)

So, we need to ask why Berkeley would resist holding that there are ideas of existence.

One reason is that Locke reckons such ideas as simple, and Berkeley thinks there are no genuinely simple ideas. I agree that this is an important reason Berkeley would have for this denial, but I here want to consider a somewhat different reason for this denial.[2] As a start, let us consider what Berkeley says about number and unity, and the abstract ideas of them. The first thing to notice in *Philosophical Commentaries* is that he denies that number is a quality, thus opposing those philosophers who had reckoned number one of the primary qualities:

> Number not without the mind in any thing, because tis the mind by considering things as one that makes complex ideas of 'em tis the mind combines into one, wch by otherwise considering its ideas might make a score of w^t was but one just now. (Berkeley 1948–57, 1: entry 104, 17)

Essentially the same point is made in the *Principles* in section 12:

> That number is entirely the creature of the mind, even though the other qualities be allowed to exist without, will be evident to whoever considers, that the same thing bears a different denomination of number, as the mind views it with different respects. Thus, the same extension is one or three or thirty six, according as the mind considers it with reference to a yard, a

---

2. Berkeley's reasons for denying simple ideas are considered in detail in Winkler 1989, chap. 3.

foot, or an inch. Number is so visibly relative, and dependent on men's understanding, that it is strange to think how any one should give it an absolute existence without the mind. We say one book, one page, one line; all these are equally units, though some contain several of the others. And in each instance it is plain, the unit relates to some particular combination of ideas arbitrarily put together by the mind. (Berkeley 1948–57, 2:46)

An important point made here is that even if there are primary qualities which exist "without," number is not one of them.

Now Berkeley also thinks that number is by definition a collection of units, and he denies that he has any idea of unity.

Unity I know some will have to be a simple or uncompounded idea, accompanying all other ideas into the mind. That I have any such idea answering to the word *unity*, I do not find; and if I had, methinks I could not miss finding it; on the contrary it should be the most familiar to my understanding, since it is said to accompany all other ideas, and to be perceived by all the ways of sensation and reflexion. To say no more, it is an *abstract idea*. (Berkeley 1948–57 2:46)

Moreover, as I think the last few lines of section 12, quoted above, indicate, Berkeley also denies that unity is a quality, existing in bodies outside the mind.

In these passages we see that Berkeley regards the idea of unity as an abstract idea. He makes the same point elsewhere in his discussion of arithmetic at *Principles* 120:

Unity in abstract we have before considered in *Sect.* 13, from which and what hath been said in the Introduction, it plainly follows there is not any such idea. But number being defined a *collection of units*, we may conclude that, if there be no such thing as unity or unit in abstract, there are no ideas of number in abstract denoted by the numerical names and figures. The theories therefore in arithmetic, if they are abstracted from the names and figures, as likewise from all use and practice, as well as from the particular things numbered, can be supposed to have nothing at all for their object. (Berkeley 1948–57, 2:96)

Here Berkeley refers to the arguments of the published Introduction and to what was said in *Principles* 13 to conclude that there is no abstract idea of unity.

We can read Berkeley's comments in section 120 in either of two ways. On one reading he is saying that he has two arguments against the abstract idea of unity, viz., what is in *Principles* 13, or more strictly in sections 12 and 13, and what is in the published Introduction. The latter, I noted in the last chapter, as it applies to abstract ideas of Type I is the argument involving the No Separation Principle.³ Or, we can read section 120 as saying that Berkeley has one argument and that it is given in *both* sections 12 and 13 and in the Introduction.⁴ Of these readings I think the first captures Berkeley's point. To help see why, consider what the situation would be if he were referring just to the argument in the Introduction against type I abstract ideas. That argument makes use of the No Separation Principle; hence, if it were applied to unity, Berkeley would have to be saying that the *quality* of unity cannot exist apart from other qualities and that this is why the *idea* of unity cannot be separated from other ideas which accompany it. But this is not what he does. For, as noted, at section 12 of the *Principles* he denies that there is any quality of unity, and at section 13 he denies that there is any simple idea of unity. Hence, the No Separation Principle would simply not apply to the case of unity. For this reason I take Berkeley to be giving a different argument in sections 12 and 13. He seems to be arguing that since unity is not a (primary) quality— indeed, not a quality at all—we do not have a simple idea of unity. And, since we lack the simple idea of unity, we also lack the abstract idea of unity. Here we recall that the abstract idea of a determinate quality is numerically identical to the simple idea of that quality, an idea taken in isolation of other ideas of determinate qualities. Berkeley's explanation for why we lack the simple idea of unity, and thus why we lack the abstract idea of unity, is that there is no quality of unity for us to have an idea *of*. Further, the fact that there is no quality of unity also explains why there is no quality of number existing in bodies, and thus why number is really a "creature of the mind."

Berkeley explicitly makes all of these claims except for one: he does not outright *say* that we lack a simple idea of unity *because* there is no simple quality of unity. But it is hard to see why he would assert in section 12 that there is no simple quality of unity if he were not subsequently trying to convey the point that this is the reason there is no simple idea of unity.

I want to say much the same sort of thing about the abstract idea of existence, since Berkeley's comments on that idea parallel what he says about unity. He denies that we have a non-abstract idea of existence, just as he does with unity. In fact, his words regarding the idea of unity are nearly the same as what he says about the idea of existence. On the latter, here again is *Philosophical Commentaries* 670:

3. In his discussion of this passage, Jesseph takes Berkeley to be referring back to the Impossibility Argument. Jesseph 1993, 102–3.

4. We could also read section 120 as saying that section 13 is supplementary to that in the Introduction, though this is not apt to be Berkeley's point, as the argument of the Introduction stands by itself.

Strange it is that Men should be at a loss to find their Idea of Existence since that (if such there be distinct from Perception) it is brought into the mind by all the Ways of Sensation & Reflection; methinks it should be most familiar to us & we best Acquainted with it. (Berkeley 1948–57, 1:82)

On the idea of unity, to repeat *Principles* 13, Berkeley says,

That I have any such idea answering the word *unity*, I do not find; and if I had, methinks I could not miss finding it; on the contrary it should be the most familar to my understanding, since it is said to accompany all other ideas, and to be perceived by all the ways of section and reflexion. (Berkeley 1948–57, 2:46)

Berkeley further denies that there is an abstract idea of existence because this, too, would be numerically identical to the non-abstract idea of existence, and there is no idea of that sort. To finish the parallel with unity, then, Berkeley would contend that there is no quality of existence in bodies, and *this* explains why we lack an idea of existence and, ultimately, why we lack an abstract idea of existence.

It is not surprising that Berkeley speaks the same way about the ideas of unity and existence. He is, of course, referring directly to Locke's treatment of these same items, and we have seen that Locke holds that there are ideas of unity and existence, that both are simple and original, and that each accompanies every other idea we experience. Since Locke regards these ideas as the same on all of these counts, it is natural for Berkeley to use much the same language in his commentary on them. My suggestion is that it is also natural to think that he is giving the same sort of *argument* concerning each of these ideas. That is, we lack the abstract ideas of unity and existence, both of which would be Type I ideas, because we lack the non-abstract idea of each. And we lack the latter ideas because neither unity nor existence is a quality of things.

Thus, on the line of interpretation developed here, Berkeley has two parallel arguments against these two Type I abstract ideas, which we can set out side by side.

1. There is no quality in bodies of unity.	1. There is no quality in bodies of existence.
2. So, we have no idea of unity.	2. So, we have no idea of existence.
3. Hence, we have no abstract idea of unity.	3. Hence, we have no abstract idea of existence.

We know from remarks he makes in the *Philosophical Commentaries* that Berkeley thinks he has made an important discovery regarding existence or, as he sometimes puts it, regarding the meaning of the word 'exists.' On the reconstruction given here, the important discovery regarding existence is that it is not a quality or property of things.

This account of Berkeley's argument against the abstract idea of existence has the further merit that it helps to explain what he says about this abstract idea. We have noted already what Berkeley says in the correspondence with Johnson:

> Abstract general ideas was a notion Mr. Locke held in common with the Schoolmen, and I think all other philosophers; it runs through his whole book of Human Understanding. He holds an abstract idea of existence; exclusive of perceiving and being perceived. I cannot find I have any such idea, and this is my reason against it. (Berkeley 1948–57, 1:293)

Here it is noteworthy that Berkeley does *not* say that the abstract idea of existence is impossible, something he does say about other abstract ideas. He claims only that he does not have this idea and he means, I take it, not that *he* does not have it but rather that it does not exist. Indeed, in all of his comments on the abstract idea of existence, Berkeley never mentions that he regards this idea as impossible. The strongest claim he makes is that it is the "most incomprehensible of all others," (*Principles*, 81), which is a statement about how hard it is to understand what such an idea might be and not a claim about its being impossible.

We associate the thought that existence is not a property of things with Hume and Kant, and rightly so since each of those philosophers puts that idea to important use. However, if the reconstruction presented here of Berkeley's argument against the abstract idea of existence is correct, it may be fairly taken as some evidence that Berkeley should be credited with first having noted that existence is not a property or, as he would have said, a quality. This is Berkeley's important discovery about existence, as he conceived of things. Moreover, as intimated earlier in the discussion of *Principles* 4 and 5, the contention that there is no abstract idea of existence is important to Berkeley's presentation and defense of the master argument for the *esse is percipi* thesis. Insofar as my reconstruction is on the right track, what ultimately helps to fuel the master argument is the insight that existence is not a quality.[5]

To sum up thus far: our investigation of the abstract idea of existence has uncovered four significant points. First, this abstract idea, along with those of sensible objects, is directly related to the deepest principle in

---

5. Charles McCracken (1983, 232–33) has clearly noted the importance of the abstract idea of existence, and its connection to the *esse is percipi* thesis (what McCracken calls "immaterialism").

Berkeley's philosophy, viz., the *esse is percipi* thesis. This is true because in one of his main arguments for this principle, the master argument, he needs to be able to deny the existence of both of these sorts of abstract ideas if his points about conceivability are to be sustained. Second, denying abstract ideas generally is necessary if Berkeley is to stave off an argument for metaphysical realism which, if successful, would effectively demolish his metaphysics. If one had both the abstract idea of existence and the abstract idea of a sensible object, then metaphysical realism would be true. Third, Berkeley has a special argument against the abstract idea of existence and that of unity, one that finds no representation in the arguments of the published or Draft Introductions. This argument issues in the conclusion that there are no abstract ideas of existence and unity, not that there cannot be such ideas. And, fourth, Berkeley's ultimate reason for thinking there is no abstract idea of existence is that existence is not a quality; it is this which explains why we have no simple and original idea of existence. In this respect Berkeley should be credited with first noticing that existence is not a quality.

Abstract Ideas and the Heterogeneity Thesis

Perhaps the primary consequence of the theory of vision worked our by Berkeley in the *Essay Towards a New Theory of Vision* (*New Theory*) is the heterogeneity thesis (H-thesis). This thesis has two parts: (1) Each idea immediately perceivable by means of a given sense is numerically distinct from each idea immediately perceivable by means of any other sense. (2) Each idea immediately perceivable by means of a given sense is specifically distinct from each idea immediately perceivable by means of any other sense. The point of the first proposition is to deny numerical identity between ideas of each sense. The ideas of taste, for example, are not immediately perceived by touch, hearing, smelling, or seeing. And the ideas immediately perceived by means of any of the latter senses are in no case numerically identical to one another or to those of taste.

The second proposition goes further in saying that ideas of any one sense are different in kind from the ideas of each of the other senses. The ideas immediately perceivable by taste, then, are different kinds of things from the ideas immediately perceivable by smell, hearing, touch and sight. And each idea immediately perceivable by any of the latter senses is different in kind from the ideas immediately perceivable by means of the others.[6]

---

6. Berkeley sometimes writes as though the H-thesis is this: *Nothing* immediately perceived by one sense is numerically or specifically identical to *anything* immediately perceived by means of another sense. I discuss this possibility, and reject it, in chapter 6.

Both parts of the H-thesis are quite plausible and intuitive when applied to ideas of taste, smell, and hearing. Tastes are numerically and specifically distinct from smells or odors and sounds, as are smells and sounds from each other. However, the H-thesis, or at least one part of it, was denied by Locke with regard to sight and touch.

> The *Ideas* we get by more than one Sense, are of *Space*, or *Extension*, *Figure*, *Rest*, and *Motion*: For these make perceivable impressions, both on the Eyes and Touch; and we can receive and convey into our Minds the *Ideas* of the Extension, Figure, Motion, and Rest of Bodies, both by seeing and feeling. (Locke 1975, II V, 127)

Locke does not tell us whether he means numerical or specific identity, or perhaps both, so we cannot be sure of the exact disagreement between Locke and Berkeley on this point.

I will not investigate in depth the arguments Berkeley uses to try to establish the H-thesis, except to make the following points: first, Berkeley is quite clear that he takes the first part of the H-thesis to follow directly from the theory of visual depth and distance perception that he elaborates in the first half of the *New Theory*.[7]

> From what we have at large set forth and demonstrated in the foregoing parts of this treatise, it is plain there is no one self same numerical extension perceived both by sight and touch; but that the particular figures and extensions perceived by sight, however they may be called by the same names and reputed the same things with those perceived by touch, are nevertheless different, and have an existence distinct and separate from them: (Berkeley 1948–57, 1:220)

It is not altogether clear whether Berkeley thinks that the second half of the H-thesis follows from his theory of vision, because he gives three arguments for that part, and two of them are independent of the theory of vision. Only the first, given at *New Theory* 128, seems to be directly related to the theory of vision he propounds. That theory, he had claimed, entailed that a man born blind and later given sight would be able at first to tell by sight whether the things he sees are of the same nature as the things he touches. From this Berkeley infers that this man

> would not call them by the same name, nor repute them to be of the same sort with anything he had hitherto known.

7. Good discussions of these arguments, though with different estimates of their worth, are in David Armstrong 1960 and Margaret Atherton 1991.

This, of course, is not a statement of the second part of the H-thesis, because the claim here says only that this man would not *take* these objects to be the same in nature or kind, not that they would not *be* the same in kind. However, Berkeley may see the matter differently. Here is how he starts the section:

> When upon perception of an idea I range it under this or that sort, it is because it is perceived after the same manner, or because it has a likeness or conformity with, or affects me in the same way as, the ideas of the sort I rank it under. In short, it must not be intirely new, but have something in it old and already perceived by me. It must, I say, have so much at least in common with the ideas I have before known and named as to make me give it the same name with them. (Berkeley 1948–57, 1:223)

Putting the points made in these two quoted passages together yields an argument for the second part of the H-thesis:

(1) If the ideas of sight and touch were the same in kind, then any person who experienced both could tell that they were the same in kind.

(2) The formerly blind but newly sighted man cannot at first tell whether the ideas of sight and touch are the same in kind.

(3) Hence, the ideas of sight and touch are not the same in kind.

Now Berkeley does think that premise (2) is entailed by his theory of vision. Hence, if the foregoing is his argument from section 128, he would also have an argument for the claim that that his theory of vision entails the second part of the H-thesis.[8]

If this is Berkeley's conviction, then his view is that both parts of the H-thesis are entailed by his theory of vision. This point has important implications if abstract ideas are related to the H-thesis in the manner indicated by Berkeley.

> the question is not now concerning the same numerical ideas, but whether there be any one and the same sort or species of ideas equally perceivable to both senses; or, in other words, whether extension, figure, and motion

8. The argument here is straightforward: If the theory of vision is correct, then the newly sighted person cannot tell whether the ideas of sight and touch are the same in kind. Thus, if the newly sighted person *can* tell that these ideas are the same in kind, then the theory of vision is incorrect. Coupling this with premise (1) yields the result that if the ideas of sight and touch are the same in kind, then the theory of vision is false. Contraposition yields that if the theory of vision is correct, then the ideas of sight and touch are not the same in kind, which is component 2 of the H-thesis.

perceived by sight are not specifically distinct from extension, figure, and motion perceived by touch.

But before I come more particularly to discuss this matter, I find it proper to consider extension in abstract: For of this there is much talk, and I am apt to think that when men speak of extension as being an idea common to two senses, it is with a secret supposition that we can single out extension from all other tangible and visible qualities, and form thereof an abstract idea, which idea they will have common to sight and touch. (Berkeley 1948–57, 1:220)

In this second passage, Berkeley argues that if there are abstract ideas of extension, then there are ideas common to sight and touch. And of course as we have seen he does deny that there is an abstract idea of this sort. But Berkeley is not merely denying the antecedent of this conditional and then fallaciously concluding that no ideas are common to sight and touch. Rather, I think he is best interpreted here in the *New Theory* as offering an argument that is structurally very similar to the argument for metaphysical realism cited at *Principles* 5 which is available to his opponent. That is, he is saying that an opponent can use the abstract ideas thesis as part of an argument against the H-thesis. The argument, then, would have this structure:

(1) If there are abstract ideas of extension, then there are ideas of sight and touch which are the same in kind.
(2) If there are ideas of sight and touch which are the same in kind, then the H-thesis is false.
(3) Thus, if there are abstract ideas of extension, then the H-thesis is false.
(4) There are abstract ideas.
(5) Hence, the H-thesis is false.

As this argument makes clear the main consequence of Berkeley's theory of vision is threatened by the doctrine of abstract ideas. Hence he needs to be able to refute premise (4) in order to stave off this result. But this is not all. If Berkeley really does argue, as I have suggested above, that his theory of vision entails each component of the H-thesis, then the threat posed by abstract ideas is broader still. For then, if the H-thesis is false, so also is Berkeley's theory of vision. Thus, the abstract ideas thesis is a double threat: first to the H-thesis, by which Berkeley puts great store, and then by way of this to the theory of vision itself. The abstract ideas thesis, if it could be secured, would scuttle the core positive ideas of the *New Theory*.[9]

9. This argument has been discussed in Atherton 1991, 177–183, and in Rudolf Metz 1925, 64ff. See, too, Geneviève Brykman 1993, 181–188.

Why would Berkeley suppose that premise (1) of this argument is true? Here we have to engage in reconstruction. Imagine one sees and touches the square-shaped facing surface of a box. In the case of touch, we suppose that one traces the square shape with one's fingers while one is also looking at that same surface. Thus, one immediately sees a particular visual idea of square shape, and immediately feels a particular tangible idea of the same shape. Berkeley assumes that he has established that these particular ideas are numerically distinct in section 121.

Now from these two particular ideas, imagine that one engages in an act of abstraction. Berkeley thinks, as we have seen, that this involves mental separation. Hence, one leaves out whatever is peculiar to these respective ideas, and one attains an idea of extension, or perhaps one of mere shape. This abstract idea is not common to sight and touch; after all, *it* is not sensed. What I think Berkeley means is that the *particular* ideas of sight and touch, the particular ideas of square shape, are the same in kind. The reason is that *each* enables one to reach a *single* abstract idea. That is, Berkeley must be asuming something like this:

> If an abstract idea can be achieved by abstracting (separating) from two or more particular ideas of some quality, then those particular ideas are the same in kind.

Berkeley does not indicate why he would think such a statement is correct, but a likely argument for it can be devised.

Consider the two particular ideas, of sight and touch, on which our imagined act of abstraction is performed. In abstracting by separation one leaves out features specific to each particular idea and retains that feature or features which are shared. Imagine there is one such feature, F, that

---

It is also possible to read *New Theory* 121–22 as saying that the existence of certain sorts of abstract ideas is a necessary condition for the truth of the H-thesis. On this reading, with the successful rejection of abstract ideas, Berkeley would gain directly the truth of the H-thesis, a dramatic and short route to an important conclusion. This reading would be structurally parallel to a reading of *Principles* 5, discussed above, in which metaphysical realism is held to be true only if there are abstract ideas, so that with abstract ideas rejected, Berkeley immediately reaches the result that metaphysical realism is false, and thus that the EIP principle is true. My reason for not endorsing this tempting reading of *New Theory* 121–22 is that if it were correct, one would expect Berkeley to indicate that he regards the H-thesis as established once he has had his say about abstract ideas of extension in sections 123–25. But this is not what he does; rather, he goes on to offer additional arguments in favor of the H-thesis, in 128–31, and then he tops it off with an account of the Molyneux problem which he treats as "further confirmation" of the H-thesis (section 132). While not, perhaps, conclusive, this is some reason to think that Berkeley takes the existence of some abstract ideas as a sufficient condition for the statement that some ideas are common to sight and touch, and thus for the falsity of the H-thesis.

remains after this process. This is a feature had by both of the particular ideas. It does not follow that F is a feature which defines the type of which these two ideas are instances, for F may be an accidental feature. But it is at least plausible to conjecture that the shared feature defines the type, for it will sometimes be true that the feature shared will type identify the particulars.[10] This conjecture, I think, lies behind Berkeley's argument.

What we have seen so far in this section is that Berkeley regards the abstract ideas thesis as a threat to the H-thesis and, as well, to his theory of vision. Small wonder, then, that he attacks abstract ideas, both in *NTV* and then a year later in the published Introduction. The latter, as we saw in preceding sections, has even greater significance, what with its connections to fending off metaphysical realism and the master argument for the thesis of *esse is percipi*. However, Berkeley thought there was still more to be said about abstract ideas.

Primary and Secondary Qualities

Berkeley thought that the H-thesis, or perhaps just one of its components, was also related to the distinction between primary and secondary qualities. In the *Theory of Vision Vindicated* he writes:

> It hath indeed been a prevailing opinion and undoubted principle among mathematicians and philosophers that there were certain ideas common to both senses: whence arose the distinction of primary and secondary qualities. But I think it hath been demonstrated that there is no such thing as a common object, as an idea, or kind of idea perceived by both sight and touch. (Berkeley 1948–57, 1:257)

Berkeley does not further elaborate on these intriguing comments, in *Theory of Vision Vindicated* but it is certainly worth asking what the connection might be. Naturally one asks what Berkeley means by the phrase 'whence arose?' One thing he might mean is that the thesis that some ideas are

10. Why just sometimes? Suppose I am painting the wall with green paint, and a few drops of paint splatter off the roller, some onto my hand and some on a nearby table. Then there is a feature, that of having drops of green paint, shared by both me and the table. Should we say, then, that this feature of drops of green paint type identifies me and the table? We will say *yes* if by 'type' we mean merely 'entities having some feature in common.' We will say *no* if 'type' means, instead, something like 'what the essence of the thing is.' Berkeley's H-thesis in its second component is talking about this second notion of type, or kind, and so this is what the above argument for his assumption requires. But shared features will only sometimes be essential features, so Berkeley's argument as I have represented it is at best a plausibility argument.

common to sight and touch provides some evidence for the primary quality and secondary quality distinction.[11] Another thing he might mean is
that the two theses are the same at bottom, not in the sense that they mean
the same thing, but rather in the sense that they pick out the same sets of
ideas: common ideas coincide with the ideas of primary qualities, and
proper ideas, or those specific to a given sense, coincide with the ideas of
the secondary qualities. On this reading the two theses are different in
sense but equivalent in extension.[12]

To defend the latter claim of extensional equivalence Berkeley would
have to deal with what Locke says about solidity which, for him, is a primary quality but not a common sensible. So, the idea of solidity, for
Locke, is not common to sight and touch. This is certainly something
Berkeley would have known, as he was a close student of the *Essay*. There
is some slight evidence, however, that Berkeley would argue that solidity
is really hardness, in which case it would still be a proper sensible but no
longer a primary quality.[13] If Berkeley could make a case for this contention, then the claim of extensional equivalence would be better supported.

I think that the evidential link is the more likely sense of Berkeley's
statement. He gives no indication that he finds any sort of identity here,
and the phrase 'whence arose' strongly suggests something weaker. So,
let us consider how the matter of abstract ideas would come into this picture, assuming that Berkeley is talking about an evidential connection. As
we have already seen, Berkeley thinks that the abstract ideas thesis entails
the falsity of the heterogeneity thesis, because it entails that ideas of one
sense are the same in kind as ideas of another sense. This is one reading of
the claim that ideas of different sense are common. This latter point, in
turn, is said to provide evidence for the primary and secondary quality
distinction, and we may suppose that Berkeley would draw the inference
that therefore the abstract ideas thesis provides evidence for the primary
and secondary quality distinction. If so, he would be making use of a principle of the form "If P entails Q, and Q is evidence for R, then P is evidence
for R," which I think is an acceptable principle under some conceptions of
evidence. In this case, then, the rejection of abstract ideas, if successful, is
important insofar as it effectively removes some of the evidence for the

---

11. Margaret Atherton (1991) suggests such a reading of this passage. "Berkeley holds
the notion that there are common sensibles to be widespread and to be responsible for the
prevailing distinction between primary and secondary qualities" (174–75).

12. This reading of the passage is suggested in Rolf Sartorius 1969, 318–23.

13. At one point Berkeley has Philonous say: "Then as for *solidity*; either you do not
mean any sensible quality by that word, and so it is beside our inquiry: or if you do, it must
be either hardness or resistance." Berkeley 1948–57, 2:191.

primary and secondary quality distinction.[14] But this is as far as the argument goes; rejecting abstract ideas is not suffcient to completely undercut the distinction of primary and secondary qualities.

So far we have seen that the denial of abstract ideas, and in one context the abstract idea of existence, is vital for Berkeley's metaphysics and his theory of vision. This denial is necessary if he is to stave off defeat of two principles which are fundamental to his philosophy. Next we consider how the denial of abstract ideas functions in positive arguments for the *esse is percipi* principle.

14. Berkeley also discusses a connection between abstract ideas and the primary and secondary quality distinction at *Principles* 10, but his argument there is clouded by the fact that he gives an incorrect statement of the latter distinction.

CHAPTER 5

The *Esse Is Percipi* Principle

In this chapter the *esse is percipi* principle (hereafter, EIP principle) and its supporting arguments are examined. Berkeley has a number of interesting arguments for this principle, and each is worth examination. There are also two broad interpretations of Berkeley that bear on the EIP principle. These two interpretations, the adverbial account of Berkeley's ideas of sense, and the inherence interpretation according to which perceived ideas inhere in the minds that perceive them, are discussed with an eye to exactly how they bear on the EIP principle. My conclusion for each of these interpretations is that they do little to help establish the principle. The master argument for the EIP principle is discussed, as well, and its connection to the abstract idea of existence, briefly noted in the preceding chapter, is investigated anew.

Berkeley often says that the EIP principle is a necessary truth, something whose denial is a contradiction or a manifest repugnancy. However, in a number of places he says something else, namely, that the denial of the principle is meaningless, while in still other passages he says that *either* the denial of the principle is a contradiction *or* the denial is meaningless. I try in this chapter to explain what lies behind Berkeley's different pronouncements concerning the status of the EIP principle. The principle will be seen as a necessary truth, I suggest, so long as we think of existence in a *Lockean* way. However, Berkeley himself rejects this way of thinking of existence, and it is when we substitute what he regards as the correct account of existence for the Lockean one that the EIP principle emerges as a contingent truth, one whose denial is meaningless rather than contradictory.

The EIP Principle

Berkeley states the EIP principle in many places, but also in a number of ways. Two initial and intertwined questions arise: what exactly does the principle say, and what is its scope? That is, over what range of things does the principle apply?

Often Berkeley expresses himself by saying that things exist in minds and nowhere else. For instance, in the first *Dialogue*, he says that individual qualities exist in and only in the mind. After reviewing arguments pertaining to each of the sensible qualities, Hylas, the spokesman for the position opposed to Berkeley's concedes:

> You need say no more on this head. I am free to own, if there be no secret error or oversight in our proceedings hitherto, that all sensible qualities are alike to be denied existence without the mind.

Berkeley also expresses EIP in a different way by saying that sensible qualities and sensible objects, such as trees, exist when and only when they are perceived. However, we know that Berkeley intends these claims as equivalent, for he takes being in a mind to be perception by a mind. Philonous Berkeley's spokeman, expresses the point:

> Look you, Hylas, when I speak of objects as existing in the mind or imprinted on the senses; I would not be understood in the gross literal sense, as when bodies are said to exist in a place, or a seal to make an impression upon wax. My meaning is only that the mind comprehends or perceives them; and it is affected from without, or by some being distinct from itself. (Berkeley 1948–57, 2:194, 250)

He also points out that he does not mean some specific mind or perceiver. In saying that something exists only in a mind, or only when perceived by a mind, he does not mean some one mind, e.g., his own or that of some other individual. Here is Philonous again:

> The question between the materialists and me is not, whether things have a real existence out of the mind of this or that person, but whether they have an absolute existence, distinct from being perceived by God, and exterior to all minds.

There is also *Principles* 48, which makes the point more narrowly, as God's perception is not brought into the picture:

> For though we hold indeed the objects of sense to be nothing else but ideas which cannot exist unperceived; yet we may not hence conclude they have no existence except only while they are perceived by us, since there may be some other spirit which perceives them, though we do not. Wherever bodies are said to have no existence without the mind, I would not be understood to mean this or that particular mind, but all minds whatever. (Berkeley 1948–57, 2:235, 61)

So, to exist in a mind is to exist in, or be perceived by, some mind or other.

At many points Berkeley expresses the EIP principle in terms of *ideas*. That is, he says in *Principles* 2 that an idea exists in and only in a mind, or an idea exists when and only when it is perceived.

> This perceiving, active being is what I call *mind, spirit, soul,* or *my self.* By which words I do not denote any one of my ideas, but a thing entirely distinct from them, wherein they exist, or, which is the same thing, whereby they are perceived; for the existence of an idea consists in being perceived.

However, at many other points the scope of the principle is much broader. In the first of the *Three Dialogues*, for instance, he is plainly talking about sensible qualities such as figure and color as entities that exist in and only in minds. This we have have already noted in the first passage quoted in this section. He says much the same in the *Principles*, but also makes it clear that he is referring, as well, to sensible objects like trees and chairs. Thus, *Principles* 4:

> It is indeed an opinion strangely prevailing amongst men, that houses, mountains, rivers, and in a word all sensible objects have an existence natural or real, distinct from their being perceived by the understanding. But with how great an assurance and acquiescence soever this principle may be entertained in the world; yet whoever shall find in his heart to call it in question, may, if I mistake not, perceive it to involve a manifest contradiction. For what are the forementioned objects but the things we perceive by sense, and what do we perceive besides our own ideas or sensations; and is it not plainly repugnant that any one of these or any combination of them should exist unperceived? (Berkeley 1948–57, 2:41–42, 42)

It is clear, then, that Berkeley is talking of every sensible thing: every idea of sense, every sensible quality, and every sensible object (every macro physical object, as we might say). Using this information, we can state the EIP principle:

EIP Every idea of sense, every sensible quality, and every sensible object exists if and only if it is perceived.

Omitted from this statement of the principle is any mention of ideas of imagination, memory, and reflection. They exist, surely, in and only in minds; but it is unclear whether Berkeley would hold that when such an idea is attended to it is thereby perceived. He *may* hold that, since in opening the main part of the *Principles* he writes:

> It is evident to any one who takes a survey of the objects of human knowledge, that they are either ideas actually imprinted on the senses, or else such as are perceived by attending to passions and operations of the mind, or lastly ideas formed by help of memory and imagination, . . . (Berkeley 1948–57, 2:41)

Here he says that ideas of reflection are perceived; they are simply not perceived by sense, that is, by being imprinted from without. This suggests that all ideas of whatever sort exist in the mind in so far as they are perceived by the mind. I will take Berkeley to mean this, so that his terms 'by sense,' and 'by reflection,' and 'of memory,' and 'of imagination,' when applying to ideas, refer to causal eitiology rather than any differences in mental acts wherein such ideas are concerned. Then Berkeley's principle is more general:

> EIP. Every idea, every sensible quality, and every sensible object, exists if and only if it is perceived.

As stated, EIP makes no claim about everything existing if and only if it is perceived, for it makes no mention of perceivers. This is Berkeley's express intent: EIP is to range over all and only non-perceivers. He puts it this way:

> . . . all the unthinking objects of the mind agree, in that they are entirely passive, and their existence consists only in being perceived: whereas a soul or spirit is an active being, whose existence consists not in being perceived, but in perceiving ideas and thinking. (Berkeley 1948–57, 2:105)

Elsewhere he states a still more general principle, namely, that to be is to be either a perceiver or to be a thing perceived.

> [T]here are only things perceiving, and things perceived. (Berkeley 1948–57, 2:236)

So the general principle would be that all things which exist are either perceivers or perceived things. Things which are neither pereivers nor perceived things simply do not exist. I will take the EIP principle to be dealing just with non-perceivers, with the understanding that a full statement of Berkeley's views on existing entities must advert to the more general principle just noted.

Another complication is that Berkeley sometimes states the EIP principle disjunctively:

> An idea, sensible quality, and sensible object exists if and only if either it is actually perceived, or it would be perceived were such and such conditions to obtain.

The phrase 'such and such conditions' refers variably to such things as whether the perceiver attends in the requisite manner, or moves position, and the like. We can call this version of the principle the *disjunctive version*, and the last statement above of EIP we can refer to as the *actual perception version*. The former finds expression in *Principles* 3 and 58, and *Philosophical Commentaries* 293a.

> The table I write on, I say, exists, that is, I see and feel it; and if I were out of my study I should say it existed, meaning thereby that if I was in my study I might perceive it, or that some other spirit actually does perceive it.

> The question, whether the earth moves or no, amounts in reality to no more than this, to wit, whether we have reason to conclude from what hath been observed by astronomers, that if we were placed in such and such circumstances, and such or such a position and distance, both from the earth and sun, we should perceive the former to move among the choir of the planets, and appearing in all respects like one of them. (Berkeley 1948–57, 2:42, 65–66)

> Bodies taken for Powers do exist w^n not perceiv'd but this existence is not actual. w^n I say a power exists no more is meant than that if in ye light I open my eyes & look that way I shall see it i.e. ye body &c. (Berkeley 1948–57, 1:36)

The difference between the actual perception and the disjunctive versions of EIP is not trivial, for the latter allows that a sensible object exists even when not actually perceived by any perceiver whatever.

Over against these passages which indicate the disjunctive version of EIP are other passages that assert the actual perception version. For instance, in *Principles* 3, a section quoted earlier in support of the disjunctive version, we find two comments supporting the actual version:

> It seems no less evident that the various sensations or ideas imprinted on the sense, however blended or combined together (that is, whatever objects they compose) cannot exist otherwise than in a mind perceiving them.

> There was an odour, that is, it was smelled; there was a sound, that is to say, it was heard; a colour or figure, and it was perceived by sight or touch. This is all that I can understand by these and the like expressions. For as to what is said of the absolute existence of unthinking things without any relation to their being perceived, that seems perfectly unintelligible. Their *esse* is *percipi*, nor is it possible they should have any existence, out of the minds or thinking things which perceive them.

These two comments come immediately before and immediately after the passage quoted above in support of the disjunctive version. A few sections later Berkeley repeats the point dramatically:

> Some truths there are so near and obvious to the mind, that a man need only open his eyes to see them. Such I take this important one to be, to wit, that all the choir of heaven and furniture of the earth, in a word all those bodies which compose the mighty frame of the word, have not any subsistence without a mind, that their being is to be perceived or known; that consequently so long as they are not actually perceived by me, or do not exist in my mind or that of any other created spirit, they must either have no existence at all, or else subsist in the mind of some eternal spirit. (Berkeley 1948–57, 2:42, 43)

Moreover, in favor of actual perception as the right account of EIP is the role Berkeley finds for God. In his account, objects not perceived by finite spirits are nonetheless perceived by God, and this fact underwrites their existence. This is part of the point in the passage from section 6 just quoted.[1]

There are problems for the actual perception version of EIP, however. First, it has been questioned whether Berkeley's God actually perceives anything.[2] The reason is that God is not affected by ideas in the way persons are when they perceive, and so it is concluded that God cannot properly be said to perceive at all. True, God knows and causes ideas, but this is not perception. Hence, we should question the actual perception version of EIP.

---

1. There are other places where Berkeley mentions God's perception; one is at *Principles* 6, where he speaks of perception by an eternal spirit.
2. See George Thomas 1976, 163–68, and George Pitcher 1977, 163–79.

This objection is not decisive, however. What it shows, at most, is that God's perception is different from perception in finite spirits or, as Kenneth Winkler puts it, God does not perceive "by sense."[3] So, while this objection does raise a very important point about God, it does not prove conclusive as an objection against the actual perception version of EIP.

The second problem for this version of EIP concerns what Berkeley says about the creation, a point that seems more forceful. What Berkeley says about creation, in short, seems flatly inconsistent with the actual perception version of EIP. The issue comes up graphically in the third *Dialogue*:

HYLAS: Are you not satisfied there is some peculiar repugnancy between the Mosaic account of the Creation, and your notions?

PHILONOUS: If all possible sense, which can be put on the first chapter of *Genesis*, may be conceived as consistently with my principles as any other, then it has no peculiar repugnancy with them. But there is no sense you may not as well conceive believing as I do. Since, besides spirits, all you conceive are ideas; and the existence of these I do not deny. Neither do you pretend they exist without the mind.

HYLAS: Pray let me see any sense you can understand it in.

PHILONOUS: Why, I imagine that if I had been present at the Creation, I should have seen things produced into being; that is, become perceptible, in the order described by the sacred historian. I ever before believed the Mosaic account of the Creation, and now find no alteration in my manner of believing it. When things are said to begin or end their existence, we do not mean this with regard to God, but His creatures. All objects are eternally known by God, or which is the same thing, have an eternal existence in his mind: but when things before imperceptible to creatures, are by a decree of God, made perceptible to them; then are they said to begin a relative existence with respect to created minds. (Berkeley 1948–57, 2:251–52)

Three points of importance are made in these passages. First, Berkeley holds that there is a sense in which objects exist eternally, as ideas in God's mind. One might wonder, then, how objects that exist eternally can also be created. Second, these objects existing eternally in God's mind might be thought of as unperceived, since they are claimed to exist in God's mind only insofar as God knows, or knows about, such objects. God's merely knowing or knowing about such objects is not perceiving them. Third, Berkeley explicitly allows for relative or conditional existence with respect to finite perceivers. Hence, an object is allowed by him

3. Kenneth Winkler 1989, 205.

to exist so long as some person would perceive it under the right conditions and that, it certainly seems, is squarely at odds wih the actual perception version of EIP.

The first point is of great interest, though it is not directly connected to the EIP principle. There are two sub-points here. In the first, Hylas is asking how Berkeley has made room for creation at all, since objects exist eternally. The answer is that objects are created *relative to finite perceivers*. Relative to God, objects are not created. Rather, creation is an event which is defined relative to finite perceivers, a fact that Berkeley finds perfectly consistent with the Mosaic account in the *Old Testament*. The second sub-point is different and concerns the fact that the eternal existence of objects as ideas in God's mind should give Berkeley pause, since he is himself critical at one point of matter on precisely this ground. That is, he contends that if matter is allowed, then it will have to be reckoned as co-eternal with God, and Berkeley finds this fact objectionable. So, parity of reasoning should dictate that it is also objectionable to suppose that objects exist eternally along with God.[4]

Hylas is brought to concede that there is nothing objectionable in saying that objects exist eternally in God's mind. The exchange goes this way:

> PHILONOUS: And are not you too of opinion, that God knew all things from eternity?
>
> HYLAS: I am.
>
> PHILONOUS: Consequently they always had a being in the Divine Intellect.
>
> HYLAS: This I acknowledge.
>
> PHILONOUS: By your own confession therefore, nothing is new, or begins to be, in respect of the mind of God. So we are agreed in that point. (Berkeley 1948–57, 2:253)

However, one might think that Hylas has given in too easily. If the eternal existence of matter is a problem, then the eternal existence of objects ought also to be a problem.

Berkeley has a way out of this problem by noting a crucial difference between co-eternal (with God) matter and co-eternal objects or ideas. The former would have *absolute* real existence, and it is this that he really opposes and finds objectionable about matter. That is, matter would exist and its existence would be wholly unconnected to God and to God's ideas or thoughts in the following sense: matter would exist at all momemts God exists, and would exist at every one of those moments even if God

---

4. Berkeley speaks of matter being co-eternal with God in *Principles* 92.

were to have no thought of it. But this is not true of co-eternal objects or ideas.

> By what we have premised, it is plain that very numerous and important errors have taken their rise from those false principles, which were impugned in the foregoing parts of this treatise. . . . Particularly, *matter* or the *absolute existence of corporeal objects*, hath been shewn to be that wherein the most avowed and pernicious enemies of all knowledge . . . have ever placed their chief strength and confidence. (Berkeley 1948–57, 2:133)

In this sense the existence of matter is not sustained by God. It is this that Berkeley finds problematic about matter, and not the fact that it would exist eternally. Co-eternal objects would not be subject to this criticism, because they would exist at all moments as ideas in God's mind.

The second point we might derive from Berkeley's comments on creation concerns the fact that objects would exist prior to creation, as ideas in God's mind, but they would not then be perceived. This point, certainly, does impinge directly on the actual perception version of EIP. We should ask, however, why we should think that these objects would not be perceived. True, they would not be perceived by finite spirits, and so would not be perceived by sense. But, as we have seen, God's perception is different from that of finite spirits in precisely this way. Hence, the real point behind this objection can only be that God does not really perceive at all; that is why objects would exist unperceived prior to the creation. Once we see this, however, we notice that this objection is simply a version of the criticism considered earlier, viz., the criticism that Berkeley's God does not perceive. This contention, we found, turns on the fact that God's perception is different from that in finite spirits, a fact which may be granted, but which is by itself insufficient to establish that God does not perceive.

The third point raised by Berkeley in his creation comments concerns relative or conditional existence. This does seem at odds with the actual perception version of EIP. To see if it is, we need to be clear about conditional existence. Berkeley himself expresses the relevant conditional for us:

> Were I (someone) to have been present at the creation, I (someone) would have perceived objects "produced into being." (Berkeley 1948–57, 2:251)

This conditional seems to allow objects to exist unperceived. For it allows objects to be produced into being even if nobody were present to perceive them.

However, I do not think that Berkeley's endorsement of this conditional causes any trouble for the actual perception version of EIP. Endorsement of this conditional is not the same as claiming that the truth of the conditional is by itself sufficient for the objects brought into being to exist. To see this point, we can compare what Berkeley says with John Stuart Mill's famous view of objects as "permanent possibilities of sensations." In Mill's view, an object such as a chair exists if and only if either certain sensations are actually had, or such sensations would be had were certain conditions to obtain. So, an object exists when no sensations are actually had just in case relevant sensations would be had were certain conditions to obtain. Hence, for Mill, that certain sensations would be had were certain conditions to obtain is both a necessary and sufficient condition for existence of an object in a case when no sensations are actually had. Thus, for Mill, the truth of a conditional such as,

> Were certain conditions to obtain, then such and such sensations would be had.

is in some cases sufficient for the truth of a statement such as is expressed by "There is a chair in the room." However, Berkeley is not endorsing a view like this. For in the envisioned circumstance, when the chair is not perceived by any finite spirit, Berkeley (but not Mill) maintains that the chair is perceived by God. So, although for Berkeley the relevant conditional is true ("Were someone to have been present at the creation, he would have perceived objects produced into being"), this fact does suffice to underwrite the existence of the objects then produced into being. Unlike Mill, Berkeley's God perceives these objects all along from eternity. So, the creation comments in the third *Dialogue* generate no special problem for the actual perception version of EIP.

In sum we have uncovered no reason to switch to the disjunctive version of EIP, since the most important pieces of evidence supporting that reading have not been found compelling. In particular, nothing in the comments Berkeley makes about creation counts decisively against the actual perception version of EIP. Moreover, there is an additional point favoring the actual perception version. All of the arguments Berkeley gives *for* the EIP principle are arguments that support the actual perception version. It would be decidedly odd to argue, in several different ways, for a conclusion one does not hold.

Arguments for EIP

Berkeley has four arguments for the EIP principle that are all to be found in the *Principles*. The fourth of these, the so-called master argument, is also stated in the *Three Dialogues*.

The first argument occurs in the first three sections of the *Principles.* Two of the ingredients of this argument are supplied by section 1, where Berkeley gives two different ways of thinking about objects. In the first statement, an object is a "collection" of qualities; in the second, an object is a "collection" of ideas.

> A certain colour, taste, smell, figure and consistence having been observed to go together, are accounted one distinct thing, signified by the name *apple.* Other collections of ideas constitute a stone, a tree, a book, and the like sensible things; which, as they are pleasing or disagreeable, excite the passions of love, hatred, joy, grief, and so forth. (Berkeley 1948–57, 2:41)

Then, in section 2 Berkeley notes for the first time that "the existence of an idea consists in being perceived." In section 3, he says that,

> That neither our thoughts, nor passions, nor ideas formed by the imagination, exist without the mind, is what every body will allow. And it seems no less evident that the various sensations or ideas imprinted on the sense, however blended or combined together (that is, whatever objects they compose) cannot exist otherwise than in a mind perceiving them.
>
> . . . as to what is said of the absolute existence of unthinking things without any relation to their being perceived, that seems perfectly unintelligible. Their *esse* is *percipi,* nor is it possible they should have any existence, out of the mind or thinking things which perceive them. (Berkeley 1948–57, 2:42)

Section 1, quoted first, makes reference to objects as collections in two different ways, in terms of qualities and then as ideas. The clear presumption is that Berkeley thinks of qualities as ideas. It is clear from section 2 that he holds that no idea exists unperceived, or without the mind; and then section 3 finds him extending this same conclusion to the objects which are made up of collections of these ideas. The argument overall can be given this way:

(1) Each sensible quality is an idea.
(2) Each sensible object is a collection of sensible qualities.
(3) Hence, each sensible object is a collection of ideas.
(4) No idea exists unperceived, without the mind.
(5) Hence, no sensible object exists unperceived, without the mind.

Of course, from premises (1) and (4) one can also infer that no sensible quality exists unperceived, or without the mind. This statement, together with (3) and (5), make up what we have stated as EIP. In the very sections from which this argument is taken, however, Berkeley gives no argument whatever for premises (1) and (2), and these are important omissions. Certainly neither of those premises is a necessary nor an obvious truth.

Something of an argument for premise (1) is given in section 10; it utilizes what we have called (in chapter 3) the No Separation Principle. It also utilizes a statement Berkeley must suppose that everyone would accept, namely, that secondary qualities exist only in the mind. Here is what he says in section 10:

> They who assert that figure, motion, and the rest of the primary or original qualities do exist without the mind, in unthinking substances, do at the same time acknowledge that colours, sounds, heat, cold, and such like secondary qualities, do not, which they tell us are sensations existing in the mind alone, that depend on and are occasioned by the different size, texture and motion of the minute particles of matter. . . . Now if it be certain, that those original qualities are inseparably united with the other sensible qualities, and not, even in thought, capable of being abstracted from them, it plainly follows that they exist only in the mind. (Berkeley 1948–57, 2:45)

The argument here can be read in two ways: first, the assumption Berkeley takes as uncontroversial might be that secondary qualities exist only in the mind; the second would say instead that secondary qualities are sensations (or ideas). In these opening sections, though, Berkeley treats these as equivalent. Having noted this, we can state his argument for premise (1):

(a) Secondary qualities are sensations (ideas).
(b) The primary, original qualities cannot be separated from the secondary qualities.
(c) Hence, each primary quality has the same status as the secondary qualities, viz., it is an idea.

If we then take for granted that the primary and secondary qualities make up all of the sensible qualities, an assumption we may safely suppose Berkeley would make, then from (c) and this assumption we may derive premise (1)—that each sensible quality is an idea.

This method of arguing for premise (1), however, suffers from the drawback that (a) was not likely to have been taken as uncontroversial. Locke, for example, would not have accepted (a), since Locke's official view is that secondary qualities are powers existing in bodies. Ideas *of* secondary qualities, for Locke, are things which exist only in the mind, of course, but the secondary qualities themselves do not. Now it is part of Berkeley's argument in section 10 to claim that (a) is widely shared and uncontroversial. Since that is not true, this case for premise (1) in his argument for the EIP principle does not have much force.

We can find a different argument for premise (1) in sections 11 and 14. In those sections he notes that philosophers have used arguments from perceptual relativity to establish that some qualities do not exist in bodies, but rather exist only in the mind. Then he points out that these same arguments can be extended to all other sensible qualities. Here is part of section 14:

> I shall farther add, that after the same manner, as modern philosophers prove certain sensible qualities to have no existence in matter, or without the mind, the same thing may be likewise proved of all other sensible qualities whatsoever. Thus, for instance, it is said that heat and cold are affections only of the mind, and not at all patterns of real beings, existing in the corporeal substances which excite them, for that the same body which appears cold to one hand, seems warm to another. Now why may we not as well argue that figure and extension are not patterns or resemblances of qualities existing in matter, because to the same eye at different stations, or eyes of a different texture at the same station, they appear various, and cannot therefore be the images of any thing settled and determinate without the mind?

Strictly, Berkeley is talking about the thesis that ideas are sometimes copies of qualities in bodies. But the argument he gives supports the claim that each sensible quality is an idea, which is premise (1).

In this argument, too, Berkeley is assuming that relativity arguments were widely used and endorsed as a means to establishing that secondary qualities exist only in the mind or as ideas. And again one might question whether this is really so. Moreover, even if philosophers did argue this by way of relativity arguments, one might question whether such arguments succeed, as does Berkeley in the very next section, thereby undermining the argument he provides for premise (1). That is, in section 15, Berkeley holds that relativity arguments do not suffice to establish that qualities exist only in the mind, but only support the epistemic point that we cannot tell by sense which qualities are really in bodies.

> Though it must be confessed this method of arguing doth not so much prove that there is no extension or colour in an outward object, as that we do not know by sense which is the true extension or colour of the object. (Berkeley 1948–57, 2:47)

Berkeley probably realized that he had not adequately supported premise (1), and so he devoted a good bit of the first *Dialogue* to arguments for just this claim. Interestingly, he reverts to perceptual relativity arguments for this end, the very sort of argument whose effectiveness for this purpose he had disparaged just three years earlier.[5]

Even if a case for premise (1) can be made, there is still premise (2) to consider. This, too, is a premise he does not argue for in the statement of the argument for the EIP principle in the first few sections of the *Principles*. However, an argument for something akin to premise (2) does surface later in section 7. This argument, which itself presumes the truth of premise (1), is indicated by these remarks:

> From what has been said, it follows, there is not any other substance than *spirit*, or that which perceives. But for the fuller proof of this point, let it be considered, the sensible qualities are colour, figure, motion, smell, taste, and such like, that is, the ideas perceived by sense. Now for an idea to exist in an unperceiving thing, is a manifest contradiction; for to have an idea is all one as to perceive: that therefore wherein colour, figure, and the like qualities exist, must perceive them; hence it is clear there can be no unthinking substance or *substratum* of those ideas. (Berkeley 1948–57, 2:43–44)

Part of the argument, then, is this:

(d) Each sensible quality is an idea. (= premise (1)).
(e) Ideas exist only in the mind.
(f) Thus, sensible qualities exist only in the mind.
(g) Hence, sensible qualities do not exist in an external substratum.

This is as far as *Principles* 7 will take the argument. However, from (g) Berkeley can immediately derive:

(h) Objects do not consist in qualities inherent in a substratum.

If (h) is true, Berkeley would likely feel there is nothing left as an option but to identify objects with the groups of qualities. So, given (h) Berkeley may reach premise (2) by elimination.[6]

Before commenting further on this argument, it will be helpful to consider Berkeley's second argument for the EIP principle. This argument is presented in section 4, which I here quote in full:

> It is indeed an opinion strangely prevailing amongst men, that houses, mountains, rivers, and in a word all sensible objects have an existence nat-

---

5. Winkler 1989 has a good discussion of *Principles* 15, on 172ff.
6. I take Berkeley to regard premise (4)—No *idea* exists unperceived, without the mind—as uncontroversially and probably necessarily true.

ural or real, distinct from their being perceived by the understanding. But with how great an assurance and acquiescience soever this principle may be entertained in the world; yet whoever shall find in his heart to call it in question, may, if I mistake not, perceive it to involve a manifest contradiction. For what are the forementioned objects but the things we perceive by sense, and what do we perceive by sense besides our own ideas or sensations; and is it not plainly repugnant that any one of these or any combination of them should exist unperceived? (Berkeley 1948–57, 2:42)

This argument stresses what is sensed or perceived in a way that the first argument did not, and it has a bold simplicity:

(6) Sensible objects are perceived by sense.
(7) Things perceived by sense are ideas.
(8) No idea can exist unperceived.
(9) Hence, no sensible object exists unperceived.

This argument makes no mention of sensible qualities, but we may presume that Berkeley thought he had covered that topic in the first argument and in the support he thought he could muster for its premise (1).

In what sense are sensible objects really ideas? Berkeley sometimes writes as if sensible objects are *single* ideas, as here in section 4. However, I doubt this can be his real meaning. Single ideas are in a single individual's mind; but Berkeley is clear that he does not mean that an object exists, or is perceived by, an *individual* mind. Recall section 48:

Wherever bodies are said to have no existence without the mind, I would not be understood to mean this or that particular mind, but all minds whatever. (Berkeley 1948–57, 2:61)

He thus must mean that objects are ideas in the sense that they are groups or collections of ideas. In that case, this account from what is perceived is really a variant of the first argument, since it will presuppose that argument's premises (1) and (2), in order to reach the conclusion that objects are collections of ideas. So, we can refer to both of these arguments for the EIP principle as the *collections arguments*.

The conclusion of neither of the collections arguments is stated in a modal form as "No sensible object can exist unperceived." For Berkeley in section 4 does not say that the statement expressed by "Some sensible object exists unperceived" is *itself* a contradiction. Instead, he says that it *involves* a contradiction, a comment he makes at a number of other points. What contradiction would it involve? I think he has in mind that it is a contradiction to assert that "Some idea exists unperceived." Recall the last line of section 4: "What do we perceive but our own ideas or sensations, and is it not plainly repugnant that any one of these or any combination of them should exist unperceived?" Objects existing unperceived involves a contradiction, because objects are groups of ideas and ideas cannot exist unperceived.

Berkeley *may* think that more is involved, for he does say in this last part of section 4 that it is repugnant that any idea *or any combination of them* (i.e., an object) should exist unperceived. Further, in section # 3 where he states the conclusion of the first collections argument, a similar point is made though in different language:

> Their (unthinking things) *esse* is *percipi*, nor is it possible they should have any existence, out of the minds or thinking things which perceive them. (Berkeley 1948–57, 2:42)

So, it looks as if Berkeley thought he was entitled to the stronger conclusion; that is, he felt entitled to conclude not merely that a contradiction is *involved* in asserting that it is impossible that objects should exist unperceived, but rather that this assertion *is* a contradiction. Indeed, it is likely that he thought that both collections arguments suffice to establish that strong conclusion.

But I do not think he is entitled to claim that it is impossible for sensible objects to exist unperceived. Both collections arguments make use of clearly contingent premises, and in each case these contingent premises are essential to the argument. Each uses the premise, for example, that each sensible quality is an idea, and we have seen that this claim is supported by resort to perceptual relativity arguments. These are one and all *a posteriori* arguments, and they support only the conclusion that it is true that sensible qualities are ideas. Hence, the claim that objects are collections of ideas is itself not shown by Berkeley to be anything but a contingent truth. And this fact suffices to establish that the main conclusion of the two collections arguments is not shown to be a necessary truth, even if both arguments are sound.

Another way to see the error in both of the collections arguments, insofar as each is held to establish the strong conclusion that the denial of EIP is contradictory, is to notice what would drive that argument. We can illustrate just for the case of sensible objects in which the key element is this sub-argument:

(10) Sensible objects are collections of ideas.
(11) No idea can exist unperceived.
(12) Hence, no sensible object can exist unperceived.

It is assumed that the 'can' in both (11) and (12) is expressive of a conceptual point.

Statement (10) is surely not a necessary truth, even if it is true; and, its terms, 'sensible objects,' and 'collections of ideas,' are not rigid designators in Saul Kripke's sense. That is, these are not terms that pick out the same objects in all possible worlds. Hence, from the fact that it is true of ideas that no single idea can exist unperceived, we cannot derive that the same holds for the sensible objects that are collections of ideas. A similar criticism applies to Berkeley's inference that no sensible quality *can* exist unperceived, from the premises that each sensible quality is an idea, and no idea can exist unperceived. The premise that each sensible quality is an idea is at best contingently true, and its terms do not rigidly designate. So, it does not follow that it is a necessary truth that sensible qualities exist only if they are perceived.

This objection to the collections arguments, if successful, shows only that those arguments fail to establish the EIP principle as a necessary truth. That is perfectly compatible with the claim that Berkeley himself thought that those two arguments *did* establish that EIP is necessarily true. There is no evidence that Berkeley was aware of this error in the collections arguments. However, in other places Berkeley seems to be of two minds about this matter, sometimes saying that the denial of EIP is without meaning, rather than that it is a contradiction. To further investigate why he says such things, it will prove helpful to examine the third argument, what I will call the *meaning argument*, as it is given in section 3.

> It seems no less evident that the various sensations or ideas imprinted on the sense, however blended or combined together (that is, whatever objects they compose) cannot exist otherwise than in a mind perceiving them. I think an intuitive knowledge may be obtained of this, by any one that shall attend to what is meant by the term *exist* when applied to sensible things. The table I write on, I say, exists, that is, I see it and feel it; and if I were out of my study I should say it existed, meaning thereby that if I was in my study I might perceive it, or that some other spirit actually does perceive it. There was an odour, that is, it was smelled; there was a sound, that is to say, it was heard; a colour or figure, and it was perceived by sight or touch. This is all that I can understand by these and the like expressions. For as to what is said of the absolute existence of unthinking things without any relation to their being perceived, that seems perfectly unintelligible. Their *esse* is *percipi*, nor is it possible they should have any existence, out of the minds or thinking things which perceive them. (Berkeley 1948–57, 2:42)

In this passage, parts of which have already been quoted in connection with the first collections argument, Berkeley states the overall conclusion in two different ways. On the one hand, he says that it is impossible for sensible things to exist unperceived or without the mind. However, second, he also says that the supposition that sensible things exist without the mind is *unintelligible*. These are importantly different conclusions, and it is not obvious which Berkeley wishes to endorse.

One might think that this question can be readily resolved. After all, Berkeley often says that it is not possible for sensible objects to exist unperceived. Or, he says something which entails this, such as that it is a contradiction to think that objects exist unperceived, or that it is a manifest repugnancy, a term he used for a clear contradiction. In section 48 of the *Principles* Berkeley says that

> we hold indeed the objects of sense to be nothing else but ideas which cannot exist unperceived. (Berkeley 1948–57, 2:61)

In section 56 he says that the supposition of ideas or objects existing unperceived has a contradiction "involved in those words," and in section 91 he says that unthinking things perceived "have no existence distinct from being perceived, and cannot therefore exist in any other substance, than those unextended, indivisible substances, or *spirits*, which act, and think, and perceive them." (pp. 80–81).[7] So, there is ample textual evidence that Berkeley holds that sensible things *cannot* exist unperceived. This is tantamount to saying that by his lights, the EIP principle is a necessary truth.[8]

However, these passages do not settle the question. There are also some passages where Berkeley says either that the denial of EIP is unintelligible or meaningless, or he states a disjunction: either the denial of EIP is a contradiction or it is meaningless. Unintelligibility, or lack of meaning, is mentioned early on at section 6 of the *Principles* where, speaking of the "bodies which compose the mighty frame of the world," he says further,

> it being perfectly unintelligible and involving all the absurdity of abstraction, to attribute to any single part of them an existence independent of spirit.

The same point is made in section 45:

> If he can conceive it possible either for his ideas or their archetypes to exist without being perceived, then I give up the cause: but if he cannot, he will acknowledge it is unreasonable for him to stand up in defence of he knows

---

7. In the first of the *Three Dialogues*, Berkeley speaks of individual qualities as things that cannot exist without the mind, Berkeley 1948–57, 2:181.

8. Other passages where this point comes up are in *Principles* 15 and in the *Dialogues*, Berkeley 1948–57, 2:212, 230, 236, 244.

not what, and pretend to charge on me as an absurdity, the not assenting to those propositions which at bottom have no meaning in them.

In other places Berkeley states a disjunction: either the denial of the EIP principle is a contradiction or it has no meaning. Following the presentation of the master argument in sections 22 and 23, he says in 24:

> It is very obvious, upon the least inquiry into our own thoughts, to know whether it be possible for us to understand what is meant, by the *absolute existence of sensible objects in themselves, or without the mind*. To me it is evident those words mark out either a direct contradiction, or else nothing at all. (Berkeley 1948–57, 2:43, 59, 51)

The same point is repeated twice in the next few lines of that section. A similar disjunctive statement appears in section 54, though there with respect to both the existence of objects without the mind and with regard to matter. (Berkeley 1948–57, 2:64).

If we insist that Berkeley means only to be saying that the denial of EIP is a contradiction, then we have no ready explanation for why he does not always say that, and why he states his case disjunctively in a number of places. The same applies if we insist that his real meaning is just that the denial of EIP is without any meaning. In that case we would lack any explanation of why he says the the denial is a contradiction.

We could say, based on the last-quoted passages, that Berkeley is unsure of his own meaning, perhaps because he has a shaky grasp of the modalities, and that is why he expresses himself differently and sometimes with a disjunction. Or we could say that he just confuses the two notions (contradictoriness and meaninglessness) and mistakenly believes they come to the same thing. Then his disjunctions as in the above-quoted passage would be read as simply alternating two expressions for the same thing.

Neither of these accounts is plausible. To see why, we need only note that Berkeley is well aware of the difference between contradiction and lack of meaning, and so he neither confuses the two notions nor treats them as the same. This comes up graphically in the discussion of matter at the end of the second *Dialogue*, and is worth quoting fully.

> HYLAS: But I am not so thoroughly satisfied that you have proved the impossibility of matter in the last most obscure abstracted and indefinite sense.
>
> PHILONOUS: When is a thing shewn to be impossible?

HYLAS: When a repugnancy is demonstrated between the ideas comprehended in its definition.

PHILONOUS: But where there are no ideas, there no repugnancy can be demonstrated between ideas.

HYLAS: I agree with you.

PHILONOUS: Now in that which you call the obscure indefinite sense of the word *matter,* it is plain, by your own confession, there was included no idea at all, no sense except an unknown sense, which is the same thing as none. You are not therefore to expect I should prove a repugnancy between ideas where there are no ideas; or the impossibility of matter taken in an *unknown* sense, that is no sense at all. My business was only to show you meant *nothing*; and this you were brought to own. So that in all your various senses, you have been shewed either to mean nothing at all, or if anything, an absurdity. (Berkeley 1948–57, 2:225–26)

From this passage, it is clear that Berkeley is aware of and sensitive to the difference between a contradiction and a lack of meaning. The fact that he is talking of matter rather than the EIP principle does not affect the point.

Given this awareness on his part, it is natural to think that when Berkeley states his point variably or disjunctively, he is saying that one or the other of these is the case depending on certain other factors, or depending on how one conceives of certain things. This would be an exact parallel to how he reasons on the question of matter. Under some ways of understanding what matter is, he holds it to be contradictory; on others, including the "obscure indefinite sense" of that term he refers to in the above passage, his point would be instead that the word 'matter' has no meaning. I think Berkeley has the same sort of thought about the concept of existence. In one way of thinking about existence, the EIP principle will come out as a necessary truth because its denial will be a necessary falsehood. In another way of thinking about existence, the denial of the EIP principle will lack meaning and thus be unintelligible.

We start with the first of these two conceptions of existence. The key to understanding what Berkeley is maintaining is to notice how he has characterized a contradiction in the passage quoted above. It is a repugnancy between two ideas, as one might have with the assertion "This object is both square and round." For a repugnancy of this sort to obtain, there have to be two conflicting ideas, that of square shape and that of round shape. Thus, if the denial of EIP is a contradiction, it will be because there is a repugnancy between two ideas. Which ideas might these be? One of them, certainly, will be the idea of existence. However, as we saw in chapter 4, Berkeley holds that there is no such idea, contrary to what Locke had claimed. Thus, Berkeley's point in saying that the denial of EIP is a contradiction has to be something like this: *If* we think of existence in a certain way, namely as something about which we can have ideas, *then* the denial of EIP is a contradiction. That is, if we think of existence along Lockean lines, then the denial of EIP is a contradiction.

We can see why Berkeley would have held this. If there is an idea of existence of the sort Locke described, one which is a simple and original idea, then it will "conform to" some feature of reality, doubtless a feature in most cases of bodies. This is a simple application of what Locke tells us about the *reality* of all simple ideas. However, as we know from the discussion of abstract ideas of type I, Berkeley holds that the features of bodies cannot be separated, either in reality or in thought; they are all "blended together," as he sometimes says. Thus, by invoking the No Separation Principle, Berkeley would argue that it is impossible to separate existence from the other features of bodies with which it is "blended" together in bodies. Thought of in this way, existence is inseparable from other features of bodies, just as a determinate color is inseparable from some shape. As one cannot have an idea of just some determinate color (recall the discussion of type I abstract ideas in chapter 3), so one cannot have an idea of existence distinct from or separated from the idea of perception. One cannot separate in idea what is not separable in reality. Thus, *provided that we think of existence in this Lockean way*, existence is not separable from perception, and the denial of the EIP principle is necessarily false. Hence, EIP comes out as a necessary truth.

However, Berkeley thinks that this is *not* the right way to think of existence. He denies that we have an idea of existence, whether simple or not, and denies, too, that we have an abstract idea of existence. The correct view of existence holds that existence is not a quality or feature of bodies or of any other part of reality and that we have no idea of existence. Hence, the question of whether existence can or cannot be separated from other features of bodies, or whether the idea of existence can be separated in thought from other ideas, cannot be sensibly raised, for there is nothing there to even count as a candidate for separation. Hence, Berkeley does not conclude, given *his own view of existence*, that the denial of EIP is necessarily false or a contradiction, but rather that we cannot assign a meaning to the denial of EIP. This is because there is no idea of existence.

The parallel with what Berkeley says about material substance is very close. In that case, too, he sometimes says that the concept of matter is repugnant or contradictory. At other points he says instead that the concept of matter is without meaning or empty, and sometimes, as in the passages quoted above, he gives a disjunction: either that concept is repugnant or it is empty and without content or meaning. As we have noted, Berkeley himself is quite explicit on why he says different things about the concept of matter. On one understanding of that concept, namely as a substratum of qualities, he holds matter to be repugnant, and so matter is impossible; it cannot exist. On another understanding of that concept, namely as an obscure, indefinite cause of our ideas, he holds that the concept of matter is without meaning, because we have no idea or notion of this concept. On the reading given above, Berkeley has very much the same divided strategy with regard to existence and the EIP principle. In one understanding of the concept of existence, the denial of EIP is a contradiction. In the other, correct Berkeleyan understanding of the concept of existence, the denial of EIP is empty and without meaning.

Now we can go back to the two collections arguments. Berkeley does not notice the error in those arguments diagnosed above, i.e., the error of thinking that what holds true of ideas must also hold true of sensible qualities and sensible bodies because they are ideas. Given those arguments, he feels entitled to conclude, that the denial of EIP cannot be true, and thus that nothing sensible can exist when not perceived. But even early on in the *Principles* he is aware that he is not really entitled to make this strong claim, given his own way of thinking of existence. This is why I am suggesting he makes the remark about unintelligibility in section 3. It is further noteworthy that he makes this remark in the conclusion of the meaning argument, the very place where one would most expect Berkeley to conclude that the denial of EIP is impossible.[9]

The remaining major argument Berkeley gives for the EIP principle is the master argument of sections 22–23. Before turning to the discussion of that argument, however, we turn to two broad interpretations of Berkeley, the adverbial account of Berkeleyan ideas, and the inherence account of ideas. These are taken up first, because each promises to show how the EIP principle comes out as a necessary truth after all.

Two Interpretations of Ideas

The adverbial view of Berkeleyan ideas, or more strictly the ideas of sense, changes what has been the usual interpretation of these items. In the latter view, sensible ideas are objects of some sort, perhaps images, which themselves have phenomenal qualities such as determinate color. It also assimilates the usual act-object model from ordinary discourse for purposes of describing or expressing our mode of awareness of sensible ideas. In saying that someone sees the chair across the room, we typically

9. I do not mean to suggest that Berkeley lost confidence in his collections arguments.

distinguish the act or event of seeing from the object seen, in this case, the chair. So also with Berkeley on the usual interpretation. The event or act of immediately perceiving is one thing, which is to be distinguished from the object of this event or act, namely a sensible idea. The act-object model, familiar from ordinary perceptual discourse, is also used in Berkeley's account of our perceptual awareness of sensible ideas.

The adverbial view of sensible ideas denies that ideas are objects of perceptual awareness, and it also rejects the act-object model as an account of Berkeley's talk of immediately perceiving ideas. Instead, according to this interpretation, sensible ideas are events (or states) of sensing. When Berkeley talks of immediately perceiving a red idea, or an idea of red, the adverbial view takes this to be sensing in a certain manner, or just (in Roderick Chisholm's way of putting it) sensing red-ly. The term 'red-ly' functions as an adverb modifying the perceptual verb 'senses.' Since ideas, in this view, are events of sensing, they are not objects of which we are aware, and neither do they have phenomenal qualities such as determinate color or shape.[10]

There is some textual support for the adverbial account of sensible ideas. George Pitcher cites the exchange in the *Dialogues* where Berkeley seems to reject, or to collapse, the act-object model as it would apply to ideas. Hylas says, initially,

> To return then to your distinction between *sensation* and *object*; if I take you right, you distinguish in every perception two things, the one an action of the mind, the other not.

To this, after some discussion, Philonous says that,

> Since therefore you are in the very perception of light and colours altogether passive, what is become of that action you were speaking of, as an ingredient in every perception? (Berkeley 1948–57, 2:195, 197)

There are also some passages in the *Philosophical Commentaries* that Pitcher brings up:

> . . . . wherein I pray you does the perception of white differ from white. (entry 585)

> The distinguishing betwixt an idea and perception of the idea has been one great cause of imagining material substances. (Berkeley 1948–57, 1:73, 75) (entry 609)

10. Defenders of this adverbial account of Berkeleyan ideas include George Pitcher (1969) and Philip Cummins (1975, 55–72). See, too, Alan and David Hausman 1995, 60–62.

These passages, Pitcher claims, show that Berkeley subscribes to proposition C, which is,

> C The alleged distinction between (I) the perceiving of an idea and (ii) the idea perceived, is a bogus one; there is no such distinction.[11]

Pitcher does not deny that there is plenty of textual support for treating sensible ideas as objects, and for thinking we should understand immediate perception of sensible ideas by means of the act-object model. However, he argues that the adverbial account helps us to make sense of the fact that Berkeley regards it as a necessary truth that an idea exists if and only if it is perceived. Suitably recast so that the verb 'perceives' is not used (the use of 'perceives' here presumes the act-object model) we would have "Necessarily, each sensible idea exists if and only if it exists in the mind." An event of sensing *cannot* exist apart from a sensing agent. Hence, a premise which we have seen is needed in both versions of collections arguments is nicely underwritten by the adverbial account. Indeed, the account explains why Berkeley felt so confident that this premise expresses a conceptual truth.

The passages from the *Commentaries*, it seems to me, do support the adverbial view. However, I think the supposed collapse of the act-object model in the *Dialogues* passage is overblown. Berkeley's concern there is not to dispute that model, but rather to distinguish between the mind's being active in perception and the mind's being passive. Consider, again, the very part of the exchange quoted by Pitcher:

> Since therefore you are in the very perception of light and colours altogether passive, what is become of that action you were speaking of, as an ingredient in every sensation? (Berkeley 1948–57, 2:197)

Here it is evident that the contrast is between an active and a passive mind in cases of perception. There is no claim that the event of perceiving and the object perceived are identical, and so no claim that the act-object model is being rejected for the perception of ideas. Moreover, a long exchange between Hylas and Philonous on this point stresses the active-passive distinction. Here is another element of that exchange:

PHILONOUS: When is the mind said to be active?

HYLAS: When it produces, puts an end to, or changes any thing.

---

11. G. Pitcher 1969, 198.

PHILONOUS: Can the mind produce, discontinue, or change, any by an act of the will?

HYLAS: It cannot.

PHILONOUS: The mind therefore is to be accounted active in its perceptions, so far forth as volition is included in them.

Philonous then continues by bringing up specific instances of perception, and stresses for each that the mind is passive rather than active. Hence, there is no act-object collapse in these passages from the *Dialogues* since those passages concern another point altogether.

Moreover, there are passages where Berkeley announces his acceptance of a position contrary to the adverbial account.

> This perceiving, active being is what I call *mind, spirit, soul* or *my self.* By which words I do not denote any one of my ideas, but a thing entirely distinct from them, wherein they exist, or, which is the same thing, whereby they are perceived; for the existence of an idea consists in being perceived.

> *Thing* or *being* is the most general name of all, it comprehends under it two kinds entirely distinct and heterogeneous, and which have nothing in common but the name, to wit, *spirits* and *ideas*. The former are *active, indivisible substances*: the latter are *inert, fleeting, dependent beings*, which subsist not by themselves, but are supported by, or exist in minds or spiritual substances. (Berkeley 1948–57, 2:196, 44–42, 79–80)

To his credit, Pitcher notes these passages, as well as several others, all of which indicate Berkeley's acceptance of the act-object model and rejection of Pitcher's statement C. (Pitcher 1969, 198). So, his point is not that the texts decide the case for the adverbial account, because they do not. Rather, his idea is that it is preferable to interpret Berkeley as holding the adverbial account because that account, and perhaps only that account, explains the fact that it is a necessary truth that an idea cannot exist apart from a mind. (Pitcher 1969, 205). Indeed, the act-object model, he says, allows that ideas can exist unperceived. Hence, that model conflicts with Berkeley's premise in the collections arguments to the effect that an idea cannot exist unperceived. Extricating Berkeley from this inconsistency is what is achieved by the adverbial account. (Pitcher 1969, 205).

As has already been indicated, Berkeley was of two minds about the modal status of the EIP principle. I have tried to explain why he sometimes says that this principle is a necessary truth, while at other points he says that its denial has no meaning. So, I do not think the question of inconsistency is troubling if one is thinking of the EIP principle, since, on a certain reading, Berkeley is content to say that it is not a necessary truth. However, he is not content to say that an individual idea can exist apart from a mind. That each individual idea exists only in a mind is, for him, a necessary truth. This claim appears as a premise in both versions of the collections argument, though Berkeley gives no argument in its support.

However, the adverbial account is itself in conflict with other elements of Berkeley's philosophy. In particular, it conflicts with the remarks Berkeley makes in his attack on abstract ideas. There, as we noted in chapter 3, Berkeley takes ideas to be objects with determinate phenomenal content, something they are not if the adverbial theory is the correct interpretation. For adverbial events of sensing do not themselves have determinate phenomenal content. Hence, there is good reason also to resist accepting the adverbial account, since the attack on abstract ideas is of fundamental importance.[12]

An alternative interpretation of Berkeleyan ideas and their relationship to minds is provided by the inherence account. Berkeley acknowledges at *Principles* 91 that all qualities are in need of a "support," and so it follows that all sensible qualities are likewise in need of a support. Traditionally, qualities were said to be supported by substances, where the notion of support was regarded as the special relation of inherence. Accordingly, for Berkeley it is claimed that each sensible quality must inhere in some substance. On this point, Berkeley is made out as accepting the substance-accident model of the Aristotelians and scholastics.[13]

Now Berkeley denies that there are any material substances. Hence, if each sensible quality must inhere in a substance, it would have to inhere in a mental substance, and this the inherence account attributes to Berkeley. Then, since he also held that each sensible quality is an idea, we could also say that according to this account, each sensible idea must inhere in some mental substance. Of course, Berkeley did not hold that sensible qualities (ideas) are qualities *of* a mental substance. In fact, he emphatically rejects such a view as absurd. So, proponents of the inherence account must construe their position in a way that does not saddle Berkeley with the result that some mental substance is red, or bitter, or fragrant, or

12. Other objections to the adverbial view are given in Winkler 1989, chap. 1. Especially important is his point that Berkeley needs ideas as objects in order to explain the content of thought.

13. This interpretation was urged by Edwin Allaire (1963, 229–44) and Philip Cummins (1963, 204–414). It was also defended by Richard Watson (1963, 381–394), and by Alan Hausman (1984, 421–443). I have critically discussed the inherence account in my "Ideas, Minds and Berkeley." (1980, 181–194.) See, too, Muehlmann 1992 for further criticism, and his *Berkeley's Metaphysics*, which contains a useful survey of the topic by Muehlmann and further references.

square-shaped. This is done by noting that Berkeley does not resort to the substance-accident model as an explanation of predication. Instead, it is claimed, he accepted a part-whole model for predication. To say that a die is hard is, on that view, just to say that the sensible quality of hardness is a part of the collection of qualities which makes up the die. Sensible qualities, though inherent in mental substances, are not *parts* of that mental substance, and for that reason Berkeley escapes the absurd result that sensible qualities are qualities of minds.[14]

There is some textual evidence for at least part of the inherence account, because Berkeley does sometimes speak of sensible qualities or sensible ideas needing a support. It comes up four times in the *Principles*, at sections 76, 89, 91, and 135, and Berkeley also *seems* to endorse the view at *Commentaries* # 637 where he says,

> Say you there must be a thinking substance. Something unknown wch perceives & supports & ties together the Ideas. Say I, make it appear there is any need of it & you shall have it for me. I care not to take away any thing I can see the least reason should exist. (Berkeley 1948–57, 1:78)

In the *Dialogues* Berkeley once speaks of minds as the *subjects* of ideas, and in contrasting material and mental substance he says,

> . . . I know what I mean, when I affirm that there is a spiritual substance or support of ideas, that is, that a spirit knows and perceives ideas. But I do not know what is meant, when it is said, that an unperceiving substance hath inherent in it and supports either ideas or the archetypes of ideas. (Berkeley 1948–57, 2:234)

None of these passages actually endorses inherence as what is meant by 'support' so in that sense they do not fully endorse the inherence account. Still, it can be granted that they do provide some evidence for that account.

The inherence account bears on the status of the EIP principle just as the adverbial account does, namely by giving support for the statement that no idea can exist unperceived. In that way, it helps to buttress each of the collections arguments, because each of those arguments has that statement as an essential premise. We can readily see why this buttressing is supplied. On the substance-accident model, it is a conceptual truth that accidents cannot exist apart from substances. A given accident can exist apart from some specific substance, of course, but it cannot exist apart from all substance. If the substance-accident model applies to Berkeleyan

---

14. Defenders of inherence say that Berkeley was forced into these tight quarters by not fully understanding the substance-accident ontology.

minds and ideas, the same conceptual truth will obtain. Sensible ideas, of necessity, will not exist apart from some mind or other. Indeed, Berkeley himself endorses the claim that it is a conceptual truth that accidents require substances, and goes it one further in *Principles* 67.

> It seems no less absurd to suppose a substance without accidents, than it is to suppose accidents without a substance. (Berkeley 1948–57, 2:70)

There is a considerable bit of textual evidence against the inherence account, however. Not insignificant, first, is the fact that Berkeley is sharply critical of the notion of inherence, even to the point of ridiculing that concept in connection with material substance. Hylas suggests that maybe material substance is spread under its accidents, which would be absurd since it would make material substance extended, and that would lead to an infinite regress since the extension of that substance would also need a support. Nor can material substance stand under its accidents, since that too would imply that material substance is extended. In sum, Philonous finds no meaning in the notion of inherence in this context.

> I am not for imposing any sense on your words: you are at liberty to explain them as you please. Only I beseech you, make me understand something by them. You tell me, matter supports or stands under accidents.
>
> How! is it as your legs support your body?
>
> HYLAS: No; that is the literal sense.
>
> PHILONOUS: Pray let me know any sense, literal or not literal, that you understand it in. (Berkeley 1948–57, 2:199)

Since Berkeley finds the notion of inherence without any meaning, it would be quite amazing if he were to adopt it in his account of the relationship of minds to ideas. Hence, even though Berkeley uses the word 'support' in speaking of the relation between minds and ideas, it is doubtful that he means 'inherence' by this word.

Further, Berkeley is quite clear about the relation between minds and ideas; he says that ideas are in minds in the sense that they are perceived by and known by minds. This is precisely what he means by 'support.' This is the point of one of the passages earlier cited in support of the inherence account,

> . . . I know what I mean, when I affirm that there is a spiritual substance or support of ideas, that is, that a spirit knows and perceives ideas. (Berkeley 1948–57, 2:234)

Here his meaning is unmistakable: 'support' means 'is perceived or known by.'

There is also *Principles* 49, where Berkeley explicitly considers the inherence view and rejects it as not his account.

It may perhaps be objected, that if extension and figure exist only in the mind, it follows that the mind is extended and figured; since extension is a mode or attribute, which (to speak with the Schools) is predicated of the subject in which it exists. I answer, those qualities are in the mind only as they are perceived by it, that is, not by way of *mode* or *attribute*, but only by way of *idea*; and it no more follows, that the soul or mind is extended because extension exists in it alone, than it does that it is red or blue, because those colours are on all hands acknowledged to exist in it, and no where else.

The same sentiment is expressed in the *Dialogues*:

It is . . . evident there can be no *substratum* of those qualities but spirit, in which they exist, not by way of mode or property, but as a thing perceived in that which perceives it. (Berkeley 1948–57, 2:61, 237)

In these two passages we have two points being made: first, Berkeley does not think that ideas are in the mind the way modes or attributes are in substances, viz., by inhering; and, second his positive meaning for the term 'in the mind' or 'supported by the mind' is merely 'is perceived or known by the mind.' In short, the inherence account was expressly anticipated by Berkeley as a way his readers might interpret his remarks, and in the passages lately quoted he explicitly takes steps to distance himself from that account, and to indicate another. So, although the inherence account, like the adverbial account, would underpin a crucial premise in the collections arguments, and thus help to support the case for EIP, it is ultimately not acceptable as an interpretation of Berkeleyan minds and ideas.[15]

The Master Argument

The master argument is given at *Principles* 22–23, and then repeated in the first of the *Dialogues*.[16] Here is the passage which sets up the argument:

I am content to put the whole upon this issue: if you can but conceive it possible for one extended movable substance, or in general, for any one

15. The inherence account is discussed further in Colin Turbayne 1982, 295–310.
16. The term 'master argument' comes from Andre Gallois, 1974, 55–69.

idea or anything like an idea, to exist otherwise than in a mind perceiving it, I shall readily give up the cause. And as for all that *compages* of external bodies which you contend for, I shall grant you its existence, though you cannot give me any reason why you believe it exists, or assign any use to it when it is supposed to exist. I say the bare possibility of your opinion's being true, shall pass for an argument that it is so. (Berkeley 1998–57, 2:50)

This passage first seems to say that Berkeley's sole concern is with the mind-dependence of *ideas*; these, he says in the first part of the passage, cannot exist otherwise than in a mind which perceives them. However, later in the passage he makes it clear that his interest is in sensible objects generally, and not just in ideas; this is the import of the phrase " . . . *compages* of external bodies . . . " Granting, then, that he is talking of sensible objects generally, the overall point of the preceding passage is that Berkeley is willing to grant that if one can conceive the possibility of an object (any sensible object) existing unperceived, then such objects do exist unperceived. However, he is confident that one cannot succeed in this conceiving.

But say you, surely there is nothing easier than to imagine trees, for instance, in a park, or books existing in a closet, and no body by to perceive them. I answer, you may so, there is no difficulty in it: but what is all this, I beseech you, more than framing in your mind certain ideas which you call *books* and *trees*, and at the same time omitting to frame the idea of anyone that may perceive them? But do not you your self perceive or think of them all the while? This therefeore is nothing to the purpose; it only shows that you have the power of imagining or forming ideas in your mind, but it doth not show you can conceive it possible, the objects of your thought may exist without the mind: to make out this, it is necessary that you conceive them existing unconceived or unthought of, which is a manifest repugnancy. When we do our utmost to conceive the existence of external bodies, we are all the while only contemplating our own ideas. But the mind taking no notice of itself, is deluded to think it can and does conceive bodies existing unthought of or without the mind; though at the same time they are apprehended by or exist in it self. (Berkeley 1998–57, 2:50–51)

In the first of these passages, Berkeley speaks of conceiving a possibility: conceiving the possibility of a sensible object existing unperceived. If one can do this conceiving, he tells us, he will concede the falsity of the EIP principle. However, as he says in the second passage, we cannot do this conceiving, because to accomplish it we would have to conceive an unperceived but existing sensible object, and this is a manifest repugnancy. We can represent what he is saying in a simple argument, which I will refer to as the *First Version* of the master argument:

(1) If one can conceive the possibility of a sensible object existing unperceived, then the EIP principle is false.

(2) One can conceive the possibility of a sensible object existing unperceived only if one can conceive a sensible object existing unperceived.

(3) One cannot conceive a sensible object existing unperceived.

(4) Hence, one cannot conceive the possibility of a sensible object existing unperceived.

One cannot pass directly from (4) to an affirmation of the EIP principle,
since doing that would be a logical error: (4) is the denial of the antecedent
of (1). The argument can be continued, however, with a premise Berkeley
seems to have accepted, viz.,

(5) If something is inconceivable, then it is impossible.[17]

Now from (4) and (5) we can derive the result that

(6) A sensible object existing unperceived is impossible.[18]

This argument is stated in terms of sensible objects, such as the trees
and books spoken of in the passage quoted from section 23. Presumably a
corresponding argument would apply to sensible ideas and sensible qualities, though as we have seen in the collections arguments, Berkeley does
not think he needs an argument for the case of sensible ideas. Generalizing the argument across all sensible things reaches the conclusion that the
EIP principle is a necessary truth.

Premise (1) is about a certain *de dicto* conception. By speaking of conceiving a possibility, Berkeley is speaking of conceiving that it is possible
that a sensible object exists unperceived. At least this is a natural reading
of those comments. However, when he responds to this point as in
premise (2), he switches to talk of a different sort of conceiving, what we
may think of as a kind of *de re conceiving*. That is, the consequent of (2)
claims that a certain *de re* conceiving (conceiving a sensible object existing
unperceived) is necessary for there to be the relevant *de dicto* conceiving
(conceiving that it is possible that a sensible object exists unperceived).
This same switch occurs in the *Dialogues* version of the argument:

PHILONOUS: . . . I am content to put the whole upon this issue. If you can
conceive it possible for any mixture or combination of qualities, or

17. K. Winkler 1983 discusses this principle, 63–80.
18. The inference here depends on an instantiation of (5), applicable to sensible objects.

any sensible object whatever, to exist without the mind, then I will grant it actually to be so.

HYLAS: If it comes to that, the point will soon be decided. What more easy than to conceive a tree or house existing by itself, independent of, and unperceived by, any mind whatsoever? I do at this present time conceive them existing after that manner.

(Berkeley 1998–57, 2:200)

De re conception of the sort I think Berkeley has in mind can be clarified by contrasting it with *de re* belief. In the latter case, we say that a person believes of some entity E that it is F, or has the property F. John may believe of the man on the corner that he is a famous basketball player. We could have a perfectly analogous notion of *de re* conception. John may conceive of the differential equation currently vexing him that it is of type T. This notion of *de re* conception would perhaps be the natural way of thinking of the concept fully on a par with *de re* belief. But I doubt this is what Berkeley is referring to, because for him there is no predication included within *de re* conceiving. Instead, one is to conceive the object itself. The analogy would be with non-propositional direct perception of an object, as when we say "John perceives O." There the perceptual verb takes a grammatical direct object as complement. The same holds for the sort of *de re* conceiving referred to by Berkeley. One conceives *a sensible object*, rather than conceiving *of some sensible object*, that it has some property. This is non-propositional conceiving or what I call *pure de re* conceiving— said to be pure because there is no predication or propositional content within its scope.

It should go without saying that Berkeley does not talk about conceiving in either a *de dicto* or a *de re* sense. These words never appear in his text. Rather, the interpretive point is that use of these concepts helps to understand what Berkeley is driving at in the master argument when he talks, in quite different ways, of conceiving.

Given this clarification, we can evaluate the argument by looking critically at premise (2). Its antecedent says that a necessary condition for conceiving the possibility of the proposition that a sensible object exists unperceived is that one *purely de re* conceive some sensible object existing unperceived. This seems to be clearly false. We can see this with a different proposition, say, the proposition that there are mermaids. Then the counterpart to the antecedent of (2) would be conceiving or thinking the thought that the proposition expressed by "There are mermaids" is possibly true. To think or conceive that proposition, one need not *purely de re* conceive a mermaid, for the latter seems to require that there be mermaids. More generally, even if one supposed that *de dicto* conceiving requires that one *purely de re* conceive something or other, it will not follow that one must *purely de re* conceive the very content of the proposition one then considers. That would be an intolerable condition on thinking or on *de dicto* conception, as the mermaid example illustrates.[19]

There is another plausible interpretation of Berkeley's meaning in the remarks where he states the master argument. That is, he may be read as saying that the apparent *de dicto* conception just *is* the sort of *pure de re* conceiving we have described. This reading would derive from the fact that Berkeley specifies what one would have to do in order to succeed in the relevant conceiving, namely, engage in *pure de re* conceiving. Given that he says this, as a success condition, it is reasonable to think that he was thinking of *pure de re* conception all along. This interpretation results in a simpler, Second Version, of the master argument:

(1) If one cannot conceive a sensible object existing unperceived, then the EIP principle is true.
(2) One cannot conceive a sensible object existing unperceived.
(3) Thus, the EIP principle is true.

Ultimately, I think, this argument will also fail, but for reasons which differ from that which we found operative in the First Version.

Why can we not conceive a sensible object existing unperceived, as claimed in premise (2)? Berkeley's answer, as given in his statement of the master argument, is that when one tries to accomplish this feat, one is *eo ipso* conceiving that very object. One might wonder why this would matter, since even if conceived, surely the object might still exist unperceived. Berkeley anticipates this response, and rejects it on the ground that by so conceiving the object one is thereby *perceiving* it; hence, it does not exist unperceived. Recall *Principles* 23:

But do not you your self perceive or think of them all the while?

His point, further, is general. He is not talking about himself trying, but failing, to conceive a sensible object existing unperceived. Were anyone to engage in such conceiving, or try to, that person would conceive, and thus perceive, the sensible object in question, and thus fail to conceive it existing unperceived.

This sort of reasoning has seemed to many commentators to be an elementary blunder on Berkeley's part, since it collapses and runs together

19. On this critical point, see Arthur Prior 1955, 117–22, and Ian Tipton 1974, 158ff.

conceiving and perceiving. These two mental operations are surely distinct, even when the former is *pure de re* conceiving; yet, Berkeley treats them as the same. Hence, the Second Version of the master argument fares no better than the first, though the error it makes is different.

I agree that Berkeley is in error on the relationship between conceiving and perceiving, but I think we have not fully uncovered the nature of the error, nor what drove him into it. In order to to see why this is so, we may note that premise (2) does not require anything so wide as the claim that *all* conceiving of sensible objects is perceiving. After all, one can have a *de dicto* conception of an object in which one conceives that some object is behind the opaque wall before one when in fact no such object is behind the wall. Premise (2) needs to be construed as dealing just with *pure de re* conceiving. In that case, Berkeley's defense of the premise rests on the claim that,

(2a) All *pure de re* conception of sensible objects is perception.

Even so, why would Berkeley have accepted (2a), a claim that seems only marginally more plausible than the statement that all conceiving is perceiving? In the *Principles* statement of the master argument, Berkeley says that when one tries to conceive a sensible object existing unperceived, one ends up conceiving one's own ideas. He makes the same point, through Hylas, in the *Dialogues*: "But now I plainly see that all I can do is frame ideas in my own mind. I may indeed conceive in my thoughts the idea of a tree, or a house, or a mountain, but that is all." (Berkeley 1948–57, 2:200). He is claiming that,

(2b) If one has a *pure de re* conception of a sensible object, then one conceives one or more ideas.

Presumably the conceiving of these ideas is also *pure de re* conceiving, for it is this very conceiving which Berkeley regards as perception. Further, if he is to derive (2a) from (2b), Berkeley must think that *pure de re* conceiving of ideas amounts to perceiving those ideas.

This last statement would not be true, however, if the ideas thus conceived were abstract. Attending to abstract ideas, even if the attending is *pure de re* conceiving, is not perceiving. Hence, the assumption that the conceived ideas are not abstract must play a role in this argument. In particular, to derive (2a) from (2b), Berkeley must be assuming that if one *purely de re* conceives some non-abstract ideas, then one perceives those ideas.

Even with (2a) established, however, Berkeley has not done enough to adequately defend premise (2). The argument just given for (2a) shows only that what is perceived is one or more non-abstract ideas. Berkeley's defense of premise (2), however, states that when one *purely de re* conceives a sensible object, then one perceives *that object*, and not merely that one perceives some non-abstract ideas. The desired connection, I believe, is supplied by another of Berkeley's assumptions, and it is here that his real error finally surfaces. We can see what it comes to in some passages from the *Commentaries*:

> Whatsoever has any of our ideas in it must perceive, it being that very having, that passive reception of ideas that denominates the mind perceiving. That being the very essence of perception, or that wherein perception consists.
> Consciousness, perception, existence of Ideas seems to be all one. (Berkeley 1948–57, 1:37, 72)

These passages indicate that Berkeley accepts the claim that,

(2c) To perceive just is to have (non-abstract) ideas.

From (2c), then, he can readily derive that perceiving a sensible object just is having (non-abstract) ideas. From this Berkeley can conclude that *pure de re* conceiving of an object amounts to perception of that object, and this ultimately is his support for the premise that one cannot conceive a sensible object existing unperceived.

Here is the reasoning which encapsulates the defense of premise (2):

(a) If one *purely de re* conceives a sensible object, then one *purely de re* conceives one or more ideas.
(b) If one *purely de re* conceives one or more ideas, and these ideas are not abstract, then one perceives those ideas.
(c) There are no abstract ideas.
(d) Thus, if one *purely de re* conceives a sensible object, then one perceives one or more (non-abstract) ideas.
(e) Perceiving something consists in having (non-abstract) ideas.
(f) Thus, *pure de re* conceiving of a sensible object is perception of that object.

From (f), of course, we can easily derive that one cannot *purely de re* conceive a sensible object existing unperceived, which is pemise (2).

Statement (a) is motivated, as we have seen, by comments explicitly made in Berkeley's statement of the master argument. Certainly Berkeley holds (c), as the analysis of the last two chapters indicates. We have lately noted that there is textual support for attributing (e) to Berkeley. These are the three assumptions on which this reconstruction of Berkeley's case for premise (2) is built, and if the reconstruction is correct, they are the assumptions, too, that underwrite the Second Version of the master argument. Further, we have seen that Berkeley accepts (f); it is endorsed as part of his argument in *Principles* 23. Statement (b) lacks explicit textual support, but in its defense we can at least say that if one were contemplating or attending to abstract ideas, then one would not be perceiving; and we can also say that it is needed as a link which connects other steps all of which are textually supported, namely (a) and (c) through (f). In other words, the case for (b) is not *ad hoc* because everything which motivates its inclusion is explicitly supported in the relevant texts.[20]

This reconstruction applies as well to the First Version of the master argument, despite the different character of that argument. The reason is that the First Version also uses the premise that one cannot conceive a sensible object existing unperceived. Hence, both versions of the master argument considered depend squarely on the three assumptions noted above. In that respect, they are equivalent.

Statement (e) is of special importance in this reconstruction. It is that statement that allows Berkeley to hold that when one *purely de re* conceives a sensible object, one perceives one or more ideas and one's perception of those ideas constitutes perception of the object. This looks like his deepest defense of the premise that one cannot conceive a sensible object existing unperceived. However, this defense has the corresponding critical drawback of making it virtually impossible for Berkeley to distinguish between imagination and perception. After all, one might engage in *pure de re* conception of some ideas in the process of imagining some object. The reasoning reconstructed here, especially with (e), would drive one to the conclusion that in so imagining, one is thereby perceiving that object, certainly an unwelcome result.[21]

Berkeley is aware that (e) is a dubious claim, for elsewhere in the *Commentaries* he says that,

> The having Ideas is not the same thing with Perception. A Man may have Ideas when he only Imagines. But then this Imagination presupposeth Perception. (Berkeley 1998–57, 1:72)

---

20. Recall the discussion of a philosopher being interpreted to hold a proposition, in chapter 1, and the discussion of what a philosopher was committed to. The argument here would be that Berkeley explicitly holds the master argument in something like the forms given here; he holds, too, the defense here provided for a key premise in those arguments; that defense requires premise (b); hence, Berkeley is committed to (b).

21. This point is also made in Ian Tipton 1987, 85–102.

On the other hand, unless he were accepting (e) it is very hard to see why Berkeley would claim *both* that in trying to conceive an object existing unperceived, one ends up perceiving one's own ideas *and* ends up perceiving the object one is trying to conceive.[22]

It may be that we have located the stress in the master argument in the wrong place, and if so Berkeley can avoid the problem of conflating imagination and perception. We have supposed Berkeley to be talking of conceiving an object existing unperceived, and we have found him saying that in trying to do this one perceives it, i.e., perceives that very object, so that one's attempt fails. The conceived object would not be *unperceived.* Perhaps what Berkeley is stressing is the notion of existence, and not that of something being unperceived. So construed, his point would be that one cannot conceive the *existence* of an unperceived object, not because in the attempt to do so one would end up perceiving it by attending to relevant ideas, but rather because one altogether lacks what one needs to be successful in such a conceiving, namely, an idea of existence. In such a reading the Second Version of the master argument would stay the same; however, the support one would find Berkeley giving for its second premise would be different.

The point would be that the only access one has to the existence of a non-perceiver is through perception. One can think of some object, e.g., one's former house in a distant location, but that is not thinking of an *existing* house in a distant place. One is merely thinking of the house. We cannot succeed in thinking of an existing house in that distant location because to do this requires that one has an idea of existence, and there is no such idea. Access to existence is through and only through perception. It is still true, that one cannot conceive an unperceived existent object, but it is not its status as unperceived which does the work, so to speak; it is its status *as existent* that Berkeley finds suspect. Thus, the support for the second premise of the Second Version would be quite simple:

(g) One can conceive a sensible object existing unperceived only if one has an idea of existence.
(h) There is no idea of existence.
(i) Hence, one cannot conceive a sensible object existing unperceived (= premise (2)).

One attraction of this reading is that it does not require Berkeley to make use of (e), a statement Berkeley elsewhere rejects; and neither does it

---

22. Suppose Berkeley were to hold that individual ideas are objects, as he sometimes says, so that perception of the right idea would be perception of an object. This would enable him to derive (f) and thus premise (2); but it would have the same result about the indistinguishability of perception and imagination.

have the consequence that Berkeley cannot sustain a distinction between perceiving and imagining objects. Further, we know that Berkeley accepts (h), and does so on grounds that are independent of the master argument. The textual support for (g), in fact, would be the same passages given in support of the reconstruction contained in (a)–(f), but the interepretation would focus on Berkeley's speaking of an *existing* but unperceived object, rather than an *unperceived* but existing object. Of course, if one objects to the former, one *eo ipso* objects to the latter. What the present reading suggests is just a different reason for that objection.

Abstraction Again

We have found two ways of stating Berkeley's master argument, and in both of them there is the premise that one cannot conceive a sensible object existing unperceived. This is premise (3) in the First Version and premise (2) in the Second. We have now also considered and motivated two different defenses of that premise that Berkeley may have had in mind. The first, via statements (a) through (f), has the unfortunate consequence that Berkeley is left with no adequate way to distinguish between perception and imagination, despite the fact that all three of the assumptions that support this defense are statements made by Berkeley. The second defense proceeds through the claim that in order to conceive a sensible object existing unperceived one would need to have an idea of existence, and there is no such idea. It is in the first defense that Berkeley needs to reject abstract ideas.

Rejection of abstract ideas is explicit in the first defense at statement (c). There, I believe, Berkeley needs to be rejecting all the different types of abstract ideas, that is, types I through IV. In attending to one or more abstract ideas, one is not thereby perceiving those ideas. Perception for Berkeley is always perception of ideas that are determinate and that have some degree of complexity. The former point would mean that attending to abstract ideas of types II and III would not qualify as perception of those ideas, for they would be ideas with merely determinable features. Nor would attending to abstract ideas of types I and IV amount to perceiving them. These are ideas that are determinate, but also simple. The type I abstract idea of determinate red color, for example, is simple in that it is not an idea of a red shape, but merely of determinate red. The type IV abstract idea of existence is similar, at least for Locke, since it is simple as well. Hence, in attending to any one of these abstract ideas one would not be engaging in perception.

Consider perception of an idea of determinate red color. This is always, for Berkeley, an idea of shape as well; there is no idea of merely determinate red color, nor an idea of mere shape of some specific configuration. A visual idea of color is always shaped, too, and a visual idea of a shape always has a color. This is the manner in which such an idea is complex. An abstract idea of mere determinate red, therefore, differs from the sorts of ideas one typically has in visual perception, and so in attending to this abstract idea one would not be perceiving it. An abstract idea of existence has a similar footing; it is a simple idea that, when attended to, would not be perceived, since it there occurs separated from other ideas in a way that never occurs in genuine perception.

It must be granted that this reasoning is a reconstruction, because Berkeley never considers the question of whether attending to abstract ideas constitutes perception of those ideas. This is not surprising, of course, because he holds that there are no abstract ideas of any sort. He would have to consider the counterfactual, "if there had been abstract ideas, attending to them would not constitute perception of them," and there is no textual evidence that I can find which indicates that Berkeley did this. In support of this reconstruction we may note that it is based entirely on points we know Berkeley held concerning ideas and perception, and in that sense it is textually based and motivated. While we do not know whether Berkeley would have drawn the inference from those agreed on points that has been drawn here, viz., that attending to any abstract idea is not perceiving that idea, it is reasonable to think that he would, since he accepted everything from which the inference is based. Insofar as that is true we may say that the master argument for the EIP principle depends on the rejection of abstract ideas including the abstract idea of existence.

These comments apply to the Second Version of the master argument, and then only to the first defense of its second premise. However, these comments are likewise apposite in connection with the First Version, since that argument also makes use of the premise that one cannot conceive a sensible object existing unperceived. Both versions of the master argument, then, via the first defense, would require the rejection of all types of abstract ideas.

Impossible Performances

Supposing that the first defense is Berkeley's support for the key claim that one cannot conceive a sensible object existing unperceived, we may ask what the argument establishes if we suppose it to be sound. What I think it shows is that any attempt to actually conceive a sensible thing existing unperceived is doomed to fail. This sort of conceiving is an impossible performance. The reason is clear from the first defense: the very attempt to engage in this sort of conception guarantees its own failure. The sense of 'guarantees' here is worth notice. The very event or activity of attempting to *purely de re* conceive an unperceived existent sensible thing *just is* the perception of that thing. The attempt, then, is self-defeating. This is because the first defense implies that,

> (2d) If one has a *pure de re* conception of a sensible object, then one perceives one or more ideas, and perception of those ideas constitutes perception of that sensible object.

In fact, given (2d) we can even see why Berkeley speaks of contradictions in this context. Suppose one attempts the relevant conception of a sensible object. Then one would be *purely de re* conceiving an existent sensible object and, *ex hypothesi*, that object is unperceived. But so conceiving that object, given (2d), is perception of that object. The object would thus be perceived and unperceived. Small wonder that Berkeley would speak of contradiction or impossibility in this context.

However, we should notice where the impossibility lies. The proposition expressed by "person S *purely de re* conceives an existent but unperceived sensible object" does not of itself imply a contradiction. Rather, it is the conjunction of this proposition and (2d) that implies a contradiction; hence, this conjunction is inconsistent. From this, of course, we cannot infer that either conjunct is inconsistent. Indeed, we know the contrary. We have noted that the first conjunct does not imply a contradiction, and certainly (2d) is a contingent proposition. Hence, when Berkeley claims that one cannot conceive a sensible object existing unperceived, the term 'cannot' does not have a logical sense but expresses something weaker.

Berkeley provides a clue as to the correct interpretation of that premise in the second of the *Three Dialogues*:

> The things, I say, immediately perceived are ideas, or sensations, call them what you will. But how can any idea or sensation exist in, or be produced by anything but a mind or spirit? This indeed is inconceivable; and to assert that which is inconceivable is to talk nonsense: is it not? (Berkeley 1948–57, 2:215)

Here we see that Berkeley infers lack of meaning or nonsense from inconceivability.[23] If we apply this line of thought to the claim that one cannot

---

23. In this passage Berkeley draws the conclusion regarding lack of meaning from *de dicto* inconceivability; I assume he would do the same with *pure de re* inconceivability.

conceive a sensible thing existing unperceived, then the proposition expressed by "some sensible thing exists unperceived." would be regarded by him as lacking in meaning. This would be the real point expressed by the second premise in the Second Version. We could thus draw the conclusion that this first defense of the master argument, in either version, yields the result that the denial of the EIP principle has no meaning.

Now we can return to the second defense which, we recall, derives inconceivability of a sensible thing existing unperceived from the fact that there is no idea of existence. Here, too, the relevant conceiving amounts to an impossible performance, but for a different reason. Lacking an idea of existence, one lacks the wherewithal by which the conception of a sensible object existing unperceived might be accomplished. Once again we see that this is an action in which one cannot succeed. This is not because the attempt to do the action is self-defeating, but rather because one lacks the means for success in the endeavor.

We noted earlier that faced with a similar position regarding material substance, Berkeley infers that the very concept of material substance is empty or lacking in meaning. Parity would dictate that he do the same in this context. He should conclude that the proposition expressed by "Some sensible object exists unperceived" is meaningless. This result would be mediated by the statement that conceiving a sensible object existing unperceived cannot be accomplished, because one lacks the idea of existence. Here, again, Berkeley would draw the conclusion that the denial of the EIP principle is meaningless from the premise that we cannot conceive a sensible thing existing unperceived. Both defenses of this last statement, then, lead to the same conclusion by different routes. In either defense, the denial of the EIP principle is shown to have no meaning. In that case, the master argument does not suffice to show that the EIP principle is a necessary truth.[24]

It might be wondered, however, how the EIP principle can have a meaning if its denial is meaningless. What, indeed, would the meaning of the principle derive from if, as Berkeley notes, we have no idea of existence? The answer that Berkeley is prepared to give, I believe, is suggested by this passage from *Philosophical Commentaries* 408:

> I must be very particular in explaining what is meant by things existing in Houses, chambers, fields, caves etc when not perceiv'd as well as when Perceived. & show how the Vulgar notion agrees with mine when we Narrowly inspect into the meaning & definition of the word Existence Which

24. These points may be taken to show that there is a notion of inconceivability, used by Berkeley, which does not imply impossibility.

is no simple idea distinct from perceiving and being perceiv'd. (Berkeley, 1948–57, 1:51–52.)

His point is that the word 'existence' does have a meaning, despite the fact that there is no idea of existence for the word to designate. The meaning of 'existence' is given by the term 'perceived.'

Dispensing with Arguments

We have seen that Berkeley gives four arguments for the EIP principle, and the last of these, the master argument, can be read in different ways. But Berkeley sometimes writes as though he regards the EIP principle as an obvious necessary truth, one for which these various arguments are not needed. This is really Berkeley's message in the meaning argument, where he says that we can see that EIP is a necessary truth just by reflecting on the meaning of the word 'exists' as it applies to anything sensible. Sometimes he makes the same point about the obvious, truistic character of the EIP principle, but he states things disjunctively in *Principles* 24.

> It is very obvious, upon the least inquiry into our own thoughts, to know whether it is possible for us to understand what is meant, by the *absolute existence of sensible objects in themselves, or without the mind*. To me it is evident those words mark out either a direct contradiction, or else nothing at all. And to convince others of this, I know no readier or fairer way, than to entreat they would calmly attend to their own thought: and if by this attention, the emptiness or repugnancy of these expressions does appear, surely nothing more is requisite for their conviction. (Berkeley 1948–57, 2:51)

It is striking that Berkeley says that the EIP principle is an obvious truth, maybe even an obvious necessary truth, and that we can discover this by reflective attention of the right sort. By recalling a distinction made earlier in this chapter, I believe we can explain why Berkeley speaks in this manner and why it would have seemed quite plausible, to him, to have done so.

Berkeley thinks he has discovered something quite new about the notion of existence. This is clearly brought out in an entry in the *Commentaries*:

> Mem: Diligently to set forth how that many of the Ancient philosophers run into so great absurditys as even to deny the existence of motion and those other things they perceiv'd actually by their senses. This sprung

from their not knowing w^t existence was and wherein it consisted this the source of all their Folly, 'tis on the Discovering of the nature & meaning & import of Existence that I chiefly insist. This puts a wide difference betwixt the Sceptics & me. This I think wholly new. I am sure 'tis new to me. (Berkeley 1948–57, 1:61–62)

I find two things of importance in this passage: first, there is the claim that something new about the notion of existence has been discovered; but, just as important, there is the point that this discovered fact about existence contrasts with a view of existence attributed to the Sceptics.

Now Berkeley may be referring to actual sceptics such as Montaigne, or even ancient sceptics such as Sextus Empiricus. It is more likely, however, that his reference is to philosophers who do not profess scepticism but whose doctrines, Berkeley thinks, have sceptical consequences. These would include philosophers such as Malebranche and, especially, Locke. Berkeley would thus be saying that in philosophers such as these there is a contrasting understanding of the concept of existence, one that differs from what he has newly discovered.

We have seen how Berkeley construes Locke's thinking on existence. Locke acknowledges an idea of existence, one that is simple and original. This has two important consequences for Berkeley. First, Locke is thereby committed to an abstract idea of existence, since he holds that there is an abstract idea corresponding to each of the simple and original ideas, a point Locke makes in his discussion of nominal essences for simple ideas. Second, given what Locke says about the reality of simple ideas, there is some feature of the world to which all simple ideas conform. Locke would thereby be committed to thinking of existence as a quality, or as some feature of external reality.

If this is how one understands the notion of existence, then Berkeley would say that a moment's reflection suffices to show that the EIP principle is a necessary truth. The qualities of bodies, Berkeley holds, cannot be separated either in reality or in thought. Red color, for instance, cannot be separated from some shape or other. If existence were a simple quality, it, too, would not be separable from other features; it would be subject to the same constraint as other simple qualities. So, if Locke's way of thinking about existence is at issue, a moment's reflection should suffice to convince us that the "quality" of existence cannot be separated from the "quality" of perception, any more than the quality of red color can be separated from shape. Further, given the No Separation Principle, the idea of existence could not be separated from the idea of perception. Hence, the EIP principle would be a necessary truth. Locke's way of construing existence would lead directly to this result; existence and perception would be logically related, something one could come to see by calm reflection on the meaning of the relevant terms.

Suppose, however, that the notion of existence is not as given in Locke, but rather it is thought of along Berkeleyan lines. In that situation, one simply altogether lacks any idea of existence, so that the action of separating one's idea of existence from any other idea simply does not arise. In that sense, such separation is an action one is in no position to carry out. In that case, calm reflection on one's understanding of the term 'existence' or 'exists' will reveal that one has no understanding of this which is separate from the concept of perception. The question of the separation of one's idea of existence from one's idea of perception cannot be sensibly raised. Here, the denial of the EIP principle will appear as a statement that makes no clear sense, because, lacking an idea of existence, one cannot sensibly entertain the thought "some sensible thing exists but is not at all perceived."

These two lines of thought, making use of Berkeley's two ways of thinking about existence, are designed to illuminate why he sometimes says that the status of the EIP principle is quite obvious, something one can divine simply by "sounding one's own thoughts." If he right about this, arguments for the EIP principle are not really needed, strictly speaking, though there is nothing wrong with providing them. A moment's reflection of the right sort will yield an easily knowable result depending on which notion of existence one considers.

CHAPTER 6

Perception

The concept of perception figures prominently in Berkeley well beyond the central role it plays in the EIP (*esse is percipi*) principle. His account of perception is also importantly related to what Berkeley says about scepticism and to his defense of common sense. This is especially true of the concept of immediate perception, and so it will be important to clarify this notion. There is also the vexing question of just what Berkeley regarded as the objects of immediate perception, for without coming to a conclusion about that issue, no special results concerning scepticism and common sense can be reached. Of course, Berkeley accepted a version of the theory of ideas, and so he held that in every perception some ideas are experienced. It might be thought, then, that he also holds that *only* ideas are ever immediately perceived; these would make up the only objects of immediate perception. Physical objects, then, would either be mediately perceived or not perceived at all.

Opposed to this way of thinking about Berkeley's objects of immediate perception is the direct realist, or common sense realist, account of Berkeley, historically associated with the work of Luce and Jessop.[1] In their view, Berkeley holds that physical objects are immediately perceived, and that as a result we often acquire immediate and certain knowledge of the existence and nature of physical objects by immediately perceiving them.

---

1. See A. A. Luce 1963, 1966 and T. E. Jessop 1953. Especially relevant in the latter is Jessop's introductory comments.

Immediate perception of physical objects along with these epistemic contentions would be crucially related to Berkeley's comments on scepticism, and especially to its supposed refutation.

In this chapter and the next, a limited defense of the Luce-Jessop interpretation is proposed and defended. It is limited in that it deals just with the perceptual components of common sense realism. Metaphysical and epistemic elements of common sense realism are taken up later (chapters 7 and 8), as is the question of just how we are to understand the notion of common sense in Berkeley.

Immediate Perception

At one point in the *Dialogues*, Philonous, speaking for Berkeley, asks Hylas:

> Are those things only perceived by the senses which are perceived immediately? Or may those things properly be said to be "sensible" which are perceived mediately, or not without the intervention of others? (Berkeley 1948–57, 2:174)

Two points are raised in this passage: first, is immediate perception the only genuine perception, or is mediate perception genuine as well? This question, on which Berkeley says different things at various points, will be taken up later. For now, the important thing is the other point raised in this passage, namely that mediate perception requires some intermediary item. The presumption then would be that immediate perception would not require such an intermediary.

Berkeley uses exactly this sort of idea in the *New Theory*:

> It is evident that, when the mind perceives any idea not immediately and of itself, it must be by the means of some other idea. . . . [T]he passions which are in the mind of another are of themselves to me invisible, I may nevertheless perceive them by sight; though not immediately yet by means of the colours they produce in the countenance. (Berkeley 1948–57, 1:172–73)

Here the notion of an intermediary is also stressed, and it is clear that it is to be a perceived intermediary. In the passage, colors are taken as the intermediary through which one is said to perceive by sight the passions in another person's mind, and these colors need to be perceived.

This information concerning Berkeley's understanding of mediate perception points the way towards an initial definition of immediate perception: it is that perception which does not require or proceed through a perceived intermediary. If we focus initially on seeing, as Berkeley does in the *New Theory*, we would have this:

(1) An object O is immediately seen by an observer S at time t = (i) O is seen by S at t, and (ii) it is false that O would be seen by S at t only if S were to see some object R at t, where R is not identical to O.

Here the term 'object' has wide scope and should not be read in a strict way. It can range over objects properly speaking, such as ideas or physical objects, but also over events or states, as in Berkeley's example of the state of passion in another person. This is not to say that all of these things *are* immediately perceived, but only that the definition leaves it an open question whether they are. This definition would directly yield a related definition of mediate seeing, thus (reference to time is deleted for convenience):

(2) Object O is mediately seen by S = (i) O is seen by S, and (ii) O would be seen by S only if S were to see some object R, where R is not identical to O.[2]

Definition 2 can be understood through Berkeley's example. The passions in another person (O) are seen, but only *by seeing* something else (R), namely, the colors in the countenance of the other person. The passions are seen mediately *by seeing* the colors in the face. This helps us understand definition 1 as well. In that case the colors in the face can be taken as O, and one does not see those colors *by seeing* something else—by seeing some intermediary. Since one does not see the colors through some seen intermediary, the colors are immediately seen. In the specific context of the *New Theory*, Berkeley's question is whether distance is immediately seen, and he thinks the answer is it is not. Distance, he holds, is seen mediately, something one accomplishes by seeing or otherwise perceiving something other than distance.

These two definitions can also be understood by considering an indirect realist theory of the sort traditionally attributed to Locke. On that theory, seen physical objects are always mediately seen, through the intermediary

2. In these definitions and in those to follow, the term 'perceives' or 'sees' appears in the definiens. This will not produce circularity unless we (or Berkeley) were to go on to define 'perceives' or 'sees' by means of 'immediately perceives,' something neither he nor I will do. Berkeley, I think, takes the term 'perceives' as undefined.

of something else that one sees, namely an idea of sensation. It is under-stood, of course, that this idea is distinct from the physical object. The idea, however, is immediately seen, since seeing it is not dependent upon seeing any intermediary entity distinct from the idea.

Though definition 1 is suggested by comments made in the *New Theory*, it is not adequate to the theory presented there, because Berkeley seems to allow that seeing might be immediate not only when it lacks dependence on some *seen* intermediary, but more generally when it lacks dependence on any *perceived* intermediary. For instance in section 11 he writes:

> Now, from sec. 2, it is plain that distance is in its own nature impercep-tible, and yet it is perceived by sight. It remains, therefore, that it be brought into view by means of some other idea that is itself immediately perceived in the act of vision. (Berkeley, 1948–57, 1:173)

This passage suggests that Berkeley would have us replace clause (ii) of definition 1 with something else (here I give just the corresponding sec-ond clause and suppress reference to observer and time):

(3) It is false that O would be seen only if some object R, not identical to O, were to be perceived.

That Berkeley had definition 3 in mind is indicated by the account he gives of seeing distance. With many others he assumes that distance is not itself immediately seen, though it is in some sense seen. Berkeley isolates three other perceptions on which the visual perception of distance is de-pendent: a feeling one gets as distance between the pupils of the eyes widens or contracts (sect. 16); perception of the degree of confusion in the visual image (sect. 21); and the sensation one experiences when the eye muscles are strained as an object is brought closer and closer to the eyes (sect. 27). Of these, only the second is a case of seeing; the other two per-ceptions involve feeling. So, definition 3 is preferable to definition 1 in that it more closely matches what Berkeley requires in the delineation of his own theory of vision.

When Berkeley comes to actually use his theory of distance perception, he appeals only to the second of the above three operations. For example, his explanation of the Barrow case proceeds along these lines. However, there are still reasons for preferring definition 3 over definition 1. First, in a discussion in which Berkeley juxtaposes his own theory to one proposed by Wallis, he explicitly cites the sensations resulting from straining the eyes as a perception on which the visual perception of distance and mag-nitude is dependent (*NTV*, sec 77). Moreover, Berkeley elsewhere cites sensations of feeling as those on which, in some cases, visual perception of distance depends. (*Theory of Vision Vindicated*, sect. 66) Further, Berkeley's theory generally needs definition 3. Imagine that a person experiences a single visual idea X, and that this idea suggests some tangible idea Y. Then by an obvious analogue of definition 1, clause (ii) for touch, Y would be immediately perceived by touch, for its "perception" would not depend on any other tangible idea. Yet we know that this is contrary to Berkeley's view; ideas or other entities that are merely suggested in this way are just *mediately* perceived. Thus, Berkeley needs definition 3 rather than 1.[3] Even so, there is a way in which even definition 3 is not specific enough. Imagine a case in which an observer immediately sees several visual ideas at once, perhaps a cluster of visual shapes. We want to say that she immediately sees both the cluster and the individual ideas that make it up. But definition 3 causes a problem. For it is true that the observer would see the cluster only if she were to see something other than the cluster, viz., its elements or components. The converse is also true; the observer would see the several ideas in the cluster only if she were to see the cluster.

To deal with this cluster problem we should amend definition 3:

(4) It is false that O would be seen only if some other object R were to be perceived, where R is not identical to O and where R is not an element or part of O, or a group of elements or parts of O, nor is O of R.

With definition 4, we allow Berkeley to get the desired results; both the cluster of ideas and the constituents of that cluster are immediately seen.

There is another notion of immediate perception (seeing) which can be found in the *New Theory*; it comes up in section 16.

It being already shown that distance is suggested to the mind by the mediation of some other idea which is itself perceived in the act of seeing, it remains that we inquire what ideas or sensations there be that attend vision. (Berkeley, 1948–57, 1:174)

Here the point is that mediate perception is dependent on and perhaps is brought about by an element of suggestion; immediate perception, then, would be that perception not thus dependent on suggestion. Philonous says:

3. This example assumes that mediate perception is genuine perception, a point taken up below.

> In reading a book, what I immediately perceive are the letters, but medi-
> ately, or by virtue of these, are suggested to my mind the notions of God,
> virtue, truth, etc. Now, that the letters are truly sensible things, or per-
> ceived by sense, there is no doubt; but I would know whether you take the
> things suggested by them to be so too. (Berkeley 1948–57, 2:174)

Is this "no suggestion" notion one that picks out a separate concept of immediate perception, distinct from that already supplied by definition 4?
Consider a perception which is reached by an act of suggestion. It occurs,
as mediate perception, only if some other perception occurs. Mediate per-
ception is then some perception that would occur only if some other per-
ception were to occur. In contrast, immediate perception would not be dependent on some other perception. The no suggestion notion, then,
implies that already on hand. Nevertheless, the no suggestion notion is
richer, because it includes a new element which, applying to vision, we
should add to definition 4:

> (iii) It is false that perception of some thing R, not identical to O, suggests
> O to the observer.

Definition 4 as enriched by this clause (iii), I think, is what Berkeley actually makes use of in the *New Theory*.[4]

The notion of suggestion raises important issues. As Berkeley uses the
term it seems to be restricted to entities that have been associated with
each other in some manner. For example, in the *New Theory* visual ideas
and ideas of touch are held to be associated with one another, so that the
former often suggests the latter. Association of this sort, however, requires that associated entities each be perceived in some manner at some
time. Thus, things such as God, virtue, and truth, which Berkeley speaks
of as suggested by the visual perception of letters on the page, are not the
sorts of things that are really perceptually suggestible, since none of those
things is ever perceived. The example of suggestion given in the *Dialogues*,
in other words, is not supported by the manner in which suggestion is
characterized in the *New Theory*. Another important point is that suggestion is not to be construed as a judgment, or a judging, and neither is it for
Berkeley an inference or act of inferring. He says in *Theory of Vision Vindicated* 42,

---

4. Here I diverge from the insightful account given by George Pitcher (1977, 2–24). As I
see it, suggestion is Berkeley's positive account of just what is involved when the perception of an entity is dependent on the perception of an intermediary. That is, the notion of
suggestion is supposed to explicate the sort of dependence Berkeley has in mind, and is
thus not brought in to express a different concept of immediate seeing (perception).

To perceive is one thing; to judge is another. So likewise to be suggested is one thing, and to be inferred is another. Things are suggested and perceived by sense. We make judgments and inferences by the understanding. (Berkeley 1948–57, 1:265)

As this passage indicates, neither perception proper (immediate perception) nor mediate perception reached by suggestion is judgmental or inferential, nor indeed, a conceptual activity of any sort, since it is not discharged by the understanding. We thus need to understand definition 4 along these lines.

The last-quoted passage, along with the theory defended in *New Theory* requiring that distance be mediately seen, indicate that Berkeley believes their mediate perception is a legitimate type of perception done "by sense." However, this way of thinking conflicts with Berkeley's characterization of perception in the *Dialogues*, where perception is several times restricted to immediate perception. Further, even if mediate perception is genuine perception, comments made in the *Dialogues* make it out to include an element of inference or of inferring, contrary to what is indicated in the passage from *Theory of Vision Vindicated*. We look first at those passages where genuine perception is restricted to immediate perception.

Hylas: . . . I tell you once for all, that by *sensible things* I mean those only which are perceived by sense, and that in truth the senses perceived nothing which they do not perceive immediately: Philonous: This point then is agreed between us, that *sensible things are those only which are immediately perceived by sense*. (Berkeley 1948–57, 2:174–75)

This exchange is unclear as to its bearing on the issue at hand. Hylas says that everything actually perceived is immediately perceived, and this certainly is relevant since it implies that all perception is immediate perception. Whatever mediate "perception" would be, then, it would not be genuine perception. However, Philonous does not agree; instead, he is searching for agreement on a definition of 'sensible thing,' and what he asserts is quite different, namely that if something is a sensible thing then it is immediately perceived. He gives, in other words, only a necessary condition for something's being a sensible thing. This reading of Philonous's comment is reinforced by a comment he makes later: "But the causes of our sensations are not things immediately perceived, and therefore not sensible." (Berkeley 1948–57, 2:191) Here Berkeley takes the denial of the above necessary condition (not being immediately perceived) to imply the denial of the antecedent (not being a sensible thing). This tells us we are right in thinking that Philonous is agreeing merely to a statement of a necessary condition for counting something as a sensible thing.

Stronger support for the claim that all genuine perception is immediate perception can be found in two other passages:

> PHILONOUS: How! is there any thing perceived by sense, which is not immediately perceived?

> PHILONOUS: How often must I inculcate the same thing? You allow the things immediately perceived by sense to exist no where without the mind: but there is nothing perceived by sense, which is not perceived immediately. (Berkeley 1948–57, 2:203, 215)

In the *New Theory* Berkeley puts things differently. His theory of vision holds that distance is not itself immediately perceived by sight, but that it is somehow seen nevertheless. His solution to how this can be is to introduce suggestion founded on past experience; this is the hallmark of mediate perception.

> Now from sect. 2 it is plain that distance is in it own nature imperceptible, and yet it is perceived by sight. It remains, therefore, that it be brought into view by means of some other idea that is it self immediately perceived in the act of vision. (Berkeley 1948–57, 1:173)

Here the phrase 'and yet it is perceived by sight' is important, because the manner in which distance is perceived by sight is through suggestion, that is, by means of mediate perception. In the theory of vision, then, mediate perception certainly counts as perception, though it is different from immediate perception. We have seen, too, that the same position is indicated by remarks made in *Theory of Vision Vindicated*.

The same issue is addressed in *Alciphron*, where the theory of visual distance perception is briefly reconsidered. There Berkeley's spokesman, Euphranor, says,

> To me it seems that a man may know whether he perceives or no; and if he perceives it, whether it be immediately or mediately; and if mediately, whether by means of something like or unlike, necessarily or arbitrarily connected with it. (Berkeley 1948–57, 3:152)

Moreover, the two last-cited works were each written more than twenty years after the publication of the *New Theory*, and it is clear that Berkeley had not changed his mind, at least as far as the message of those two works is concerned. It would be odd, though not out of the question, if he had changed his position in *Three Dialogues*, only to return to it many years later.

Evidence that Berkeley had not changed his mind comes from another passage in the *Dialogues*. Hylas had said that when he looks at a picture of Julius Caesar, he mediately sees the man himself. To this Philonous demurs.

> PHILONOUS: Tell me, Hylas, when you behold the picture of Julius Caesar, do you see with your eyes any more than some colours and figures with a certain symmetry and composition of the whole?
>
> HYLAS: Nothing else.
>
> PHILONOUS: And would not a man, who had never known any thing of Julius Caesar, see as much?
>
> HYLAS: He would.
>
> PHILONOUS: Consequently, he hath his sight, and the use of it, in as perfect a degree as you.
>
> HYLAS: I agree with you.
>
> PHILONOUS: Whence comes it then that your thoughts are directed to the Roman Emperor, and his are not? This cannot proceed from the sensations or ideas of sense by you then perceived; since you acknowledge you have no advantage over him in that respect. It should seem therefore to proceed from reason and memory: should it not? (Berkeley 1948–57, 2:203–4)

What Hylas had spoken of as seeing Caesar *by* seeing the picture, Philonous calls "having your thoughts directed to the Roman Emperor." He goes on to assign this procedure to reason and memory, thus making it seem that he takes mediate perception to involve reasoned inference. But we should also consider how the exchange continues:

> PHILONOUS: Consequently it will not follow from that instance, that any thing is perceived by sense which is not immediately perceived. Though I grant we may in one acceptation be said to perceive sensible things mediately by sense: that is, when from a frequently perceived connexion, the immediate perception of ideas by one sense suggests to the mind others perhaps belonging to another sense, which are wont to be connected with them.

Two things are important about this passage. First, Philonous agrees that mediate perception is actually perception dependent on suggestion; he even says that mediate perception is "by sense." Second, he characterizes mediate perception in a way that does not involve reason and memory, and also does not involve inference. Mediate perception, then, is something different from what is applicable in the case of seeing Caesar by seeing the picture of him. The latter involves inference, while the former does not.

There is, however, another passage where Berkeley seems to take all this back.

> PHILONOUS: Either you perceive the being of matter immediately, or mediately. If immediately, pray inform me by which of the senses you perceive it. If mediately, let me know by what reasoning it is inferred from those things which you perceive immediately. So much for the perception.

Here he seems to allow that mediate perception counts as perception, but he also includes an element of inferring in it, thereby distinguishing it from immediate perception. However, there is something special about this passage as well, in it Berkeley is talking about whether *matter* is in any sense perceived. This is like the Caesar case, only still further removed from perception by sense. Matter is not at all perceived, but is instead something to which our thoughts might be directed by some reasoning from what is immediately perceived. It is appropriate to bring up reasoning because matter is in principle imperceptible. Nor need this passage be read as endorsement of the claim that mediate perception includes or has as an ingredient an element of inference. Its last sentence can just as easily be read as asserting that if something is mediately perceived, then if we know something about it, we do so by means of inference. With just this one sentence to go on, interpretible in more than one way, a conservative approach would opt for the latter interpretation, thereby leaving mediate perception open to be thought of as Berkeley elsewhere characterizes it. Support for such a reading can be further supplied from the passage earlier considered. Berkeley contrasts the Caesar case with things that are mediately perceived. Things perceived immediately and strictly, he says, are those which "are actually and strictly perceived by any sense, which would have been perceived, in case that same sense had then been first conferred on us" (Berkeley 1948–57, 2:204). He then says,

> As for other things, it is plain they are only suggested to the mind by experience grounded on former perceptions. But to return to your comparison of Caesar's picture, it is plain, if you keep to that, you must hold the real things or archetypes of our ideas are not perceived by sense, but by some internal faculty of the soul, as reason or memory. (Berkeley 1948–57, 2:204, 221)

Here the "other things" are things that are mediately perceived by way of suggestion, and these things are made out to be different from Caesar. One comes to have knowledge of Caesar, not by suggestion, but instead by means of an inference that probably engages both reason and memory. The case of matter is on a par with that of Caesar; neither is strictly mediately perceived at all, but instead both are things we can come to have knowledge of solely on the basis of some reasoned inference.

On balance, then, the several passages of the *Three Dialogues* do not suffice to motivate interpreting Berkeley so that mediate perception includes an element of inference and fails to count as perception. On the contrary, his considered view seems to be that neither immediate nor mediate perception includes judging or inferring, and that both count as genuine perception. It is true that immediate perception has priority, because mediate perception is, as he says, "grounded on former perceptions." That is, it is based upon there having earlier been immediate perception of the presently mediately perceived items. But from this Berkeley does not infer that mediate perception is not really a form of perception.

We noted earlier that definition 4 defines a notion of immediate perception which is non-conceptual. That is, immediate perception is an event that does not include the application of a concept as a constituent element, and neither does it include a judging or inferring. We should also notice that, as Berkeley uses the term, 'immediately sees' ('immediately perceives') is non-propositional in that the verb takes a grammatical direct object as complement rather than a propositional clause. Thus, he is not discussing the act of *perceiving that* something is or is not the case, nor perceiving one thing *as* another nor *as* having some property. Numerous passages support this construal of Berkeley's concept; here is a representative example.

> PHILONOUS: . . . You will further inform me, whether we immediately perceive by sight any thing beside light, and colours, and figures: or by hearing, any things but sounds: by the palate, any thing beside tastes; by the smell, beside odours; or by the touch, more than tangible qualities. (Berkeley 1948–57, 2:175)

This range of sensible qualities comes within the scope of immediate perception, rather than facts or propositions about what is sensible.

Since for Berkeley the concept of immediate perception is both non-conceptual and non-propositional, it is reasonable to think that it will support certain inferences. For example, if a person immediately sees the man in the corner, and the man in the corner is the dean of the college, then the person immediately sees the dean of the college. Substitution of co-referential expressions in sentences using 'immediately sees' ('immediately perceives') will yield a sentence with the same truth value. I think the same may be said for the term 'mediately sees' (or 'mediately perceives'). Thus if a person mediately sees the man in the chair, and the man in the chair is drinking water, then the person mediately sees a man drinking water.[5]

Amending the Definition

Although Berkeley actually makes use of definition 4, it will not fully serve his interests. There are two sorts of problem cases to consider, one aimed at its second clause and the other at its third. The former can be brought out by a case of a person who sees two non-adjacent visual ideas simultaneously. These ideas are not elements of one cluster of visual ideas, perhaps because one is to the left of the visual field and the other is to the right. We want to be able to say that the person immediately sees *both* of these visual ideas simultaneously. But the second clause of definition 4 is not satisfied. The ideas in question are distinct and not related to each other as part or element to whole. Nonetheless, the person would not see the one idea if he were to fail to see the other, assuming all else is held constant.

The problem for clause (iii) of definition 4 arises when we have a person who sees two visual ideas and it happens that each suggests the other to him and at the same time. In this case, even if the second clause is met, we would have to conclude that each of these ideas is mediately seen. But we

---

5. Berkeley himself does not discuss inferences of this sort. The point is just that his concept of immediate seeing (perception) allows for them. Later we see that he needs to allow for these and related inferences.

An especially fascinating case, raised by an anonymous reviewer, concerns *mediate* perception. Suppose I look at the facing side of College Hall, and so, on my reading of Berkeley, we say that I immediately see College Hall. Imagine, though, that this event suggests to me the hidden back side of College Hall, so that the back side of that building is mediately seen. In this case it would seem that I also mediately see College Hall, so that the same object is both immediately and mediately seen on the same occasion.

This example requires an inference of this form: If person S mediately perceives object O, and O is a part of object R, then S mediately perceives R. As I note later, inferences of this very sort succeed in many (but not all) cases where we are talking of *immediate* perception. The example forces us to ask: do inferences like this work in some cases for mediate perception as well? I am inclined to think the answer is YES, because for Berkeley mediate perception is not an inferential, conceptual activity any more than is immediate perception. Hence, I think Berkeley must acquiesce and accept that the very same object can be simultaneously immediately and mediately perceived.

For an illuminating account of Berkeley's notion of mediate perception, see Jody Graham 1997, 397–423.

do not want to rule out simultaneous immediate seeing of two ideas, not even when, coincidentally, each suggests the other.[6]

We can solve the problem raised by the first case by thinking of the person's seeing the two visual ideas as a complex perceptual event, one that takes simpler perceptual events as components. As an illustration, consider an event of a person raising her hand to ask a question. This event may be thought of as complex, because it has as a component the simpler event of moving her hand from her lap to a position six inches from her lap. Similarly, the complex perceptual event has as a simpler component the event of seeing the visual idea to the left. It also has as a simpler component the event of seeing the visual idea to the right. The complex perceptual event, further, has these two visual ideas as constituents So, for example, the relatively simple event of seeing the idea on the left has that idea as a constituent. And both ideas are constituents of the complex perceptual event. Again the example of raising one's hand may be used to illustrate the point. In that example, the woman's hand is a constituent of the event of raising her hand.[7]

What we want to rule out is a situation in which the event of seeing a distinct entity is part of, or included in, the event of seeing an object O. That sort of entity would be precisely the sort which would lead to mediate seeing. On the other hand, we want to allow for a case in which an entity is not a constituent of the event of seeing object O. That sort of situation is just what we have in simultaneously immediately seeing two non-adjacent visual ideas. We can handle this problem by amending the second clause of definition 4 so that it speaks of perceptual events. The problem of coincidental suggestion can also be accomodated, but it requires an additional amendment, namely by changing the third clause so that it is a subjunctive. The full definition that results is this rather complex one:

5. S immediately sees O = (i) S sees O; and, (ii) it is false that S would see O only if S were to perceive R, where R is not identical to O, and where R is not a part or element or group of parts or elements of O, nor is O of R, and where R is a constituent of an event which is a component of the event of seeing O; and, (iii) it is false that S would see O only if O were to be suggested to S by R.[8]

6. These cases were brought to my attention by Tom Downing and James van Cleve.

7. These points are accomodated easily if we think of events as Kim-events, i.e., as an ordered triple consisting of an individual taking a property at a time. See Jaegwon Kim 1993, especially chap. 1.

8. Discussions with Martha Bolton were helpful in coming up with these amendments.

This definition captures all of what Berkeley uses of in the theory of vision and elsewhere, but also more. It is shielded from the two problem cases in a way that Berkeley's actual definition is not. We cannot say, then, that definition 5 is really Berkeley's account of immediate seeing, since he never considered the problem cases and never was moved to amend the preceding definition. The most we can say, not overly generously, is that had Berkeley thought of the foregoing two problem cases, he would have been moved to make some changes in his definition, and the amendments made here are in the direction he would need to have taken.[9]

By making use of definition 4, we could easily state counterpart definitions of immediate smelling, hearing, tasting, and touching. We could just as easily do the same for the improved definition given in 5. Then we could say that immediate perception is just the disjunction of the preceding five definitions. More exactly, we could say that immediately perceiving something is either immediately seeing it, or immediately touching it, or immediately hearing it, or immediately tasting it, or immediately smelling it. We could also form counterpart definitions of mediate smelling, hearing, tasting and touching, and use the same sort of disjunction to accomodate the notion of mediate perception.

Epistemic Concepts

It may seem that the last definition, as well as definition 4, leaves something out, or at the least fails to stress, viz., an explicitly epistemic element to the concept of immediate perception. We can see the point here by stepping out of the context of Berkeley's philosophy and considering a definition of the notion of immediate perception once attributed to Moore:

> An object O is immediately perceived by a person S at time t = S's assertion that he perceives O at t could not be mistaken at t.[10]

This definition is framed in terms of one of the usual concepts of certainty, and this is a concept Berkeley sometimes uses, as we see in this exchange:

9. A problem I will not pursue here has to do with univocity. Direct realists, indirect realists, and philosophers of Berkeley's idealist or phenomenalist stripe dispute with each other over what the objects of immediate (or direct) perception are. Hence, in formulating a definition of this concept, one should take care to come up with a definition acceptable to all parties to the dispute. Further amendments to definition 5 would be called for if we were to make the definition fully acceptable to the indirect causal realist. For steps in this direction, see James Cornman 1975, chap. 1.

10. See Norman Malcolm 1963, 88, for this sort of definition.

HYLAS:. . . . How can a man be mistaken in thinking the moon a plain lucid surface, about a foot in diameter, or a square tower, seen at a distance, round, or an oar, with one end in the water, crooked?

PHILONOUS: He is not mistaken with regard to the ideas he actually perceives, but in the inference he makes from his present perceptions. Thus, in the case of the oar, what he immediately perceives by sight is certainly crooked, and so far he is in the right. . . . His mistake lies not in what he perceives immediately and at present (it being a manifest contradiction to suppose he should err in respect of that), but in the wrong judgment he makes concerning the ideas he apprehends to be connected with those immediately perceived. (Berkeley 1948–57, 2:238)

This passage hints at a definition of the notion of immediate perception like that framed by Malcolm. It also would yield a straightforward definition of the notion of mediate perception. It would just be that perception about which the relevant assertion could be mistaken.

One might also think that another epistemic concept is part of Berkeley's notion of immediate perception, namely, that of immediately or intuitively knowing. To immediately perceive some thing O, on such a view, would be to acquire immediate, or intuitive, knowledge of O by perceptual means. This concept is also suggested by remarks Berkeley makes.

My own mind and my own ideas I have an immediate knowledge of; and by the help of these, do mediately apprehend the possibility of the existence of other spirits and ideas. (Berkeley 1948–57, 2:238)

These comments on epistemic matters suggest two different approaches one might take regarding the notion of immediate perception. One approach would be to amend the definition already given (both definition 4 and 5) to incorporate either or both of these two epistemic concepts. Doing that would allow us to say that Berkeley really operates with one, very complex, notion of immediate perception. A second approach would be to say that these comments on epistemic matters indicate that Berkeley has a *second*, wholly epistemic, concept of immediate perception. Here the first approach will be considered; examination of the second is deferred to a later section.

There are two reasons to resist incorporating epistemic elements into the definition of immediate perception. First, the resulting definitions would not be sufficiently general, applying to all who immediately perceive. Children and other perceivers who lack concepts appropriate to the beliefs which would presumably be certain and intuitively known in an event of immediate perception will not have such knowledge. Lacking the relevant concepts, they will fail to even acquire the correct beliefs. Yet such persons immediately perceive all the same. A second related reason takes seriously what Berkeley says in *Theory of Vision Vindicated*:

> To perceive is one thing; to judge is another. So likewise to be suggested is one thing, and to be inferred is another. Things are suggested and perceived by sense. We make judgments and inferences by the understanding. (Berkeley 1948–57, 1:265)

This passage indicates that in sense, one does not judge and thus does not apply concepts. If not, there is no means in immediate perception itself by which the requisite beliefs could be acquired.

The point being made here is actually quite narrow. What is being questioned is whether epistemic concepts such as that of certainty and intuitive knowing should be built into the definition of the concept of immediate perception. In effect, by doing this one is saying that an ingredient in every event of immediate perception is the event of acquiring certain and intuitive knowledge. This latter would be a constituitive element of immediate perception. In denying that this is the right way to understand Berkeley's concept of immediate perception, one is perfectly free to grant that certain epistemic conditional statements are true. For example, there is reason to think that Berkeley holds these two statements to be true:

> If a person immediately perceives a thing, X, then the person acquires certain knowledge of X.

> If a person immediately perceives a thing, X, then the person acquires intuitive knowledge of X.

The second of these statements is supported by a passage from the third of the *Dialogues*:

> Wood, stones, fire, water, flesh, iron, and the like things, which I name and discourse of, are things that I know. And I should not have known them, but that I perceived them by my senses; and things perceived by the senses are immediately perceived;. . . .

Berkeley does not here mention intuitive knowledge, but he does elsewhere in the same place:

> When, therefore, they (ideas) are actually perceived, there can be no doubt of their existence. . . . What a jest it is for a philosopher to question the existence of sensible things till he has it proved to him from the veracity of

God, or to pretend that our knowledge in this point falls short of intuition. (Berkeley 1948–57, 2:230)

The first epistemic conditional is different because Berkeley actually uses two quite distinct concepts of certainty. Where 'X' in the above conditional designates an idea, Berkeley is willing to utilize the concept of certainty adverted to by Malcolm:

> So long as I confine my thoughts to my own ideas divested of words, I do not see how I can easily be mistaken. The objects I consider, I clearly and adequately know. I cannot be deceived in thinking I have an idea which I have not. It is not possible for me to imagine, that any of my own ideas are alike or unlike, that are not truly so. (Berkeley 1948–57, 2:39)

In this passage it is clear that Berkeley is talking only about ideas, rather than anything else he might allow to be immediately perceived. However, in speaking of sensible things, generally, rather than just ideas, Berkeley uses a different, weaker concept of certainty in *Three Dialogues*.

> Le me be represented as one who trusts his senses, who thinks he knows the things he sees and feels, and entertains no doubts of their existence.

> I do therefore assert that I am as certain as of my own being that there are bodies or corporeal substances (meaning the things I perceive by my senses).

> I might as well doubt of my own being as of the being of those things I actually see and feel. (Berkeley 1948–57, 2:237, 238, 230)

These passages, and others in which Berkeley speaks of the trust he places in the senses (e.g., *Philosophical Commentaries*, entries 517a, 686a, and 740) make clear that he links certainty as it applies to sensible things not only with propositions that are not at all doubtful, but also with propositions it would be ludicrous to actually doubt, since there are no grounds for doubting them. There is also reason to think that Berkeley was aware of and sensitive to this meaning of 'certain,' since he says in *Commentaries* 813,

> I am certain there is a God, tho I do not perceive him have no intuition of him, this not difficult if we rightly understand w^t is meant by certainty. (Berkeley 1948–57, 1:97)

Thus, in the conditional we are considering—if one immediately perceives X, then one acquires certain knowledge of X—If 'X' designates an idea, Berkeley is prepared to be understood as using the strong concept of certainty, as given by Malcolm, in the consequent. However, where 'X' is a schematic letter with variable designation including reference to sensible things, the concept of certainty is framed in terms of there being no actual doubt and no grounds for doubting.[11]

While it is true that the lately quoted passages indicate Berkeley's endorsement of the conditionals noted above, these same passages give no support to the narrower reading according to which these epistemic elements of intuitive knowledge and certainty are partially constituitive of the concept of immediate perception. We should, then, think that Berkeley's concept of immediate perception includes no epistemic components in addition to what is stated in definition 5.

Acquaintance

Compatible with everything said thus far is an interpretation of immediate perception as acquaintance. This would accord with the observation that Berkeley's use of 'immediately perceives' is non-propositional, since when one is acquainted with some object O, one knows O itself rather than some proposition descriptive of O. Acquaintance accords, too, with Berkeley's claim that immediate perception is not judging or inferring or an operation of the understanding. Moreover, if contexts in which 'immediately perceives' are used are transparent so that inferences discussed earlier are sanctioned, no changes are called for on the acquaintance interpretation. For if a person is acquainted with O, and O is identical to R, then the person is also acquainted with R.[12]

There is some textual support for the acquaintance interpretation, since Berkeley does sometimes talk of knowing objects, typically ideas. For example,

> Colour, figure, motion, extension and the like, considered only as so many *sensations* in the mind, are perfectly known, there being nothing in them which is not perceived.

Earlier in the same book he had said,

11. I thus think that the scope of Berkeley's acceptance of the "manifest qualities thesis" is restricted. For an opposing view, see Phillip Cummins 1995, 107–25.

12. Acquaintance is endorsed as the correct account of immediate perception for Berkeley in K. Winkler 1989, 153. The non-epistemic view I defend below accords with that given in Pitcher, a view Winkler rejects as "misleading," 154.

All the choir of heaven and furniture of the earth, in a word all those bodies which compose the mighty frame of the world, have not any subsistence without a mind, that their being is to be perceived or known; (Berkeley 1948–57, 2:78, 43)

The last few words in this passage suggest that Berkeley equates perceiving objects with knowing them.

Further support for this account derives from two features of acquaintance as that notion was deployed by Bertrand Russell. In his view, there
are three elements of acquaintance: being present to or with the observer;
being presented to the observer; and certain knowledge. The first of these
is simple enough: an object of acquaintance O is present to or with an observer at a given time means that O exists at that time. Thus, distant stars
which passed out of existence many light years ago, but are still seen today because their light is just reaching us now, are not objects of acquaintance. The stars are not present to or with the observer now, though the
light from those stars might be. Second, the formulation that the object is
presented to the observer means that every feature of the object is there
for inspection. In the words of H. H. Price addressing sense-data, "all the
goods are in the shop window." That is, every feature of the object is a feature the person is aware of.[13] Berkeley seems to speak of this notion of being presented to an observer at one point in the *Principles*:

> Every particular finite extension, which may possibly be the object of our
> thought, is an *idea* existing only in the mind, and consequently every part
> thereof must be perceived.

This is not quite "being presented" to because Berkeley speaks of parts
rather than features or properties. But Berkeley's remark is quite close to
what Russell had in mind, and supports thinking of immediate perception as acquaintance. He also seems to accept the first element of acquaintance, that of "being present to or with":

> I can as well doubt of my own being, as of the being of those things which
> I actually perceive by sense: it being a manifest contradiction, that any sen-
> sible object should be immediately perceived by sight or touch, and at the
> same time have no existence in Nature.(Berkeley 1948–57, 2:98, 79)

The third element of Russellian acquaintance, that of certainty, is more
problematic because certainty is usually defined for beliefs. Beliefs,

---

13. A still richer notion would add that every feature the person is aware of is a feature
of the object, a condition I take not to be included within acquaintance.

whether *de dicto* or *de re*, have propositional content, and that is not in-cluded within the notion of acquaintance. Being acquainted with O is not being certain in one's beliefs about O. So, while Berkeley does use a notion of certainty similar to what is found in Russell—that of the impossibility of mistaken belief—it is not easy to see what it comes to if it is to be par-tially constituitive of acquaintance.

I think we can by-pass the question of how to fit the notion of belief into that of acquaintance. Besides the first two elements, already discussed, the key element in acquaintance is that of knowledge, of objects rather than propositions. Berkeley does seem to hold to such a position; indeed, he seems to say that it is because every feature of the object is presented to the observer that the object is itself known. Recall *Principles* 87:

> Colour, figure, motion, extension and the like, considered only as so many *sensations* in the mind, are perfectly known, there being nothing in them which is not perceived. (Berkeley 1948–57, 2:78)

Whatever is meant by knowing objects rather than facts or propositions, it is still something one might have even if certainty attaches not to this knowledge but rather to whatever belief one might acquire as a result of knowing the object.

With all this said in favor of interpreting Berkeley's concept of immedi-ate perception as acquaintance, however, there remain a number of rea-sons not to accept this interpretation. First, Berkeley generally follows Locke on many key points, and Locke contends that perceiving is not knowing. Locke speaks of "*Perception . . . being the first step and degree to-wards Knowledge, and the inlet of all the Materials of it*," and as the " . . . first Operation of all our intellectual Faculties, and the inlet of all Knowledge into our Minds." (*Essay*, II, X, 15) Locke is thus distinguishing between perceiving and knowing. Though not decisive, this suggests that Berke-ley's concept of immediate perception is not epistemic and thus not one of acquaintance. Moreover, the epistemic component of acquaintance is not strongly supported by Berkeley's texts. First, there are not many texts which can be read in the acquaintance manner. We have, I believe, cited all of them, and they amount to just two (*Principles* 6 and 87). More im-portantly, it may be just an incidental feature of Berkeley's wording that hints at acquaintance. We speak as though we are endorsing acquaintance when, if pressed, we would grant that we meant something else. For ex-ample, we may say that James knows football, but nobody would take this to mean that he is acquainted with football. Instead, it would be taken to mean that James knows many facts about football and, perhaps, that he knows well how to play it. The case is similar in Berkeley. He may just be falling in with a common way of speaking, but never intending to suggest acquaintance. I grant this is a very weak reason, but its importance is this: acquaintance in its epistemic component is sufficiently unusual as a point for someone to make, that we would want to see explicit acknowledgement of some sort that it is the intended meaning, as one gets in Russell. Such acknowledgement, however, is absent in Berkeley's texts.

It is true that in a couple of places Berkeley does talk of knowing objects. But there are also places where he speaks of knowing the existence of objects, as well as knowing the nature of objects, and in neither of those places are we tempted to say that he means we are acquainted with an object's existence or its nature. So, Berkeley's wording in the two passages where he talks of knowing objects should not be taken as sufficient to indicate he held to a notion of acquaintance.

Finally, and most important, I think Berkeley holds that among the objects that are immediately perceived are sensible objects such as trees and hedges. While someone might hold that trees and hedges are known, and mean by this the acquaintance sort of knowing, these things are not presented to observers in the way that objects of acquaintance are supposed to be. Trees and hedges may typically be present to or with the observer, as they typically exist at the moment of perception. But they are not presented to observers in a way required by acquaintance. Not every feature of a sensible thing is presented to an observer in a perceptual situation, not even every, or even most, non-relational feature of the object. Trees and hedges, then, are not objects of acquaintance in Russell's sense, just as Russell claimed. Yet trees and hedges, Berkeley wants to say, *are* often immediately perceived. So, Berkeleyan immediate perception is not best construed as Russellian acquaintance.[14]

Non-Epistemic Perception

Thus far I have argued that Berkeley's concept of immediate perception is not epistemic in either of two ways: first, it does not include some explicitly epistemic component as part of its *definiens;* and, second, it is not to be thought of as acquaintance. In fact, it is reasonable to think that Berkeley's concept is non-epistemic in a broader sense as well. That is, it is non-epistemic in the sense that immediately perceiving something does not imply that one thereby gains any knowledge, justified belief, or even

14. An alternative interpretation of Berkeley's notion might hold that immediate perception is *just* the epistemic component of Russellian acquaintance, that of knowing objects, though the evidence I give here runs counter to that position.

any beliefs about what is then immediately perceived.[15] So understood, we will say that Berkeley's concept of immediate perception is *fully* non-epistemic.

The argument for this interpretation takes us back to the passage from *Theory of Vision Vindicated* noticed earlier and here re-stated:

> To perceive is one thing; to judge is another. So likewise to be suggested is one thing, and to be inferred is another. Things are suggested and perceived by sense. We make judgments and inferences by the understanding. (Berkeley 1948–57, 1, 2, 65)

Since perception is taken as non-judgmental, it becomes reasonable to see Berkeley's concept of immediate perception as non-conceptual as well. It is in judgments that concepts are applied, and with no judgment involved in perception, then perception can be taken as non-conceptual, too. If perception is non-conceptual in this sense, then it is also fully non-epistemic. To show this it suffices to note that the utilization of concepts is necessary for belief-acquisition. Hence, if immediate perception does not include the utilization or application of concepts, it also does not imply or require the acquisition of belief about the immediately perceived object. Further, since belief is necessary for knowledge and for justified belief, immediately perceiving something does not imply that one thereby acquires knowledge or justified belief about what is immediately perceived. Thus, immediately perceiving for Berkeley is fully non-epistemic.

The argument here is not airtight, though it is plausible, nonetheless. It is not airtight because it assumes that the only context in which concepts are applied is in the making of judgments, and this might be challenged.[16] However, concept application in the making of judgment is the paradigm, and it is this which underwrites the inference to there being no concepts involved in immediate perception.

Two Senses of 'Immediately Perceives'

Thus far we have examined two ways in which 'immediately perceives' might have an epistemic sense: either certain epistemic concepts might be included in its definiens as additions to the clauses making up definition 4 (or 5); or, immediate perception might be identified with acquaintance.

15. This is the notion of non-epistemic perception examined in Fred Dretske 1969, chap. 1.

16. It is challenged in the theories of perception of Wilfrid Sellars and Edmund Husserl. Both are briefly sketched in my "Theories of Perception," 1996, 394–96.

Another approach, briefly mentioned earlier, is to agree that Berkeley accepts and uses a non-epistemic notion of immediate perception. However, it is held that Berkeley also uses another notion of immediate perception, and that this notion is explicitly epistemic.

This approach has been pursued by Georges Dicker, who finds a psychological and an epistemic concept of immediate perception in Berkeley.[17] The former is this:

X is immediately perceived $_p$ = X is perceived without the perceiver's performing any (conscious) inference.

Dicker finds another, epistemic, concept of immediate perception in Berkeley, which he represents as,

X is immediately perceived$_e$ = X is perceived in such a way that its existence and nature can be known solely on the basis of one's present perceptual experience. (Dicker 1982, 49)

Further, Dicker thinks that Berkeley conflates these two notions, because Berkeley holds that satisfaction of the former is a sufficient condition for satisfaction of the latter. That is, he thinks Berkeley accepts the principle (called "Q"),

For any X, if X is immediately perceived$_p$, then X is immediately perceived$_e$. (Dicker 1982, 50)

The only evidence Dicker gives for thinking that Berkeley accepted the psychological concept of immediate perception he (Dicker) defines is that Berkeley has Hylas say,

By *sensible things* I mean those only which are perceived by sense, and that in truth the senses perceive nothing which they do not perceive immediately: for they make no inferences.

It is instructive that in his reply to these comments, Philonous does not address the point Hylas makes, but instead brings up the question of how the term 'sensible thing' is to be understood:

This point then is agreed between us, that *sensible things are* those only which are immediately perceived by sense. (Berkeley 1948–57, 2:174–175)

17. Georges Dicker 1982, 48–66.

We should be wary of attributing to Berkeley a definition which is only put in Hylas' terms and which is not agreed to by Philonous.

Moreover, attribution of the above psychological notion of immediate perception to Berkeley ignores the way in which Berkeley himself characterizes that notion in the *New Theory*. That characterization, as we have seen, proceeds in terms of lack of perceived intermediaries and lack of suggestion, and no mention is there made of inference, conscious or otherwise. When lack of inference is brought up, in *Theory of Vision Vindicated*, the aim is to say something true of both immediate and mediate perception, and not to provide a definition of the former. For these reasons, I think it is safe to say that Dicker's psychological concept of immediate perception is not to be found in Berkeley.

This is a minor point for Dicker's purposes, however, because his essential claim is that Berkeley has what is basically a non-epistemic concept of immediate perception (wrongly identified, or so I claim, as Dicker's psychological notion), *and* an additional, epistemic, concept, namely immediate perception$_e$. Dicker's reason for thinking that Berkeley uses this concept is that it is needed in the argument presented in the famous passage about the coach in the first *Dialogue*. That is, he takes Berkeley in that passage to be arguing for the conclusion that the coach is "not immediately perceived by sense at all", and to reach this conclusion Berkeley *needs* both the epistemic notion of immediate perception and principle Q,

Q. For any X, if X is immediately perceived$_p$, then X is immediately perceived$_e$.

A closer look at the coach passage, however, shows that Berkeley is not arguing for the conclusion Dicker attributes to him. To see this we need to consider the main part of the passage:

When I hear a coach drive along the streets, immediately I perceive only the sound; but from the experience I have had that such a sound is connected with a coach, I am said to hear the coach. It is nevertheless evident, that in truth and strictness, nothing can be *heard* but *sound:* and the coach is not then properly perceived by sense, but suggested by experience. So likewise when we are said to see a red-hot bar of iron; the solidity and heat of the iron are not the objects of sight, but suggested to the imagination by the colour and figure, which are properly perceived by that sense. (Berkeley 1948–57, 2:204)

Berkeley is not here saying that the coach and piece of hot iron are not perceived by sense, as Dicker says, but rather that they are not *properly* perceived by sense. The difference is quite important. Proper perception is a concept Berkeley introduces in the *New Theory* to mark out those ideas that are perceivable by only one sense as opposed to those ideas, if there are any, which might be perceived by more than one sense. Color, for instance, is something he takes to be properly immediately perceivable by sight, meaning that it is immediately seen but not immediately perceived by means of any other sense. Sound operates in the same way, being properly immediately perceivable only by hearing. And of course, Berkeley is right: the coach and hot piece of iron are not *properly* immediately perceived, for there is no one sense by the sole means of which they are perceived. This is how such objects differ from sounds, in the one case, and color and figure, in the other. Since Dicker has mis-identified the conclusion Berkeley is aiming at in this passage, his argument that Berkeley needs immediate perception$_e$ breaks down. Berkeley is not endorsing the conclusion for the which the epistemic notion of immediate perception is deemed necessary.

In a more recent paper Dicker has proposed another argument for a separate epistemic notion of immediate perception in Berkeley.[18] He notes that when we look at Berkeley's arguments against indirect causal realism in the first of the *Dialogues*, we see that Berkeley makes use of the principle that whatever is perceived by the senses is immediately perceived. This principle, what Dicker calls "PPI," is then used by Berkeley in his arguments for the claim that we never immediately perceive the causes of our sensations. However, if the term 'immediately perceives' is purely non-epistemic, then the use of PPI will not fully support Berkeley's arguments. Specifically, the definition given above as definition 5 will allow that we often do immediately perceive the causes of our sensations, even if those causes are the physical objects spoken of by indirect causal realists. Hence, to block this result and to allow Berkeley's arguments to work in full generality, Berkeley must resort to an epistemic notion of immediate perception. Only such a notion will permit Berkeley to unequivocally maintain that we do not immediately perceive the causes of our sensations, and thereby refute all versions of indirect causal realism.

The key to this argument is to take seriously Dicker's reference to *all forms* of indirect causal realism. In particular, we can consider adverbial causal realism which dispenses with perceptual intermediaries such as ideas in favor of adverbial events of sensing. In looking at a chair, one is thereby caused to sense in a certain manner; one is not thereby caused to immediately see some sensible ideas. According to this theory, so long as the chair is not suggested by the event of sensing, it will follow that the

---

18. Georges Dicker 1992.

chair is immediately seen, since clause (ii) of definition 4 (and definition 5) will be satisfied because no perceived intermediaries will be involved. But the chair is the cause of the sensation, here construed as the event of sensing, and thus the cause of the sensation is immediately seen, a result Berkeley is at pains to rule out. Hence, he needs some other, epistemic concept of immediate perception. Only with such a concept will he reach the desired conclusion about the causes of our sensations.[19]

I believe that Dicker's argument is important and fully correct, though curiously irrelevant to what is being considered here. Dicker is concerned with the question "What does Berkeley need if his argument is to be fully general and plausible, applying to all forms of indirect causal realism?" Evaluating Berkeley by means of this question delivers Dicker's epistemic concept of immediate perception. However, Berkeley's arguments are not here being evaluated for their overall plausibility. Instead, the much narrower question of what *Berkeley's* concept of immediate perception amounts to is being examined, not the question of what concept would he require in order for his arguments to be fully plausible by our lights.

In fact, there is something to be said in Berkeley's behalf in this matter, even granting the correctness of Dicker's argument. The sorts of causal realist theories Berkeley was motivated to refute by means of the arguments Dicker analyzes were theories that held that in every perceptual experience at least one idea (phenomenal individual) is immediately perceived. Berkeley never considered anything like adverbial causal realism, for it was not considered part of the competition, by Berkeley or anyone else (perhaps excepting Arnauld) at this point in time. So, if we ask the question, how do Berkeley's arguments fare and what do they require, if his aim is to refute all then-extant forms of causal indirect realism, then I think Berkeley can make do with the non-epistemic notion of immediate perception which is found in his texts. It is only when we are asking a higher-level question, as Dicker is doing, that Berkeley is forced to an epistemic notion of immediate perception.

Objects of Immediate Perception

Earlier I examined one thesis concerning immediate perception, namely, that if something is perceived, then it is immediately perceived. I argued that this was not a thesis Berkeley held, though he certainly held its converse. Here an equally important but distinct thesis is explored:

---

19. I would not call this theory *indirect* causal realism, because the adverbial events or states are not perceived.

that if something is immediately perceived, then that thing is an idea. Contrary to a common and traditional interpretation, I argue that Berkeley also did not accept this latter thesis. This is not because he thinks that ideas are not items of immediate perception, but rather because they are not the *only* items of immediate perception. Berkeley held that, in addition to ideas, ordinary physical objects—what he called 'sensible objects' or sensible things'—are immediately perceived.

On this point Berkeley accepts a theory I will call 'perceptual direct realism.' (hereafter, PDR). More accurately, he accepts the perceptual part or component of PDR. In this sense, one key piece of the Luce and Jessop interpretation of Berkeley as a common sense realist is here claimed to be correct. Some other components of PDR, however, I argue were not accepted by Berkeley, so that the Luce and Jessop account cannot be fully supported.

Certainly Berkeley held that ideas are immediately perceived. This theme runs through many of his writings, and hardly stands in need of documentation. We can understand the claim that ideas are immediately perceived in several ways. First, sometimes a single idea is immediately perceived by a single sense, as when a single visual idea is immediately seen. There can also be cases in which more than one idea is immediately perceived by a single sense, either as a cluster of ideas, or as distinct ideas not in a cluster. Looking at a multi-colored and variously shaped mural, for example, would involve one in immediately seeing a cluster of visual ideas; and, simultaneously seeing two ducks fly off, one on the left of one's spot in the blind and the other on the right, would result in one immediately seeing two non-adjacent visual ideas. All of these possibilities apply as well to the other sense modalities.

A further case would be when one immediately perceives different ideas by more than one sense. One might immediately see ideas, either individually, in clusters, or as non-clustered, non-adjacent ideas, at the same moment that one immediately hears some sound or sounds. So, when we say that ideas are immediately perceived, we must mean this to reflect all of the above cases.[20]

Years ago A. A. Luce and T. E. Jessop individually argued that Berkeley believed ordinary physical objects to be immediately perceived.[21] There is, I believe, a fair bit of textual support for thinking that Berkeley did accept this view. We can divide these passages into two categories, in the first of which are passages in which objects are claimed to be *perceived*, but where

20. But at *Commentaries* 647, Berkeley says that one can have simultaneous immediate perception only with sight and touch.
21. Refer to footnote 1.

the term 'immediately perceived' is not used. We begin with *Principles* 34, where Berkeley asks:

> What therefore becomes of the sun, moon, and stars? What must we think of houses, rivers, mountains, trees, stones; nay, even of our own bodies? Are these all but so many chimeras and illusions on the fancy? To all which, and whatever else of the same sort may be objected, I answer, that by the principles premised, we are not deprived of any one thing in Nature.

Then in the next section he continues the thought:

> I do not argue against the existence of any one thing that we can apprehend, either by sense or reflexion. That the things I see with mine eyes and touch with my hands do exist, really exist, I make not the least question. (Berkeley 1948–57, 2:55)

It is clear that in section 35 Berkeley is referring back to the objects mentioned in section 34, but adding to the list of those seen and touched. Further, though he does not use the term 'immediately perceives,' it is more than likely that is his meaning, as we would expect him to use a term like 'mediately perceive' or 'suggested' if that were his point. More generally, as we saw earlier, immediate perception is the primary sort of perception for Berkeley. And when we find him dropping the prefix 'immediately,' but without also alerting us as to some special meaning, he indicates immediate perception. With this point in mind, section 34 and 35 endorse the claim that objects are immediately perceived. The point is repeated in section 84:

> If at table all who were present should see, and smell, and taste, and drink wine, and find the effects of it, with me there could be no doubt of its reality.

Again Berkeley does not use the tem 'immediately perceives,' though it is clear that is what he means.

Consider, next, a passage from the *Dialogues*:

> But to fix on some particular thing; is it not a sufficient evidence to me of the existence of this *glove*, that I see it, and feel it, and wear it?

Just before these lines Berkeley had made clear that he was talking of *sensible things*, of which the glove is one. We have noted that Philonous takes sensible things to be immediately perceived, so the point here is that the glove is immediately seen and felt. Somewhat later Berkeley says,

> Is this as strange as to say, the sensible qualities are not on the objects: or, that we cannot be sure of the existence of things, or know any thing of their real natures, though we both see and feel them, and perceive them by all our senses?

Here the context makes it clear that he is talking about objects and their qualities. It is Hylas' position he is discussing, and he is saying that it has the consequence that qualities are not on the objects, and that we lack perceptual knowledge of the existence and nature of the objects even though we perceive them by all the senses.

On the next page Berkeley says,

> If by *material substance* is meant only sensible body, that which is seen and felt (and the unphilosophical part of the world, I dare say, mean no more) then I am more certain of matter's existence than you, or any other philosopher, pretend to be.

Here the tip-off is the use of the term 'sensible body,' which, along with 'sensible thing' Berkeley uses to mean 'physical object.'

There is also a passage in which Berkeley links perception of objects with common sense:

> *Lastly*, whether the premises considered, it be not the wisest way to follow Nature, trust your senses, and laying aside all anxious thought about unknown natures or substances, admit with the vulgar for real things, which are perceived by the senses?

Berkeley's point in this passage is that it is best to side with the vulgar in several ways, one of which is to hold that real things and their qualities, as opposed to copies of things as Hylas had proposed, are perceived by the senses. In the *Dialogues* this is what Berkeley uniformly takes as immediate perception. Finally, there is a passage which also gives Berkeley's view of the nature of objects:

> I see this *cherry* I feel it, I taste it: and I am sure *nothing* cannot be seen, or felt, or tasted: it is therefore *real*. Take away the sensations of softness, moisture, redness, tartness, and you take away the cherry. . . . [A] cherry, I say, is nothing more than a congeries of sensible impressions, or ideas perceived by various senses: which ideas are united into one thing (or have one name given to them) by the mind; because they are observed to attend one another. (Berkeley 1948–57, 2:77, 224, 236, 237, 246, 249)

In the second category of supporting passages are those in which Berkeley explicitly says that objects are immediately perceived. One of them is *Principles* 38:

> It sounds very harsh to say we eat and drink ideas, and are clothed with ideas. I acknowledge it does so, the word *idea* not being used in common discourse to signify the several combinations of sensible qualities, which are called *things:* and it is certain that any expression which varies from the familiar use of language, will seem harsh and ridiculous. But this doth not concern the truth of the proposition, which in other words is no more than to say, we are fed and clothed with those things which we perceive immediately by the senses.

There is also section 88:

> I can as well doubt of my own being, as of the being of those things which I actually perceive by sense: it being a manifest contradiction, that any sensible object should be immediately perceived by sight or touch, and at the same time have no existence in Nature, since the very existence of an unthinking being consists in *being perceived.* (Berkeley 1948–57, 2:56, 79)

There are also some passages in the *Dialogues:*

> Wood, stones, fire, water, flesh, iron, and the like things, which I name and discourse of, are things that I know. And I should not have known them, but that I perceived them by my senses; and things perceived by the senses are immediately perceived.

In speaking of a legitimate use of the word 'matter,' Berkeley says,

> With all my heart: retain the word *matter*, and apply it to the objects of sense, if you please, provided you do not attribute to them any subsistence distinct from their being perceived. . . . *Matter* or *material substance* are terms introduced by philosophers; and as used by them imply a sort of independency, or subsistence distinct from being perceived by a mind: but are never used by common people; or if ever, it is to signify the immediate objects of sense.

Finally, there is a passage in the first letter to Samuel Johnson:

> I see no difficulty in conceiving a change of state, such as is vulgarly called Death, as well without as with material substance. It is sufficient for that purpose that we allow sensible bodies, *i.e.*, such as are immediately perceived by sight and touch. (Berkeley 1948–57, 2:230, 261, 282)

In all then, based on these many passages, we have ample support for the view that Berkeley holds that physical objects are immediately perceived. Of course, when one immediately perceives an object one must also immediately perceive one or more of its sensible qualities; so, these, too, will count as entities that are immediately perceived.

Luce and Jessop considered Berkeley to be a direct realist about perception. Direct realism, though, has been understood in different ways. Probably the two principal ways have been as a theory of *perception*—a theory of what perception is and what its objects are; and, secondly, as a theory of perceptual *knowledge*—generally, a theory of what perceptual knowledge is, how it is acquired, and of the objects about which such knowledge is had. It is important that we keep these two types of theories distinct. The first is what I earlier referred to as 'PDR'; I will call the latter sort of theory *epistemic direct realism* (EDR).

Luce and Jessop can be interpreted as saying that Berkeley accepted *both* PDR and EDR; and that acceptance of PDR enabled him to hold EDR. More accurately, they held that Berkeley accepted a specifically naive form of PDR, one that accords best with common sense. I think there is some truth in both of these claims, but here I want to focus on PDR alone. As usually understood, this theory includes several components. Where Luce and Jessop were right was in thinking that Berkeley accepted some of these components; but I believe they went wrong in supposing that he held all of them.

PDR certainly incorporates the thesis that physical objects are typically immediately perceived. Generally more recent philosophers have used other terms, such as 'directly perceived,' but they generally come to the same as Berkeley's 'immediately perceives.'[22] In addition, PDR includes statements concerning the existence and nature of physical objects. At a minimum, PDR includes the *existential* thesis that physical objects and some of their properties exist independently of perceivers and of events of perception. It also includes some statement concerning the properties of physical objects and an indication of which of these properties are perceivable. An example of a certain naive sort would be a theory in which objects have all of the sensible qualities they are generally perceived to have. Another, less naive, would hold that objects have only tsome of the qualities they are generally perceived to have, namely, the so-called primary ones. I will say that this sort of statement, within PDR, concerning the properties of physical objects is a *metaphysical* thesis.

The first part of PDR, that physical objects are typically immediately perceived, is a *perceptual* thesis. It makes no claim about the nature of physical objects, nor about whether they exist independently of perception. Berkeley accepts this perceptual component, as indicated in the preceding section. However, given that he accepts the EIP principle, naturally he rejects the existential component of PDR. Berkeley *says* that he

22. There are exceptions, though, among them James Gibson (1966) and David Armstrong (1968).

accepts the metaphysical component, since he asserts that objects have the full range of properties they are typically perceived to have. He says,

> It is likewise my opinion, that colours and other sensible qualities are on the objects. I cannot for my life help thinking that snow is white and fire hot. (Berkeley 1948–57, 2:229–30)

Since Berkeley accepts one of the key elements of PDR, and also says that he accepts another, we can see why one would be tempted to suppose that Berkeley is a direct realist about perception. But we can also see why this is misleading and inaccurate, because he really accepts only two elements of perceptual direct realism, and what he rejects within PDR is the existential component. It is inaccurate to say, in other words, that Berkeley *is* a perceptual direct realist, for it is clear that he is not. However, it is correct to say that some key elements within perceptual direct realism are items which he accepts. On this latter point, Luce and Jessop were right; they erred only in claiming that Berkeley is a realist.

Not Thinking with the Learned

George Pitcher has objected to the claim that Berkeley accepted a part of PDR; specifically, his criticism is aimed at the first component of PDR, and at a point implied by PDR. PDR includes the claim that physical objects and their sensible qualities are immediately perceived. Also, anyone who accepts the latter would likely also accept the claim that the same person can immediately perceive a single object by more than one sense. Moreover, PDR implies that physical objects are *public* objects, in the sense that more than one person can immediately perceive a single object. Pitcher objects to all three of these claims.[23]

These three points each face some difficulty. The first two conflict with certain texts, while the third runs into a special problem of its own. Since each Berkeleyan sensible idea is immediately perceived by at most one person, and in that sense is *private*, Pitcher concludes that no two persons ever immediately perceive the same physical object, so that physical objects would not be public after all. So, the first two claims above are in conflict with various texts, and the third conflicts with doctrines which Berkeley accepts.

23. Pitcher calls the view he criticizes the "Ayers-Pappas" theory. He cites Michael Ayers' editor's comments in his edition of *Berkeley's Philosophical Works* 1975, and my "Berkeley, Perception and Common Sense" as the guilty pieces. The criticisms are given in Pitcher 1986.

Pitcher's proposal is to solve these three problems in essentially the same way. The three claims which cause the trouble here are those which Berkeley asserts when he is speaking with the vulgar. However, each of these claims is, strictly speaking, false. The strict true position, in each case, is what is expressed when one thinks with the learned. Passages in Berkeley which support PDR, such as those marshalled earlier, are to be discounted; they apply only insofar as Berkeley is speaking with the vulgar. His *real* position, one that expresses what the learned think, is found in other texts.

Pitcher's objection to thinking that for Berkeley physical objects are public will be taken up at a later point (chapter 7). Pitcher brings up several passages as support for the contention that Berkeley rejects the claim that physical objects are immediately perceived; and, if he is right about this, it will also follow that a person never immediately perceives a single object by more than one sense.

> In truth and strictness, nothing can *heard* but *sound*: and the coach is not then properly perceived by sense, but suggested from experience. (Berkeley 1948–57, 2:204)

Pitcher also brings up some passages from *Alciphron*:

> ALCIPHRON: Do we not, strictly speaking, perceive by sight such things as trees, houses, men, rivers, and the like?
>
> EUPHRANOR: We do, indeed, perceive or apprehend those things by the faculty of sight. But will it follow from thence that they are the proper and immediate objects of sight?
>
> ALCIPHRON: I see, therefore, in strict philosophic truth, that rock only in the same sense that I may be said to hear it, when the word rock is pronounced.
>
> EUPHRANOR: In the very same. (Berkeley 1948–57, 3:154, 155)

Pitcher's idea is that when Berkeley says that physical objects are immediately perceived, as in the passages we have noted, he is speaking loosely, or with the vulgar. When he is speaking carefully and strictly, as in the passages Pitcher cites, he is speaking with the learned and giving his real position on perception and its objects. It is a merit of Pitcher's objections that he makes no attempt to deny the many passages we have cited in support of the claim that objects are immediately perceived. On the contrary, he admits all of those, but simply tries to give an alternative reading of them. They are one and all passages where Berkeley is merely speaking with the vulgar, and should not be taken at face value.

Although Pitcher does not mention this, there are other passages which support his position. For instance, in the *New Theory* Berkeley says,

> There is no other immediate object of sight besides light and colours.
> All that is properly perceived by the visive faculty amounts to no more than colours, with their variations and different proportions of light and shade:

In the *Theory of Vision Vindicated* we have,

> The proper, immediate object of vision is light, in all its modes and variations, various colours in kind, in degree, in quantity; various in their bounds or limits; various in their order and situation. (Berkeley 1948–57, 1:223, 234, 266)

These additional passages can be thought of as strengthening the position Pitcher defends, and correlatively casting further doubt on the thesis that for Berkeley physical objects are immediately perceived. In nearly all of the passages in support of immediate perception of objects, Berkeley seems to say that objects are immediately *seen*. Material quoted in support of Pitcher's view conflicts with exactly that statement.

What I think Pitcher does not notice, however, is that in all of the passages supporting his position, and thus his criticism, Berkeley is speaking of objects that are *properly* and immediately perceived, rather than objects that are (merely) immediately perceived. Proper and immediate perception is a concept which is deployed in the *New Theory*, where Berkeley defends the old Aristotelian idea that some ideas are proper to a given sense. Light and colors, he says, can only be immediately seen, smoothness can only be immediately felt. It is in this spirit that he says that sounds, strictly speaking, can only be heard. Thus, in the passages Pitcher cites, and in the additional ones here supplied for him, Berkeley is affirming that

> What is immediately and properly perceived by one sense is not immediately perceived by another sense.

This claim is not at all in conflict with the thesis that

> Physical objects are immediately perceived.

especially when we notice that what is properly and immediately perceived by a given sense is always an *idea* and never a physical object. So,

Pitcher's objection does not point to any genuine conflict with ascribing key components of PDR to Berkeley.[24]

There is another facet of Pitcher's criticism that deserves notice, namely the degree to which it compromises Berkeley's committment to common sense. One of the key elements of common sense, for Berkeley, is the claim that physical objects are immediately perceived. Pitcher's position, therefore, would push one to the view that strictly speaking Berkeley does not really defend common sense at all. He only seems to be doing this when he is speaking loosely. His real view, at least on perception and its objects, is actually opposed to common sense. This way of reading Berkeley is reinforced once we notice that rejection of the public character of physical objects is also part of Pitcher's objection. That different people immediately perceive the same physical object is surely part of what common sense affirms, and thus Pitcher's position would further erode Berkeley's adherence to common sense. But this is a very hard consequence to accept. Berkeley says repeatedly that he is a champion of common sense, and indeed that his primary aim is to bring people back from metaphysical dead-ends and absurdities to common sense. This is *the* prominent theme in the *Dialogues*, but it also surfaces in the *Principles* and in the *Commentaries*. Pitcher's view requires that we not take seriously all of these pledges of adherence to common sense.

What shall we say of the heterogeneity thesis that Berkeley defends in the *New Theory* and in *Theory of Vision Vindicated*? That thesis may seem to conflict with the second item raised by Pitcher, the thesis that a single physical object is both immediately seen and immediately touched or felt. In the preceding section we noted a number of passages in which Berkeley claims that the same object is immediately seen and felt. However, the heterogeneity thesis maintains that no idea which is immediately seen is numerically or even specifically the same as an idea immediately perceived by touch. Hence, since the heterogeneity thesis can hardly be questioned as an item Berkeley held, both early and late, we would have to say that nothing is both immediately seen and felt or touched.[25]

This reasoning, I believe, rests on a misunderstanding of the scope of the heterogeneity thesis. We can bring this out by noting a distinction between two statements:

24. This way of avoiding G. Pitcher's criticism is also in K. Winkler 1989, 156ff. Correspondence with Winkler in 1985 helped shape my thinking on this point. The difference between immediate perception and its objects and proper immediate perception was first, and still earlier, brought to my attention by Joseph Tolliver.

25. Bertil Belfrage (1992) defends this interpretation.

(1) No idea which is immediately perceived by sight is numerically or specifically identical to an idea which is immediately perceived by touch.
(2) Nothing which is immediately seen is also immediately touched.

The first of these two statements expresses Berkeley's heterogeneity thesis in the *New Theory*.

> The extension, figures, and motions perceived by sight are specifically distinct from the ideas of touch called by the same names, nor is there any such thing as one idea or kind of idea common to both senses. (Berkeley 1948–57, 1:222–23)

However, the second statement, above, has much greater scope, claiming not that no *idea* immediately perceived by sight is also immediately touched or felt, but rather that *nothing at all* is both immediately seen and touched. Once this distinction is made, it should be clear that the first statement above, expressing the heterogeneity thesis, does not imply the second. The reason the implication fails is simply that the scope of the latter is much broader than that given in the heterogeneity thesis. Hence, there is no conflict between the common sensical statement that a single object is both immediately seen and touched, and the heterogeneity thesis.[26]

In effect, this issue of scope amounts to the point made earlier in discussing Pitcher. Berkeley distinguishes between ideas which are *proper and immediate* objects of sense, and ideas which are merely *immediate* objects of sense. Proper and immediate ideas are those entities discussed throughout the *New Theory*, and it is these with which the heterogeneity thesis is concerned. The later more philosophical works are more generally concerned just with the immediate objects of sense, not with proper and immediate objects of sense. Once this distinction is observed, it should be clear that on the question of immediate perception and its objects, there is no conflict between the doctrines of the *New Theory* and the account of perception defended in the later philosophical works. The thesis that both ideas and objects, considered as "collections" of ideas, are immediately perceived is perfectly compatible with all of the important positive points contained in the *New Theory*.

26. The same scope distinction suffices to show that there is no conflict between the H-thesis and the claim that physical objects are immediately perceived.

CHAPTER 7

Commonsense Realism

Perceptual direct realism, as I have called it, is one of the main elements in the commonsense realist interpretation of Berkeley. Commonsense realism (hereafter, CSR), as I understand that concept, includes a version of PDR, but also something more. The extra element is *epistemic direct realism* (EDR), briefly alluded to earlier. This chapter will address the question of whether Berkeley accepted CSR, and that will naturally direct attention to whether he accepted EDR. While I will try to show that he did accept the latter, this will not be enough to show that he accepted CSR. The reason for this has already been established. Because there are some elements of PDR that Berkeley did not accept, he did not fully subscribe to CSR. Nevertheless, it will be instructive to review this ground again, for it will help reveal just how close Berkeley came to really accepting commonsense realism. This will show how far one can go in supporting the Luce and Jessop interpretation of Berkeley.

While we may be able to show that Berkeley said he accepted some of the elements making up CSR, it might be argued that there is a sense in which he cannot be said to have accepted those elements after all. This is because those parts of CSR, it is argued, are logically inconsistent with core elements of Berkeley's philosophy, and so though Berkeley said he accepted those parts of CSR, he really could not do so, at least not if he is to remain consistent. The second half of this chapter will take up this consistency question. Here I will try to establish that there is more to be said on Berkeley's behalf than many commentators have allowed.

Commonsense Realism

Commonsense realism includes two broad sets of claims, one perceptual (PDR), and the other epistemic (EDR). More exactly, CSR includes *specific versions* of PDR and of EDR, versions that philosophers have generally said are "naive." We start with PDR where we will set out a fuller statement than the minimal version considered in chapter 6.

PDR has three sub-parts into which we can group its several elements; I earlier identified these as *existential, metaphysical,* and *perceptual* parts. The first of these can be stated this way:

> PDR, existential part: (1) There are ordinary (macro) physical objects; and, (2) all (macro) physical objects and at least some of their qualities exist independently of and are generally unaffected by perceptions.[1]

All realist positions, whether direct or not, accept both of these existential elements of PDR. Differences between various forms of realism, on these existential points, would arise only regarding which qualities of objects would be taken as existing independently of perception.

The metaphysical part of PDR contains two elements. Here the first element is stated in its naive form, which will affect the sense of the first element. Other, non-naive versions of PDR would state this metaphysical element differently.

> PDR, metaphysical part: (1) Every macro physical object has the sensible qualities it is typically perceived to have; and (2) no macro physical object has phenomenal individuals (ideas, sensa) as constituents.

It is clear that clause (1) of this metaphysical part of PDR is "naive" since it implies that physical objects actually have such qualities as colors. They literally have what we might call *manifest* colors or colors as they are perceived. Certainly there are other versions of PDR that do not incorporate this naive metaphysical element. Another view of the qualities of objects would hold that they have only the so-called primary qualities, while still another would say that objects have only the properties attributed to them by physical theories in science. These alternative versions, though, need not be further considered, as the present concern is whether Berkeley accepted the naive, common sense version of PDR.

Fully stated, the properly *perceptual* part of PDR, in its common sense version, includes four elements:

1. For accounts of common sense realism similar to what is given here, see James Cornman 1975.

PDR, perceptual part: (1) Macro physical objects and some of their qualities are typically immediately perceived; (2) macro physical objects are
publicly perceivable; (3) when macro physical objects are immediately
perceived, they are typically immediately perceived as they are; and (4) it
is false that in every perceptual experience, at least one phenomenal individual (idea, sensum) is immediately perceived.

In this perceptual part of PDR we again have a "naive" element, in clause
(3). It is this clause that shows the connection of this common sense version of PDR to the original American school of New Realists such as Holt
and Perry, while it is clause (1) of the perceptual part which makes the
theory a version of *direct* realism.

Besides the foregoing elements of PDR, common sense realism includes
the epistemic theses I have noted make up epistemic direct realism or
EDR. We can state this part of CSR as follows:

EDR: (1) Human cognizers typically gain immediate, non-inferential perceptual knowledge of macro physical objects; and, (2) human cognizers
typically gain certain perceptual knowledge of macro physical objects.

It should be clear that this epistemic part of CSR is independent of PDR, in
the sense that one can accept the latter but reject the former. One might
consistently hold that PDR is correct, in the commonsense version given
above, but still insist that perceptual knowledge is always inferential and
consists in beliefs which are less than certain. Commonsense realism,
however, does not take this tack; instead, it accepts all of the elements of
PDR along with EDR.

Berkeley and CSR

We turn now to the question of whether Berkeley accepted CSR. If we
interpret that question to mean whether he accepted all of the elements
making up CSR, all of PDR and all of EDR, it is plain that the answer will
have to be in the negative. There are parts of PDR that Berkeley rejects.
But it is worth seeing just which parts of PDR and EDR he did accept.

Certainly Berkeley held the first existential part of PDR, Samuel Johnson to the contrary notwithstanding. In accepting the theory of ideas,
Berkeley by no means holds that there are no physical objects. The second
existential part of PDR, however, is in conflict with the EIP principle, and
so would not be acceptable to Berkeley. He says that

philosophers, though they acknowledge all corporeal beings to be perceived by God, yet they attribute to them an absolute subsistence distinct

from their being perceived by any mind whatsoever, which I do not. (Berkeley 1948–57, 2:212)

A physical object has an absolute existence, for Berkeley, just when it is an object that would exist even if there were no perceptions by any mind at all, finite or infinite. In denying that objects have an absolute existence, Berkeley is rejecting the second existential part of PDR.

He does accept something quite close to it, however. In the discussion of the account of creation, for example, Berkeley makes it clear that he holds ideas to have existed as things thought of by God before any perception by finite perceivers. Hence, he would hold the same for all combinations of ideas that are identical to physical objects. So, although he does not hold that objects have an absolute existence, he does hold that they have what we might term *absolute finite existence*:

> Macro physical objects and some of their qualities would exist even if they were not to be perceived by any *finite* perceiver.

It is because there is such a small difference between absolute existence and absolute finite existence that commentators might be tempted into thinking that Berkeley accepts the full existential part of PDR. However, though he comes close, Berkeley actually does not accept all of the existential part, because he does not really accept its second clause.

Neither does he accept all of the metaphysical part of PDR, and again it is the second clause that he rejects. Berkeley would not use the term 'sensa,' of course, but he does use the analogous term 'idea.' The important point is that he thinks that macro physical objects are "collections" of ideas, and so they have ideas as constituent elements. It is this which signals his rejection of clause (2) of the metaphysical part of PDR. Berkeley's view of physical objects is made clear in a number of places, including *Principles* 1, and in a well-known passage from the *Dialogues*:

> A certain colour, taste, smell, figure and consistence having been observed to go together, are accounted one distinct thing, signified by the term apple. Other collections of ideas constitute a stone, a book, and the like sensible things.

> I see this *cherry*, I feel it, I taste it; and I am sure *nothing* cannot be seen, or felt, or tasted; it is therefore *real*. Take away the sensations of softness, moisture, redness, tartness, and you take away the cherry. Since it is not a thing distinct from sensations; a *cherry*, I say, is nothing but a congeries of sensible impressions, or ideas imprinted by various senses: which are united into one thing . . . by the mind; because they are observed to attend one another.

In these passages Berkeley indicates that he accepts an account of physical objects which holds that ideas are constituents of such objects, in some sense of 'constituent.' He does not, then, accept the second element of the metaphysical part of PDR.

He does, however, accept the first element. We can see this clearly in a passage from the *Dialogues* in which Philonous sets out Berkeley's view:

> It is likewise my opinion, that colours and other sensible qualities are on the objects. I cannot for my life help thinking that snow is white, and fire hot. You indeed, who by snow and fire mean certain external, unperceived, unperceiving substances, are in the right to deny whiteness or heat, to be affections in them. But I, who understand by those words the things I see and feel, am obliged to think like other folks. (Berkeley 1948–57, 2:41, 249, 229–30)

This passage shows not only that Berkeley accepted the first element in the metaphysical part of PDR, but also that he regards it as a matter of common sense, i.e., something that the "other folks" believe. Acceptance of this point, however, should not be confused with its converse: that if a macro physical object has some quality, then it is perceived to have that quality. This thesis, which we could say is the thesis that every quality of a physical object is a *manifest quality*, is not endorsed by Berkeley, even though the same thesis when restricted to immediately perceived ideas is endorsed.[2]

Of the four elements in the perceptual part of PDR, I think Berkeley accepts all but the last one. We have already examined the evidence (chapter 6) in favor of thinking that Berkeley accepted the first element in the perceptual part, so that need not be rehearsed again. The question of the public nature of physical objects, noted in the second element of the perceptual part of PDR, is supported by a number of texts, including these from the *Principles*:

> The table I write on, I say, exists, that is, I see and feel it; and if I were out of my study I should say it existed, meaning thereby that if I was in my study I might perceive it, or that some other spirit actually does perceive it.

> Sensible objects may likewise be said to be "without the mind" in another sense, namely, when they exist in some other mind; thus, when I shut my eyes, the things I saw may still exist, but it must be in some other mind.

2. I take the term 'manifest quality' from Cummins 1995, though I do not think the scope of the thesis in Berkeley is as broad as Cummins makes it out.

> For though we hold indeed the objects of sense to be nothing else but ideas which cannot exist unperceived; yet we may not hence conclude they have no existence except only while they are perceived by us, since there may be some other spirit that perceives them, though we do not.

These texts clinch the point that for Berkeley physical objects are publicly perceivable things. To be sure, one might wonder how he is in a position to *consistently* accept this point; however, here I am not (yet) discussing the matter of consistency.

The third, "naive" element in the perceptual part of PDR, that when objects are immediately perceived they are perceived as they are, is a corollary of the first element in the metaphysical part of PDR: that each physical object has the sensible qualities it is typically perceived to have. As we have seen that Berkeley accepts the latter, we need adduce no additional evidence to show that he accepted the former. However, as additional support we may notice this comment from Philonous, which I think not only indicates acceptance of this element of PDR but also indicates that Berkeley regards it as a matter of common sense:

> I am of a vulgar cast, simple enough to believe my senses, and leave things as I find them. To be plain, it is my opinion, that the real things are those very things I see and feel, and perceive by my senses. (Berkeley 1948–57, 2:42, 80, 61, 229)

The fourth element in the perceptual part of PDR, of course, is one that Berkeley rejects. This rejection follows directly from his acceptance of the theory of ideas, according to which in every perceptual experience, at least one idea is immediately perceived. This latter claim is the direct contrary of the fourth element in the perceptual part. Here again a question of consistency becomes relevant. Since Berkeley rejects the fourth element in the perceptual part of PDR, how can he also accept the first element of that part of PDR? This important consistency question, as with the one concerning the public nature of objects, is deferred to the next section.

The other main ingredient in CSR, epistemic direct realism (EDR), was fully accepted by Berkeley. The first element of EDR concerns immediate, non-inferential knowledge of objects. These are not terms Berkeley used; instead, he generally adapts Locke's term 'intuitive knowledge,' but I think this is a mere terminological difference. Berkeley's usage is an adaptation of Locke, because Locke does not think that we have intuitive knowledge of physical objects. Berkeley is sensitive to this point, and even seems to boast about it in the Philosophical Commentaries at 563 and 547:

I am the farthest from Scepticism of any man. I know with an intuitive knowledge the existence of other things as well as my own Soul. This is wᵗ Locke nor scarce any other Thinking Philosopher will pretend to.

We have intuitive Knowledge of the Existence of other things besides our selves & even praecedaneous to the Knowledge of our own Existence, in that we must have Ideas or else we cannot think. (Berkeley 1948–57, 1:70, 69)

This second passage is not as clear as the first, since the term 'other things' may refer merely to ideas, and not also to objects. However, two further passages will help decide the issue.

Away . . . with all that scepticism, all those ridiculous doubts. What a jest it is for a philosopher to question the existence of sensible things, till he hath it proved to him from the veracity of God; or to pretend our knowledge in this point falls short of intuition or demonstration? I might as well doubt of my own being, as of the being of those things I actually see and feel.

We see philosophers distrust their senses, and doubt of the existence of heaven and earth, of everything they see and feel, even of their own bodies. And after all their labour and struggle of thought, they are forced to own, we cannot attain to any self-evident or demonstrative knowledge of the existence of sensible things. But all this doubtfulness which so bewilders and confounds the mind, and makes philosophy ridiculous in the eyes of the world, vanishes, if we annex a meaning to our words, and do not amuse ourselves with the terms *absolute, external, exist*, and such like, signifying I know not what. (Berkeley 1948–57, 2:230, 79)

In this last passage, I take it that when Berkeley says that all these doubts "vanish," he is claiming that, for him, we *do* gain self-evident knowledge of sensible things.[3]

The second element in EDR, regarding certain perceptual knowledge of objects, was also accepted by Berkeley, as the following makes clear:

But however oddly the proposition may sound in words, yet it includes nothing so very strange or shocking in its sense, which in effect amount to no more than this, to wit, that there are only things perceiving and things perceived; or that every unthinking thing is necessarily, and from the very nature of its existence, perceived by some mind . . . Is this as strange as to say, the sensible qualities are not on the objects; or that we cannot be sure of the existence of things, or know anything of their real natures, though we both see and feel them, and perceive them by all our senses?

---

3. This means that the usual interpretation of Berkeley as a foundationalist in epistemology for whom epistemic foundations are restricted to beliefs about ideas is a mistake.

In this passage Berkeley is contrasting his position with that of Hylas, and thus by implication saying that, according to his position but not that of Hylas, we have certain perceptual knowledge of objects. There is another passage which comes on the heels of the last:

> If by *material substance* is meant only sensible body, that which is seen and felt (and the unphilosophical part of the world, I dare say, mean no more) then I am more certain of matter's existence than you or any other philosopher pretend to be . . . I do therefore assert, that I am as certain as of my own being that there are bodies or corporeal substances.

There are also passages in the *Commentaries*, of which 517a is representative:

> N.B. I am more for reality than any other Philosophers, they make a thousand doubts & know not certainly but we may be deceiv'd. I assert the direct contrary. (Berkeley 1948–57, 2:236, 237–8, 64)

Here Berkeley does not mention objects. However, it is clear that he talking about Descartes, and the sort of "reality" of which Descartes is doubtful is that of the material world. It is this, then, about which Berkeley is claiming certain knowledge.

Let us take stock. Of the eight items making up the three parts of PDR, Berkeley accepts five and rejects three. On the other hand he accepts all of EDR, the other main ingredient in CSR. In the strict sense, then, Berkeley certainly does not count as a defender of of CSR, since there are three key elements in it, all included within PDR, that he does not accept. What he does accept are seven of the ten total elements making up CSR. Of these accepted items, Berkeley makes the most of his acceptance of three, since these are the items which most clearly mark out differences between his philosophy and that defended by others such as Locke, Malebranche, or Descartes. These three, most stressed by Berkeley, are the two elements of EDR and the thesis that physical objects are typically immediately perceived.

Digression on Direct Realism

Direct realists about perception share with Berkeley the thesis that physical objects are typically immediately perceived. They agree, that is, that objects are perceived without dependence on perceived intermediaries of specific sorts. It will prove helpful for later discussion of related themes in Berkeley to say more about immediate perception of objects as this is conceived of by direct realists. What is given here is by no means a full treatment of direct perceptual realism; rather, attention is focused on those direct realist themes which will recur in Berkeley; or where Berkeleyan counterparts to those direct realist themes will come up for discussion.

One important item is that when an object is immediately perceived, for a direct realist, there is no requirement that every *part* of the object is also immediately perceived. We can see this by taking an example of immediately seeing an object such as the Washington Monument. When a person immediately sees the Monument, she does so from some point and from some perspective; perhaps she looks at the Monument from the south. In that case she will not immediately see the side of the Monument which faces north, and it is likely that she will fail to immediately see very much of the sides which face east and west. In this case, then, she will fail to see many of the parts which make up the Monument, indeed probably most of those parts. The parts she immediately sees are those in the south wall, and some of those in the east and west walls. Nevertheless, though she immediately sees just some percentage of the total number of parts making up this object, she still immediately sees the Monument itself.

Further, this point will apply generally to immediate perception of objects. In nearly every case of immediate perception of an object, one will fail to immediately perceive some percentage of the object's parts. There may be some cases where this will not hold. Imagine a person holding a small cube in her hand. She may then both immediately perceive the cube, by touch, and immediately perceive by touch every part of the cube. Even here, however, we would have to assume a very coarse-grained individuation of parts in order to make the case. On any more fine-grained individuation of parts, even when she is immediately touching all six sides of the cube, she is not touching every part, for she would not be touching every part of the surface of each side and neither would she be touching or otherwise immediately perceiving any of the internal parts of the cube. So, even if we allow that on *some* account of parts, there will be a few cases in which a person immediately perceives all of the parts of an object, this will not be true in general. But in many of the cases in which it is not true, one will still immediately perceive the object by immediately perceiving some of its parts. In this respect, immediate perception of objects is just like the Monument case described above.

In all of these examples, the direct realist exploits the ordinary way in which we use all-purpose perception verbs. So, when we make use of 'sees' and say that Sara sees the Washington Monument, we do not require that she see every part of the Monument. The direct realist is simply adapting this to her talk of immediately seeing the Monument. Our ordinary concept of seeing, and more generally of perceiving, is being used, except that the perception verb takes the prefix 'immediately.'

A related and similar point applies if we are talking of properties rather than parts. Whenever one immediately sees an object, one will immediately see one or more of its properties. So, in immediately seeing the Monument, one also immediately sees the color of the south wall, and the shape of the south wall. But there will be many properties of the Monument one will fail to see, perhaps even most of them. For instance, one will likely not immediately see the texture of the walls, not even the south one from a certain distance, and neither will one immediately see or otherwise perceive its density. Nor will one immediately perceive the properties of the walls out of one's line of vision. But despite all of this, one immediately sees the Monument. In general, one immediately perceives objects despite the fact that one fails to immediately perceive many, maybe even most, of the object's properties. For most objects, this will even be true if we restrict attention just to non-relational properties. One might immediately perceive a greater percentage of such properties, but seldom if ever would one immediately perceive all of an object's non-relational properties. This fact, though, would not mean that one would fail to immediately perceive the object in question.

Indeed, there are some cases in which one might immediately perceive nearly all of an object's parts, and still fail to immediately perceive the object. Imagine that a car is carefully disassembled, and each of its parts is hung up on a sturdy clothesline. So one sees in a single glance the doors, wheels, fenders, front grill, windshield, and so on, and so sees in one glance nearly all of the car's parts. However, in this case we would not say that one had immediately seen the car, because the parts one immediately saw were not attached in the right way. The stress on being attached *in the right way* is important; we would not want to acknowledge that the car is immediately seen if, after disassembly, the parts were then welded together in some quite un-car-like vertical sculpture, all of which one could see in a single glance. Then one would immediately see a bizarre pirce of sculpture, but one would not immediately see the car, even though one immediately saw nearly all of its parts and they were attached.

I doubt if there is any principled way of specifying how great a percentage of parts or properties one needs to immediately perceive if one is to immediately perceive an object.[4] Cases run on a spectrum where our intuitive judgments are firmest at either end of the spectrum. If the Monument were totally hidden by dense fog except for a very small, six inch square

4. See Peter Alexander 1970.

part of the south wall which was strangely fog-free, then immediately seeing that six inch square would not be sufficient for immediately seeing the Monument. True, one would then immediately see an attached part of the Monument. However, one would have failed to immediately see enough of the Monument's parts—or enough of a single part, if one thinks of the entire south wall as a single part—and so one would fail to immediately see the Monument. Similarly, suppose that Chris is standing behind a high and solid wooden fence, in such a way that she can put her hand through a small hole in the fence. If one were to immediately see just Chris' hand, one would not thereby immediately see Chris, despite the fact that the hand is a part attached in the right way. One simply has not immediately seen enough of Chris.

Points analogous to those here discussed for the direct realist will arise in connection with an assessment of Berkeley's claim that, on his theory, physical objects are immediately perceived. However, in that discussion we will have to utilize additional examples from the direct realist repertoire to fully appreciate Berkeley's position.

Consistency

We have noted that Berkeley does not accept CSR. That doctrine is a conjunction of ten separate claims, and we have seen that there are three of them which he rejects. The rejection in each case has the same form. Thus, the CSR proposition expressed by "No macro physical object has phenomenal individuals (sensa, ideas) as constituents" is rejected by Berkeley in the sense that there is a proposition, expressed by "A physical object is nothing but a collection of ideas," which is certainly something Berkeley accepts, and this latter proposition is a contrary of and thus entails the denial of the former CSR proposition. The case is similar for the CSR proposition expressed by "Macro physical objects exist independently of all perceptions;" this proposition is a direct contrary of Berkeley's EIP principle. Also, the fourth element in the perceptual part of PDR, "It is false that in every perceptual experience, at least one phenomenal individual (sensum, idea) is immediately perceived"—is a direct contrary of a proposition Berkeley accepts. In this sense Berkeley's philosophy is inconsistent with CSR. His philosophy contains three theses which are each explicit denials of statements included in CSR.

There is another inconsistency question that one might raise, one that concerns the remaining elements in CSR that Berkeley accepts. Is any one of those elements inconsistent with Berkeley's philosophy as well? If so, then perhaps Berkeley could not even say that there are important parts of

CSR with which his philosophy is in agreement. In turn, this would mean that the Luce-Jessop interpretation of Berkeley would be on even shakier ground.

There are three ways to understand this additional inconsistency question. First, one might wonder whether each of the seven elements of CSR that Berkeley accepts is itself consistent. Or, second, one might question whether these seven items, each individually consistent, are consistent with one another. These two issues do not seem to me worthy of consideration. The seven items of CSR accepted by Berkeley, I think, are obviously individually consistent; and the fact that we take CSR to be consistent is good evidence that the seven items Berkeley accepts make up a consistent set. It is the third way of thinking of inconsistency which is important: is Berkeley's philosophy inconsistent with one or more of the seven items in CSR which he accepts? Thus, to illustrate: is the claim that macro physical objects are publicly perceivable inconsistent with Berkeley's philosophy? This is the present concern, for each of the seven elements in CSR accepted by Berkeley.

To examine this question properly, we have to take seriously the phrase "inconsistent with Berkeley's philosophy," and that requires that we be able to say what we take Berkeley's philosophy to be. Two problems arise in making that specification. First, there are just too many propositions which have a claim to being included as parts of Berkeley's philosophy, and we can hardly be interested in listing all of them. Second, and more importantly, many of the items we would want to include in Berkeley's philosophy will be irrelevant to the seven accepted elements of CSR. For example, Berkeley's claim that some highly theoretical scientific terms, what I called earlier 'wide abstract ideas,' are far removed from sense and so lack meaning, seems to me to be logically irrelevant to the seven accepted items in CSR. But Berkeley's stance on wide abstract ideas is certainly part of his overall philosophy.

The approach to take, I think, is to identify what to include in Berkeley's philosophy by using one or both of two criteria: (a) what do we think is absolutely essential to Berkeley's philosophy; and, (b) what, among things accepted by Berkeley, is most relevant to one or more of the seven items in CSR which we have seen he accepts? Joint use of these two criteria leads us to the following list as the propositions making up Berkeley's philosophy.

1. Nominalism is true, at least insofar as there are no abstract general ideas, and everything in nature is particular.
2. The EIP principle is correct.

3. The only kinds of things that exist are perceivers, which are finite spirits, and things perceived, which are ideas and groups of ideas.

4. It is false that physical objects are partially constituted by material substance.

5. The theory of ideas is correct, i.e., the cognitive acts of perceiving, remembering, and imagining are always directed at, or have among their contents, ideas.

6. There is an infinite perceiver who in some way perceives all ideas, and thus all groups of ideas.

For convenience, this set of propositions will be referred to as *set B*. I would emphasize, again, that B does not contain the full range of propositions making up Berkeley's philosophy; it contains just those propositions picked out by use of the above two criteria.

Is B inconsistent with the first element in the existential part of PDR, that is, with the claim that there are macro physical objects? Statement (3) in B is perfectly consistent with the account Berkeley gives of objects as collections of ideas; and, since ideas and collections of them exist, Berkeley is entitled to hold, too, that macro physical objects exist. However, an objection might be lodged, based on the notion of a collection of ideas. Whichever way Berkeley explicates the notion of a collection, any collection which is a physical object will have just some of its constituent ideas in existence at any one time. Indeed, at any one time *most* of the constituent ideas in the collection will not exist. So, it will not be strictly speaking true that the *object* which Berkeley takes to be this collection will exist at that moment either. Hence, this objection concludes, B is really inconsistent with the existence of physical objects after all. More exactly, it is B as supplemented with the identification of some groups of ideas, mentioned in item (3), with objects which has this result.[5]

There are two responses open to Berkeley on this point. The first, in the spirit of the objection, is to note that on the ordinary, non-collections, way of thinking of objects, many of the properties and conditions the object will eventually have or be in do not exist at any given time. However, we do not for that reason hold that the object fails to exist at that time. The "collections of ideas case" is analogous to this truth about objects ordinarily construed; so, since we do not draw the conclusion that the object fails to exist in the latter case, we should not do in the collections of ideas case either.

5. Harry Bracken (1965) urges an objection along these lines.

A second, and perhaps better response would be to refer again to the account of creation which Berkeley gives in the *Dialogues*. Part of his story is that God in some way *always* perceives, or at least *always* has as objects of his thought, all ideas, and thus all groups of ideas. Hence, it would not be true that these groups of ideas would be missing any constituent ideas at any time. The objection assumes that ideas not perceived by any finite perceiver do not exist, and this is something that Berkeley denies in his account of the creation. Set B, then, is consistent with the existence of macro physical objects.

The next item to consider is the first element in the metaphysical part of PDR: the thesis that each macro physical object has the sensible qualities it is typically perceived to have. We can again advert to the collections account of objects to help show that this thesis is consistent with B. Sometimes, as at *Principles* 1, Berkeley expresses the collections thesis by saying that an object such as an apple is a collection of sensible qualities. He feels free to switch to the claim that an object is a collection of ideas, because he thinks that every sensible quality is an idea. If this last statement were correct, then of course objects would have the sensible qualities they are perceived to have. For in perceiving an object one is thereby perceiving some of the ideas (sensible qualities) in the collection that makes up that object. Hence, set B as supplemented with the collections account of objects is consistent with the claim that objects have the sensible qualities they are typically perceived to have. It is no objection to the foregoing argument for consistency to maintain that the thesis that every sensible quality is an idea is just false. We could concede the falsity of that thesis without impugning the consistency claim.

It is reasonable to think Berkeley would use the above reasoning, especially when we remember that the thesis that every sensible quality is an idea was used as a premise in arguments for the EIP principle. However, there is another more complex answer suggested by some texts. First, we note a reason to be less than happy with the contention that every sensible quality is an idea. A sensible quality of an object, say its shape or color, are generally enduring features of the object, and so are entities which persist across time just as the object does. We will thus not want to identify a sensible quality with *an* idea, for it does not exist across time. We noted a similar point in connection with objects. Sometimes Berkeley speaks of objects as (single) ideas, but it is very doubtful that this expresses his real view and for a similar reason: objects have a sort of permanency which individual ideas lack. In the case of objects, of course, there are also texts where Berkeley tells us that an object is not an idea, but rather a collection of ideas. He does not say any such thing regarding qualities; however, he does make a related suggestive point.

In the *Principles* Berkeley speaks more fully of ideas of sense than he does elsewhere:

> The ideas of sense are more strong, lively, and distinct than those of the imagination; they likewise have a steadiness, order, and coherence, and are not excited at random, as those which are the effects of human wills often are, but in a regular train or series, the admirable connexion whereof sufficiently testifies the wisdom and benevolence of its Author. (Berkeley, 1948–57, 2:53)

He goes on to call these regular trains of ideas *Laws of Nature*, which he says we learn by experience, "which teaches us that such and such ideas are attended with such and such other ideas, in the ordinary course of things" (ibid.) Two kinds of "laws of nature," or regularities in the order of ideas, are suggested in these passages. First, there is a regularity wherein the same idea is experienced in similar circumstances ("the ordinary course of things"). When one looks at something that is brown in color and thereby experiences an idea of brown, then one will regularly experience an idea of brown in similar perceptual circumstances, "in the ordinary course of things." These passages also suggest regularities between different ideas. In looking at and touching the same brown desk, the idea of brown is regularly attended with the tactile idea of a certain smoothness, and this regularity is also reckoned a "law of nature." It is the first sort of regularity which is most relevant at this juncture.

The brown color of a desk is ordinarily a stable, ongoing feature of the desk. Berkeley's talk of regularities in the series of ideas may be indicative of a different way he thought of sensible qualities, other than identifying them with individual ideas. That is, he may have in mind that what it is for the desk to be brown is for one to regularly experience ideas of brown when one gazes at the desk in ordinary circumstances. This would be to identify the color brown with a pattern of ideas of the same sort, relative to fixed circumstances. Or, he may have had in mind something different: for an object to be brown is for one to regularly experience ideas of brown in its presence, and for it to be true that were anyone in these circumstances to attend to the object, that individual would experience ideas of brown.

These two ways of speaking of an object being brown correspond, in Berkeley's terminology, to what may be more familiar in another idiom. Some have been tempted to say that for an object to be brown is just for the object to look brown in normal circumstances of viewing. The idea is that the object is brown just in case it regularly looks brown. A somewhat different position would be that the object is brown just in case it regularly looks brown in some circumstances, and would look brown to anyone placed in those circumstances. On either of these ways of construing color in objects, it will be true that objects have the colors they are perceived to have. For the colors objects are perceived to have just are the colors they look or seem to have and, given these accounts, that just is the color of the object. Berkeley's position, as suggested in his talk of laws of nature within the realm of experienced ideas, would have the same result. The color something is perceived to have is the color one regularly receives in idea, and that would just be the color of the object, according to this way of thinking of color.

If this account of color is anything like what Berkeley has in mind with his talk of laws of nature defined over ideas, then of course it will have to be generalized to range over all sensible qualities. In the passages quoted above wherein Berkeley talks of regularities within ideas, he is not speaking merely of ideas of colors. Generalizing in the indicated way across all of the sensible qualities would then yield the result that, given either of these accounts of sensible qualities, objects would have the sensible qualities they are typically perceived to have. Hence, the first element in the metaphysical part of CSR would be consistent with Berkeley's philosophy, in the sense that it would be consistent with set B as supplemented with one of these accounts of what sensible qualities are.

The first element in the perceptual part of CSR is the thesis that physical objects are typically immediately perceived. The main reason to think that this is inconsistent with set B is that statement (5) in B seems to require that objects be at best mediately perceived. If there is always a perceived idea in every perceptual experience, then *it* (the idea) will be a perceived intermediary and any object then perceived will be mediately perceived.

To see that this argument is incorrect, we need only note, again, Berkeley's adoption of the "collections account" of objects. On that view, an object is identical to a collection of ideas. It is thus open to Berkeley to argue that *by* immediately perceiving some of the constituent ideas in the collection that makes up an object, one thereby immediately perceives the object as well. The discussion of direct realism given earlier is a useful analog. In that theory, *by* immediately perceiving some of the parts of the building, one thereby immediately perceives the building. Berkeley's case is similar, except that the ideas in the collection are not *parts* of the object.

A closer analogy from direct realism would involve an "object" that has members but not parts. Consider the professor in front of the large introductory lecture class. By immediately seeing some of the members of the class, as she gazes out over the audience, she thereby immediately sees the class. Or consider a case of a general on the reviewing stand as the troop marches past. By immediately seeing some of the members of the troop, the general also immediately sees the troop. This is so despite the fact that the general fails to immediately see all of the members of the troop; and the professor need not see all the members of the class in order to immediately see the class. These examples are analogous enough to what would hold in Berkeley's theory, given his collections account of objects, that we can readily see that set B, supplemented with the collections account, is consistent with the immediate perception of objects.[6]

While this story makes set B and the immediate perception of objects consistent, there are two reasons to withhold assent. First, immediately perceiving some constituent ideas which are members of the collection making up some object is immediately perceiving *too few* of the constituents making up that collection. This would be analogous to seeing one or two of the soldiers in the troop. By doing that, one does not thereby immediately see the troop. The situation in such an example would be like the example, given earlier, of seeing just a very limited part of a person—his hand—which is sticking through the hole in the fence, while all the rest of the person is hidden. One does not see the nearly totally hidden person by seeing just that one hand, even though it is an attached part of the person. The reason is that one does not see enough of the person, or enough of the attached parts of the person, for it to be true that one also sees the person. Another reason to be doubtful of the above account is simply that Berkeley never talks about immediate perception of objects in quite that way. He does talk about immediately perceiving objects; and, he does adopt the collections account. But generally these two are put together with allusions to perceiving the object's sensible qualities.

We know that Berkeley frequently interchanges his collections statement: a physical object is a collection of ideas, he sometimes says; or, a physical object is a collection of sensible qualities, as he says at other points. He feels entitled to do this, as we have noted, because he thinks that each sensible quality is an idea. If *that* is assumed, we can more readily see why he would have supposed that on his theory objects are immediately perceived. By immediately perceiving enough of an object's qualities, one thereby immediately perceives the object. Consider the desk again. By immediately seeing the brown color and the shape of the top, and perhaps the texture of its surface by touch, one also immediately perceives the desk. This way of viewing the matter makes Berkeley's account somewhat more analogous to direct realism than talking of idea-constituents of the collection making up an object. Further, this same sort of

6. Further development of these points is contained in my "Berkeley and Immediate Perception."

construal of his thinking on this matter would carry through if his official account of sensible qualities were given by either of the regularities and "laws of nature" positions discussed above. On each of those positions, one would immediately perceive the sensible qualities and thus immediately perceive the object. Either way, by talking of idea-constituents of collections, or by talking of qualities, one will secure the consistency of set B and immediate perception of objects. Talk of sensible qualities, however, seems to be more in line with Berkeley's thinking on the matter.

Another element in the perceptual part of CSR is the thesis that physical objects are publicly perceivable. As we briefly noted in chapter, Pitcher has argued that this element is inconsistent with Berkeley's philosophy. Although Pitcher does not talk of set B, we can understand his argument to be that statement (5) of B logically excludes the public character of physical objects.[7] Statement (5) in B implies that in every perceptual experience it, at least one idea is immediately perceived. However, every immediately perceived idea is private to the individual who experiences it, in the sense that it is impossible for anyone else to immediately perceive exactly that idea. No idea immediately perceived by one person, in other words, is numerically identical to an idea immediately perceived by another. It would follow, Pitcher says, that no two people ever immediately perceive the same physical object, because no two people ever immediately perceive the same idea-constituent of the collection which makes up the object. Hence, Berkeley's philosophy, in the form of set B, logically rules out the claim that objects are publicly perceivable, and thus deepens the inconsistency between CSR and Berkeley's philosophy.[8]

Pitcher's argument rests on the assumption that if two people do not immediately perceive the same constituents of an object, or perhaps if those two people cannot immediately perceive the same constituents, then they do not immediately perceive the same object. To test this assumption we can imagine a case of two people on either side of a large wooden fence, and suppose that each is looking at the fence. We would say, I think, that each person sees the fence, even though each is seeing different parts of the fence. Of course, this example is not fully analogous to Berkeley's account, because as already noted ideas are not parts of physical objects. However, the general on the reviewing stand example will suffice to make the point here. That is, two generals on different sections of the reviewing stand, may see different members of the troop, but still each would see the troop. Two people can see the same object even

7. George Pitcher 1986, 99–105.
8. Besides Pitcher, this line of thought has been endorsed by Richard van Iten (1962, 61–62). See, too, David Yandell 1995.

though they do not see the same parts or constituent elements of the object.

These comments will not affect Pitcher's argument if he understands his assumption to be stating a logical exclusion, i.e., to be saying what follows if two people *cannot* perceive the same constituents of an object. To deal with that point, we can consider a different example. Think of an object O as having temporal parts. Thus, O-at-time-t is a time slice of the whole of O, and O-at-time-t+1 is a different time slice of the whole of O. Imagine that person S immediately perceives O-at-time-t, and that person T immediately perceives O-at-time-t+1. In these circumstances, it is not possible for S at t to immediately perceive O-at-t+1, and neither is it possible for person T at t+1 to immediately perceive O-at-t. Nevertheless, both S and T immediately perceive O, by immediately perceiving different time slice constituents of the whole of O. Pitcher's assumption is false, even on the stronger logical reading.

There is another response to Pitcher's argument worth considering, one that questions the contention that each perceived idea is private to one perceiver. If it is true that Berkeley's God in some sense always perceives each idea, as I claimed earlier (chapter 5), then it is false that each idea is private to exactly one perceiver. Since Pitcher's argument requires this privacy assumption concerning ideas, we would thus have another independent reason to think that his argument fails. However, while strictly speaking a correct response to Pitcher, this argument will ultimately carry little weight in connection with CSR. For that theory, we may assume, is implicitly speaking only of non-divine perceivers when it claims that objects are publicly perceivable objects. To secure the consistency of the latter claim with set B, we need to undermine Pitcher's other assumption.

We should also notice that if Berkeley's real view of sensible qualities is either of the accounts we briefly considered in terms of regularities, then Pitcher's argument can be effectively blocked, even if the *idea* perceived by each individual is private to that person. Each of these private ideas would be elements of the regular series of ideas which helps to make up the sensible quality, and so though the ideas are private the quality each immediately perceives is the same, numerically the same.

Would not this manuever simply move the question one step back? We would have the ideas each be elements or constituents in the "collection" which make up the regular pattern of ideas that, we have taken Berkeley to suggest, constitutes the sensible quality. The ideas are private, while the sensible quality is public; thus, Pitcher's original argument re-emerges, this time directed at qualities rather than objects.

To see that this version of the argument is not forceful, we can consider yet another direct realist theory, the theory recently propounded by

William Alston.[9] On his account, for a brown desk to look brown and rectangular in normal viewwing conditions just *is* for one to directly (immediately) see the desk. On Alston's theory, the event of something's looking brown, is a non-epistemic, non-conceptual episode, quite analogous to what, I argued, we find with Berkeley's concept of immediate perception. Now imagine persons S and T looking at the desk. We may suppose that the desk looks brown and rectangular to S, and that it also looks brown and rectangular to T. The event of the desk's looking brown and rectangular to S is private to S; and the related event in T is private to T. But for all that we would agree that they both directly (immediately) see the brownness and rectagular shape of the desk. Berkeley's theory, thought of along the lines of the different accounts of regularities of ideas earlier described, is strictly similar to Alston's on this matter. Hence, since we would want to hold that S and T both directly see the same qualities, given Alston's theory, we should say the same for Berkeley's theory, given one of the regularity accounts of sensible qualities.

Another element of PDR is the thesis that when physical objects are perceived, they are typically perceived as they are. To see that this thesis is consistent with set B we need only note that it implies that if an object is perceived to have a sensible quality F, then it does have F. This latter statement, in turn, is implied by the statement from the metaphysical part of PDR which asserts that physical objects have the sensible qualities they are perceived to have. We noted earlier that this element of the metaphysical part of PDR is consistent with set B; hence, the present element from the perceptual part of PDR is also consistent with set B. The thesis that when physical objects are perceived, they are generally perceived as they are, is not only a thesis Berkeley accepts, but is also one that is consistent with his core philosophical doctrines as reflected in set B.

We come, then, to EDR, and here it may seem that each of its two elements is in conflict with set B, and for a number of different reasons. The first element of EDR—that we typically gain immediate, non-inferential perceptual knowledge physical objects—may be thought to be in conflict with set B, as supplemented with the collections account of objects. The argument is this: the collections account of objects really amounts to endorsement on Berkeley's part of analytical phenomenalism, that is, the thesis that every physical object statement is analyzable into statements about ideas. The latter idea-statements, which make up the analysans of any physical object statement, will include mostly subjunctive conditionals of the form "If one were to immediately perceive idea of such-and-such a sort, then one would also immediately perceive an idea of thus-

9. William Alston 1993, chap. 2.

and-so a sort." This will mean that if we really have immediate, non-inferential perceptual knowledge of physical objects, then we would have to have such knowledge of complex subjunctive conditionals of the type just indicated. However, the argument continues, we never have immediate and non-inferential knowledge of conditionals of that type and with that degree of complexity. So, we have no immediate and non-inferential knowledge of physical objects provided that set B is supplemented with this phenomenalist reading of the collections account of objects. Hence, the first part of EDR is inconsistent with set B as supplemented.[10]

One problem with this argument is that it is doubtful that analytical phenomenalism is the correct interpretation of the collections account. Consider *Principles* 3, where a phenomenalist position seems to be asserted:

> The table I write on, I say, exists, that is, I see it and feel it; and if I were out of my study I should say it existed, meaning thereby that if I was in my study I might perceive it, or that some other spirit actually does perceive it. (Berkeley 1948–57, 2:42)

There are three reasons to think this is not an expression of *analytical* phenomenalism. First, the passage concerns only existential physical object statements and so has restricted scope. Analytical phenomenalism, however, is a thesis about all physical object statements. Second, Berkeley makes use of terms referring to persons in his statement (the terms 'I' and 'other spirit'), and it is doubtful that analytical phenomenalism countenances such non-idea terms in its analysans. Third, and most importantly, Berkeley refers to the table itself in the subjunctive conditional he specifies as the meaning of the statement, "A table exists." This comes in his double use of the term 'it,' which is clearly referring to the table. If the passage were an endorsement of analytical phenomenalism, then, it would be circular, containing physical object terms in the analysans.

The latter two points apply, as well, to another passage in which Berkeley seems to endorse something like analytical phenomenalism, though not in full generality.

> The question, whether the earth moves or no, amounts in reality to no more than this, to wit, whether we have reason to conclude from what hath been observed by astronomers, that if we were placed in such and such circumstances, and or such a position and distance, both from the earth and sun, we should perceive the former to move among the choir of

10. Winkler (1989, 193ff.) defends analytical phenomenalism as an interpretation of Berkeley.

the planets, and appearing in all respects like one of them. (Berkeley 1948–57, 2:65–66)

If we take this as an analysis of the statement expressed by "the earth moves," it is certainly not an analysis that meets the demands of analytical phenomenalism. For, as with the example of the table, the suggested analysans here explicitly contains terms referring both to observers, and to physical objects and, going beyond the table case, it contains terms referring to conditions of observation. None of these sorts of terms in the analysans are permitted by analytical phenomenalism, which restricts non-logical terms in the analysans to idea-terms.

Suppose, however, that analytical phenomenalism *is* correct as an interpretation of Berkeley's notion of a physical object. I do not think it follows that what one knows, when one knows some physical object statement to be true, is some subjunctive conditional couched in the vocabulary of ideas. This would follow only if a certain deduction principle were correct:

If a person S knows that p and p entails q, then S knows that q.

However, this principle is not true, and it is not difficult to see why. If S knows p but does not know that p entails q, she need not know that q. If S knows that Jack is in Libya, and Jack's being in Libya entails that Jack is in a place which is west of Egypt, S need not know that Jack is in a place which is west of Egypt, so long as she does not know of the relevant directional relation of Libya and Egypt. Hence, even if analytical phenomenalism were correct as an account of Berkeleyan objects, it would not have the implication that immediate knowledge of physical objects is ruled out.

Another objection to this first element of EDR comes from *Principles* 59. There Berkeley tells us what knowledge of the physical realm amounts to, and his message is that it is inferential. Since we may properly think of his statement on knowledge in that passage as an official augmentation of set B, then so augmented, B is inconsistent with the thesis that we have immediate knowledge of objects. Here is the relevant passage:

We may, from the experience we have had of the train and succession of ideas in our minds, often make, I will not say uncertain conjectures, but sure and well-grounded predictions, concerning the ideas we shall be affected with, pursuant to a great train of actions, and be enabled to pass a right judgment of what would have appeared to us, in case we were placed in circumstances very different from those we are in at present. Herein consists the knowledge of Nature, which may preserve its use and certainty very consistently with what hath been said. It will be easy to apply this to whatever objections of the like sort may be drawn from the magnitude of the stars, or any other discoveries in astronomy or Nature. (Berkeley 1948–57, 2:42, 65–66)

The reference to well-grounded predictions of later ideas is the key element in this passage; coupling this with the claim that "herein consists the knowledge of Nature . . . " seems to have the immediate consequence that all knowledge of the physical is inferential.

I doubt the passage has to be read in this way. In both sections 58 and 59, Berkeley is talking about scientific knowledge, and in particular knowledge in astronomy. The phrase "knowledge of Nature" is thus referring to the knowledge we have in science, of the motions of bodies particularly those studied in astronomy. Inferential knowledge in *those* domains is perfectly consistent with immediate knowledge of perceived near-by objects. There is no indication that Berkeley is talking of the latter in the last-quoted passage. That passage, in other words, does not contain a general statement of what knowledge of anything physical consists in, but is much more restricted in scope, dealing just with some scientific knowledge.

A third objection aims at finding internal logical difficulties within the thesis that we have immediate knowledge of objects. Immediate knowledge of some proposition p, the argument runs, requires that one's belief that p be absolutely certain. However, no belief about a physical object is ever really certain, nor could it be. For a certain belief is one which cannot be in error, and this one cannot attain with respect to physical object beliefs. So, one cannot have immediate knowledge of physical objects; the very idea is logically muddled once we stop and think about it. Augmenting set B with a statement that cannot be true will produce an inconsistent set of statements, and in this sense the first element of EDR is inconsistent with set B.

This argument, too, is problematic, and for two reasons. First, the claim that immediate knowledge requires absolute certainty is dubious, both on general epistemological grounds and, more importantly in the present context, because it underestimates the epistemological situation in Berkeley's time period.[11] To understand the latter point, we need only recall Locke's discussion of sensitive knowledge. Such knowledge is had of presently perceived physical objects, but it falls short of counting as intuitive knowledge. The manner in which it falls short of being intuitive is not that sensitive knowledge is inferential. Rather, while both intuitive and sensitive knowledge are immediate, intuitive knowledge has a higher

---

11. For the general epistemological point, see my "Non-Inferential Knowledge," 1982.

degree of certainty than sensitive knowledge enjoys. Hence, for Locke it will not be true that all immediate knowledge requires absolute certainty.[12] Another shortcoming in the above argument is that it is not *logically* false that some knowledge of physical objects is absolutely certain. It does seem true, as Descartes noted, that beliefs about physical objects always can be in error. This shows that it is just false that we have absolutely certain beliefs about physical objects. But it does nothing to show that certain beliefs about physical objects are logically impossible. Hence, even if immediate knowledge did imply absolute certainty, what it would show is that Berkeley was wrong to hold that we have immediate knowledge of physical objects, not that he was inconsistent in accepting that thesis.[13]

When we look back at set B, we notice that it is statement (5)—essentially giving the theory of ideas—which is most apt to be in conflict with immediate knowledge of physical objects. Since in every perceptual experience one immediately perceives one or more ideas, it would seem that any knowledge one acquires about a physical object as a result of such perception will be inferential, and based upon the knowledge one gains of the immediately perceived ideas. However, we should also recall that though he endorses (5), Berkeley also holds that we typically perceive physical objects immediately and, we have noted, he is consistent in holding this to be true. It is this fact which undercuts the worry that statement (5) would force Berkeley into thinking that perceptual knowledge of objects is always inferential. Immediate perception of objects, even with the truth of (5), is what allows for immediate, non-inferential knowledge of objects.

The second element of EDR, and the last element in CSR, is the thesis that the (immediate) knowledge often gained of physical objects is *certain* knowledge. The primary reason to think that set B has a negative bearing on this thesis comes, again, from statement (5), and in particular from the supposition that (5) forces Berkeley into holding that perceptual knowledge of objects is always inferential. When knowledge is inferential, it will generally fall short of being certain. Hence, one would conclude that statement (5), and thus set B, rules out Berkeley's claim that we have certain perceptual knowledge of objects.

There are two reasons to regard this argument as less than conclusive. First, as we saw immediately above, statement (5) in B does not drive

12. Locke's account of non-inferential sensitive knowledge is in book iv of the *Essay*, chapters II and III. Its status as non-inferential might be contested, though in the present context I will not digress to take up that issue.

13. Ian Tipton (1974, 112) says that Berkeley cannot hold that knowledge of physical objects is immediate because such knowledge is not certain.

Berkeley to the position that all perceptual knowledge of objects is inferential. Hence, certainty would not be ruled out on grounds of *inferentiality*, since Berkeley consistently with (5) holds that we have immediate perceptual knowledge of objects. Second, we need to be sensitive to what Berkeley means by 'certainty.' Berkeley does not hold that a proposition p is certain only if one's belief that p cannot be mistaken, though he does hold that if one's belief that p cannot be mistaken, then one is certain in one's belief that p. Berkeley has two concepts of certainty, and he applies them differentially depending on the objects of one's beliefs. Consider what he says about individually perceived ideas in the Introduction to *Principles*.

> So long as I confine my thoughts to my own ideas divested of words, I do not see how I can easily be mistaken. The objects I consider, I clearly and adequately know. I cannot be deceived in thinking I have an idea which I have not. It is not possible for me to imagine, that any of my own ideas are alike or unlike, that are not truly so. (Berkeley, 1948–57, 2:39)

The relevant passages in which a different, weaker concept of certainty is deployed were noted in chapter 6 and are worth repeating here:

> Let me be represented as one who trusts his senses, who thinks he knows the things he sees and feels, and entertains no doubts of their existence.

> I do therefore assert that I am as certain as of my own being that there are bodies or corporeal substances (meaning the things I perceive by my senses) . . .

> I might as well doubt of my own being as of the being of those things I actually see and feel. (Berkeley 1948–57, 2:237, 238, 230)

> N.B. I am more for reality than any other Philosophers, they make a thousand doubts & know not certainly but we may be deceiv'd. I assert the direct contrary. (Berkeley 1948–1957, 1:64)

In these passages, it is clear firstly that Berkeley is applying the notion of certainty to physical objects and not to individually perceived ideas. Second, the concept of certainty he makes use of in these passages is not that wherein mistaken belief is impossible. Rather, here he links certainty of belief with those beliefs for which one has no doubts. This is a much weaker concept of certainty than the former, and it is when we attend to this concept that we see that the thesis that we have certain perceptual knowledge of objects is consistent with statement (5) in set B. Having immediate, non-inferential perceptual knowledge of objects, we have found, is consistent with statement (5) in B. Noticing now that such knowledge requires, for Berkeley, only that one actually have no doubts about that physical object belief, indicates that it is quite *plausible* for Berkeley to maintain that this knowledge is certain. If such a thesis regarding certainty is plausible given set B and the first element in EDR, then surely it is consistent with them, too.

Having shown that Berkeley accepted seven of the elements of CSR, and that his doing so is consistent with other core elements of his philosophy, we have achieved a partial but not insignificant vindication of the Luce-Jessop interpretation of Berkeley. These results are related to Berkeley's stated aim of defending common sense, primarily because all of the elements of CSR which we have seen Berkeley consistently accepts, he also holds to be elements of common sense. This means that not only is the part of CSR accepted by Berkeley consistent with Berkeley's philosophy, as given in set B, but so is an important portion of common sense consistent with his philosophy as represented in B. These matters, and a number of others pertaining to common sense and Berkeley's defense and use of it, form the topic of the next chapter.[14]

It should be stressed that the vindication of the Luce and Jessop interpretation proposed here is partial. This is because it has not been shown either that Berkeley's philosophy, as given in set B, is consistent with common sense, or even that his philosophy is consistent with commonsense realism. Indeed, I have said that the opposite is true. Commonsense realism is not consistent with Berkeley's philosophy, I have noted, because that philosophy contains statements in set B which are explicit denials of some of the components of commonsense realism. Further, since common sense contains commonsense realism as a part, it follows that Berkeley's philosophy, stated in set B, is inconsistent with common sense as well. What is true instead is that a core portion of commonsense realism, comprising the seven elements of it which are accepted by Berkeley, are consistent with set B and thus with his philosophy. Only in this restricted way is it true to say that Berkeley's philosophy is consistent with common sense and with commonsense realism.[15]

14. Had Kant been apprised of the degree to which Berkeley agreed with common sense realism, he would have had grounds to classify him as an empirical realist rather than an idealist.

15. A further question on which I have not touched is this: Is the class of propositions included in Berkeley's philosophy but not included in set B consistent with common sense and with commonsense realism? I believe that the answer to this question is *yes*, though I have done little to demonstrate it here.

CHAPTER 8

Common Sense

Berkeley tells us that one of the chief aims of his philosophy is to bring people back to common sense. He means back from metaphysical excess and obscurity, and from philosophical doctrines which lead to puzzles, paradoxes, and contradictions. He goes so far as to say that he is a champion of or defender of common sense, indeed one who "side(s) in all things with the Mob" (*Commentaries*, entry 405). This is definitely an overstatement on Berkeley's part, of course. Yet even if this claim *were* true, it is unclear why it would matter. That is, why should there be any *philosophical* importance attaching to agreement with common sense? In the hands of a philosopher such as Thomas Reid there is a principled answer to this question. However, Berkeley says very little about what he takes common sense to be, and little, as well, regarding why common sense is of philosophical importance.

I think that while Berkeley does attach some importance to common sense, it is actually rather less than some of his comments may indicate. Further, there are a number of important philosophical points on which Berkeley departs significantly from common sense. This means that Berkeley must not be talking about a general defense of common sense, but rather about the *degree* to which his philosophy sides with common sense. This degree of agreement with common sense is what ultimately proves to have a limited importance. The role that agreement with common sense plays in Berkeley is that of being one mark of evidence in favor of a philosophical theory, a factor which operates in the context of a number of other marks of evidence. Within this group of marks of evidence, agreement with common sense has no special epistemic status or weight, except to the extent that such agreement may be used to break ties between competing philosophical theories which come out equal relative to all other marks of evidence.

Common Sense

There are three ways in which Berkeley characterizes common sense. The first is what I will call common sense as a *disposition*. It is hinted at (but only hinted at) in the following passage from the Preface to the *Three Dialogues*:

> And although it may, perhaps, seem an uneasy reflexion to some, that when they have taken a circuit through so many refined and unvulgar notions, they should at last come to think like other men: yet, methinks, this return to the simple dictates of Nature, after having wandered through the wild mazes of philosophy, is not unpleasant.

There is a remark later in the *Dialogues* which may be making a related point:

> *Lastly*, whether the premises considered, it be not the wisest way to follow Nature, trust your senses, and laying aside all anxious thought about unknown natures or substances, admit with the vulgar those for real things, which are perceived by the senses? (Berkeley 1948–57, 2:168, 246)

In both of these passages Berkeley is linking common sense with "the simple dictates of Nature," and with "following Nature." These simple dictates of nature may be understood to be natural dispositions to trust one's senses and to believe the deliverances of the senses. Common sense would thus be this natural disposition to form beliefs in a certain manner. It is a disposition that can be thwarted or overcome, but in the absence of any reason to do so, Berkeley recommends following Nature and taking on the beliefs which one's natural disposition would lead one to acquire.

Elsewhere Berkeley speaks of common sense in different terms, referring to the *person* who is commonsensical. The two notions may be linked, of course; a commonsensical person may just be one who does follow Nature in the matter of belief acquisition, and so indulges her natural disposition. This point is suggested by the second of the two passages above, taking the term 'the vulgar' to refer to the commonsensical person. But Berkeley also characterizes the commonsensical person in other terms.

For instance, speaking of a certain notion in mathematics he says in *Principles* 123 that it is,

> the source from whence do spring all those amusing geometrical paradoxes, which have such a direct repugnancy to the plain common sense of mankind, and are admitted with so much reluctance into a mind not yet debauched by learning.(Berkeley 1948–57, 2:98)

A person not debauched by learning is elsewhere referred to as the "unphilosophical part of the world," made up of "men who had plain common sense, without the prejudice of a learned education" A person of common sense is thus a person who is uncorrupted in a certain manner, perhaps one whose natural belief forming dispositions are not clouded or inhibited by hesitancies engendered by too much "learning."

A third way in which Berkeley charactertizes common sense is just by listing *propositions* which he takes to be matters of common sense. He is also confident that the person of common sense will believe these propositions. However, there are a great many propositions of common sense, a truly vast number, and it is unlikely that Berkeley is interested in all of them. Of this large number, he really lists just a very few. Here is one such listing:

> I wish both our opinions were fairly stated and submitted to the judgment of men who had plain common sense, without the prejudices of a learned education. Let me be represented as one who trusts his senses, who thinks he knows the things he sees and feels, and entertains no doubts, of their existence;

Here Berkeley, through Philonous, lists one of the propositions making up EDR as a common sense proposition. He does not mention certainty in this passage; but, we have noted that one of his uses of that term, especially as it applies to physical objects, is linked to there being no doubt about the proposition in question. Later in the same passage, Philonous says,

> I do therefore assert that I am as certain as of my own being, that there are bodies or corporeal substances (meaning the things I perceive by my senses), and that granting this, the bulk of mankind will take no thought about, nor think themselves at all concerned in the fate of those unknown natures, and philosophical quiddities, which some men are so fond of. (Berkeley 1948–57, 2:237, 238)

Here the notion of certainty comes up explicitly, thus reinforcing our interpretation of the previous passage. Also to be noted is the claim that objects are perceived by the senses. As argued in chapter 6, when Berkeley speaks of such perception, he generally means to refer to immediate perception. Hence, accepting that line of argument, he is affirming that the thesis that objects are immediately perceived is a common sense proposition. Similarly included as a common sense proposition is the claim that there are physical objects, an element in the existential part of CSR.

Later in the *Dialogues* another listing is provided:

> . . . it is none of my business to plead for novelties and paradoxes. That the qualities we perceive are not on the objects: that we must not believe our senses: that we know nothing of the real nature of things, and can never be assured even of their existence: that real colours and sounds are nothing but certain unknown figures and motions: that motions are in themselves neither swift nor slow: that there are in bodies absolute extensions, without any particular magnitude or figure: that a thing stupid, thoughtless and inactive, operates on a spirit: that the least particle of a body, contains innumerable extended parts: These are the novelties, these are the strange noions which shock the genuine uncorrupted judgment of all mankind.

In addition to repeating the epistemic point that we have perceptual knowledge of objects, Berkeley also makes the claim that objects have the qualities they are perceived to have, thus affirming as a common sense proposition another of the elements of CSR.

In another place Berkeley speaks of what those of a "vulgar cast" believe.

> I assure you, Hylas, I do not pretend to frame any hypothesis at all. I am of a vulgar cast, simple enough to believe my senses, and leave things as I find them. To be plain, it is my opinion, that the real things are those very things I see and feel, and perceive by my senses.

This passage can be plausibly read as asserting that when objects are perceived, they are perceived as they are, still another element of CSR. Still later in the same passage, wherein Berkeley is concerned to state what those of a vulgar cast believe, he says,

> Away then with all that scepticism, all those ridiculous philosophical doubts. What a jest is it for a philosopher to question the existence of sensible things, till he hath it proved to him from the veracity of God: or to pretend that our knowledge in this point falls short of intuition and demonstration? I might as well doubt of my own being, as of the things I actually see and feel. (Berkeley 1948–57, 2:244, 229, 230)

In speaking of intuitive knowledge of objects in this passage, Berkeley is indicating that the vulgar are of the opinion that we have such knowledge. The first element in EDR, then, is reckoned by Berkeley a proposition of common sense.

We found previously (chapter 7) that Berkeley accepts seven of the ten elements making up CSR. Here we have lately seen that six of those seven are to also be counted propositions of common sense. I do not think there is any passage in which Berkeley explicitly indicates that the public character of physical objects is also a matter of common sense, but it would be incredible if Berkeley were to deny this. So, I think it is reasonable to suppose that Berkeley regards all of the seven accepted items in CSR as propositions of common sense.

The class of common sense propositions (C-propositions) contains many, maybe uncountably many, additional propositions. Included in this class are three important propositions which Berkeley rejects: that physical objects and some of their qualities exist independently of perception, that no physical object has ideas (phenomenal individuals) as constituents, and that there is real causation between events in the physical world. The first of these propositions, the thesis of metaphysical realism, is inconsistent with the EIP principle and is unacceptable to Berkeley for that reason. The second conflicts with the collections account of objects which Berkeley holds. Hence, there are two elements of CSR which seem clearly to be C-propositions, and which Berkeley rejects. The third proposition here noted conflicts with Berkeley's thesis that genuine causation flows only from spirits, particularly from God.[1] So there are some philosophically important C-propositions which Berkeley does not accept, including two which are included in CSR.[2]

There are also a great many additional C-propositions on which Berkeley is silent, at least as regards their status as C-propositions. We may safely suppose, the proposition that bushes are not trees is a C-proposition, and so is the proposition that there is water in different places, and countless others. It is likely, of course, that Berkeley both believes these propositions and would hold that they are C-propositions. But they do not seem to be of any special philosophical importance. Only a very small number of C-propositions, those in CSR which are accepted and a few others, are singled out for special attention.

We could say that these propositions are isolated and examined closely because they are disputed propositions. In the *Dialogues*, particularly,

1. Berkeley's views on causation and its restriction to spirits may be found in *Principles* 50–53.
2. What about the proposition in CSR that it is false that in every perception, at least one idea is immediately perceived? I am unsure how Berkeley thinks of this. However, if *this* proposition is an element of set C, the restricted group of common sense propositions discussed below, then the competition between Berkeley's philosophy and that of the materialist will be even closer.

there is a competition between the views of the materialist, represented by Hylas, and those of the immaterialist, represented by Philonous. Among the things the immaterialist affirms and the materialist denies are the C-propositions we have noted, and so we could say that their philosophical importance just comes to the fact that these propositions make up the content of the dispute.

I think this point is correct; these C-propositions do make up much of the disputed territory in the *Dialogues*. However, that is not the only reason for their significance. Berkeley takes the fact that the immaterialist *agrees with* or accepts a greater number of these C-propositions than does the materialist to make up one good reason to think that the immaterialist doctrines are true and those of the materialist are false. If the *only* reason this small class of C-propositions were singled out is that it contained disputed propositions, one could hardly use degree of agreement with the members of this class to count against one side of the dispute and in favor of another. Berkeley thus must think of the C-propositions in this class as special in some additional way.

As a start on saying what this special character comes to, we can distinguish between ordinary and reflective common sense propositions. By an ordinary C-proposition I mean a proposition that the typical person of common sense does believe, a proposition the person would assent to if queried. We may safely suppose that there are a great many ordinary C-propositions. A reflective C-proposition is one a typical common sense person would believe upon some unbiased reflection on the matter. Reflective C-propositions thus come in two groups. First, there will be propositions which number among the ordinary C-propositions, but which the person would continue to believe upon appropriate reflection. Second, there may also be propositions which are not counted among the ordinary C-propositions, but which the reflective person would assent to were she to engage in the needed reflection. It is thus possible that the class of reflective C-propositions will include many in the class of ordinary C-propositions, but also include some additional propositions. Berkeley hints at the reflective common sense person in *Principles* 55:

> though we should grant a notion to be ever so universally and stedfastly adhered to, yet this is but a weak argument of its truth, to whoever considers what a vast number of prejudices and false opinions are every where embraced with the utmost tenaciousness, by the unreflecting (which are the far greater) part of mankind.

There is no reason to think that Berkeley is identifying the reflective with the learned and the unreflective with those of common sense. Rather, he is talking about a division within the group of common sense persons. This is borne out by a glance at the preceding section, where it is clear that Berkeley is concerned with universal assent to a proposition, thus referring to all the common sense people, and wondering whether this counts in favor of the believed proposition. In many cases, he says, it will not. In particular, the ordinary person might say she believes that matter exists, because she has heard this term often enough. But this would not be a reflective acceptance, because

> This is not the only instance wherein men impose upon themselves, by imagining they believe those propositions they have often heard, though at bottom they have no meaning in them (Berkeley 1948–57, 2:64)

Putting these two passages together, his message would be that while the ordinary common sense person would believe that matter exists, the reflective common sense person would not. Thus, that matter exists is not a reflective C-proposition, though it may well be an ordinary C-proposition. Of course, the terminology of ordinary versus reflective is not one Berkeley deploys; it is devised here to try to state and capture a distinction he seems to regard as important.

Some reflective C-propositions are also settled propositions. By this I mean that they survive as beliefs of the reflective common sense person even after repeated events of reflection upon their truth and meaning. Settled C-propositions are not merely those propositions Berkeley refers to as "stedfastly adhered to," for the latter need not be propositions that would survive reflection but may be just those people believe on account of stubbornness and prejudice.

Sometimes Berkeley seems to identify the class of common sense persons very narrowly, as those who are unlearned and in his own country, as in *Philosophical Commentaries* 392.

> There are men who say there are insensible extensions, there are others who say the Wall is not white, the fire is not hot &c We Irish men cannot attain to these truths. (Berkeley 1948–57 1:47)

Elsewhere he specifies the class of common sense persons much more broadly, referring to all mankind.

> . . . it being a main part of our inquiry, to examine whose notions are widest of the common road, and most repugnant to the general sense of the world.

> HYLAS: But do you in earnest think, the real existence of sensible things consists in their being actually perceived? If so, how comes it that all

mankind distinguish between them? Ask the first man you meet, and
he shall tell you, *to be perceived* is one thing, and *to exist* is another.

PHILONOUS: I am content, Hylas, to appeal to the common sense of the
world for the truth of my notion. (Berkeley 1948–57, 2:182–3)

Philonous then goes on to give an unconvincing argument for the claim
that the EIP principle is a matter of common sense—unconvincing because the point he makes is just that the common sense person will give
perception as the *reason* she believes that an object exists, and this epistemic point does not imply that the existence of the object consists in being
perceived. This aside, however, it is clear that Berkeley is referring to the
whole of mankind as making up the class of common sense persons. The
class of C-propositions, then, is made up of those propositions believed by
the whole of mankind, by every person of common sense wherever that
person may be found.

The small group of C-propositions Berkeley attends to also seem to be
special in another way in that they seem to count as *basic*. We take first the
class of ordinary common sense propositions, a large class indeed. Within
this, some sub-group is basic in the sense that in coming to have belief in
any other proposition in the larger class, one presupposes belief in one or
more of the propositions in the sub-group. Imagine, next, that the large
class of ordinary common sense propositions is altered by appropriate
acts of reflection, so that we reach the class of reflective common sense
propositions. Here, too, there will be a small sub-group of C-propositions
belief in which will be presupposed should one believe any other proposition in the larger class. It is reasonable to think that these two presupposed sub-groups of C-propositions will have essentially the same mem-
bership; but if they do not, we focus on those presupposed by belief in
reflective C-propositions. This sub-group makes up the small set of basic
C-propositions. My conjecture, given that Berkeley does not speak of basic common sense propositions, is that the C-propositions Berkeley
singles out, (including those in CSR) are basic in just this way.

We come now to a proposal regarding the small group of C-propositions to which Berkeley pays special heed. First, these are all C-propositions, as noted earlier. This group includes the members of CSR, plus
some propositions that only the materialist accepts: that objects exist independently of perception and there is real causal action between events.
Second, these C-propositions are each reflective C-propositions; and they
are settled, widely or universally shared among people of common sense
who are also reflective, and basic, in the sense that they are presupposed
by belief in each of the other reflective C-propositions. In other words,
joint use of the notions of being reflective, being settled, being universally

believed, and being basic, picks out a small sub-group of C-propositions. The heart of the proposal is that this selected sub-group of C-propositions *is* just the sub-group identified and attended to by Berkeley; and, it is *because* the sub-group can be selected in the way proposed here that agreement or disagreement with that sub-group may count as a mark of evidence in favor of or against a philosophical theory.

While this proposal is conjectural, it is not wholly so. We know that Berkeley picks out a small group of C-propositions as notably important, and we can pretty well identify the members of this group. We have seen, too, that he is somewhat alert to the notion of reflective common sense and to widely or universally shared C-propositions. We know, as well, that he regards agreement with the small group of C-propositions as a mark in favor of a philosophical theory. These points are not conjectural. What are items of conjecture are the notions of settled and basic C-propositions, and the idea that *because* each of the member C-propositions picked out by Berkeley is a reflective, settled, universally believed and basic C-propositions, that agreement with that small group of propositions may count as evidence for a philosophical theory. But it is not an unreasonable conjecture, because we know that Berkeley needs *some* reason to think that agreement with his favored set of C-propositions counts as a positive mark of evidence.

For convenience, I will refer to the C-propositions of most concern to Berkeley as set C. It consists of the seven statements in CSR which Berkeley accepts, but, to be complete and fair to Berkeley's opponents, we should also include the two elements from CSR that Berkeley rejects—metaphysical realism and the statement that no physical object has ideas (phenomenal individuals) as constituents. We should also include the statement that there is genuine causation between events in the physical world. Thus, set C consists of ten propositions, though only some of them were accepted by Berkeley.

Competition in Metaphysics

We have noted that Berkeley takes agreement with common sense to be important, and we have indicated that generally he means agreement with a small sub-group of the propositions of common sense. The first point finds expression in the beginning of the *Dialogues*.

> Philonous: Well then, are you content to admit that opinion for true, which upon examination shall appear most agreeable to common sense, and remote from scepticism?

Hylas: With all my heart. Since you are for raising disputes about the plainest things in Nature, I am content for once to hear what you have to say.

Then near the end of the *Dialogues*, Philonous reminds Hylas of their earlier agreement:

After all, is there any thing farther remaining to be done? You may remember you promised to embrace that opinion, which upon examination should appear most agreeable to common sense, and remote from *scepticism*. (Berkeley 1948–57, 2:172–73, 259)

To evaluate what Berkeley is saying, we need to know what he means by 'agreement.' The best clue on this point comes from elsewhere in the *Dialogues* where he explains, through Philonous, the nature of Hylas' disagreement with common sense.

It is none of my business to plead for novelties and paradoxes. That the qualities we perceive, are not on the objects: that we must not believe our senses: that we know nothing of the real nature of things, and can never be assured even of their existence: that real colours and sounds are nothing but certain unknown figures and motions: that motions are in themselves neither swift nor slow: that there are in bodies absolute extensions, without any particular magnitude or figure: that a thing stupid, thoughtless and inactive, operates on a spirit: that the least particle of a body, contains innumerable extended parts. These are the novelties, these are the strange notions which shock the genuine uncorrupted judgment of all mankind; and being once admitted, embarrass the mind with endless doubts and difficulties. And it is against these and the like innovations, I endeavor to vindicate common sense. (Berkeley 1948–57, 2:244)

In this passage Berkeley tells us that Hylas accepts some doctrines that are direct contraries of propositions in C. In saying that, for Hylas, we have no knowledge of objects and cannot be assured of their existence, Berkeley is saying that Hylas accepts propositions that are inconsistent with the two elements of EDR, both of which are included in C. Hylas also accepts, says Berkeley, the claim that qualities which we perceive are not in objects. Thus Hylas is made to accept a propositions that conflicts with another proposition in C: that objects have the sensible qualities we perceive them to have. With respect to Hylas' doctrines, disagreement with common sense means accepting propositions that are inconsistent with some C-propositions. By the same token, agreement with common sense will mean accepting propositions which are consistent with C-propositions because, in the case of the three propositions cited in the passage above, they *are* C-propositions. More generally, though, agreement with common sense would be accepting propositions which are consistent with the propositions of common sense.[3]

Which C-propositions does Berkeley have in mind when he says that his doctrines are consistent with (agree with) more of these C-propositions than is the case with the doctrines of the materialist? He could be referring to *all* C-propositions, all propositions the common sense person believes. That is, when Berkeley has Philonous identify propositions that conflict with doctrines Hylas accepts, they happen to be propositions in C. But it is *possible* that when he speaks of greater agreement than in the case of the materialist, between his philosophical doctrines and common sense, he means agreement with all C-propositions, and not just those in C. In other words, the proposal made earlier would be in error. Agreement with common sense is not restricted to agreement with members of set C.

I grant the possibility of this point correct. At neither the beginning nor the end of the *Dialogues*, when Berkeley speaks of agreement with common sense, does he ever mention *specific* C-propositions. However, we must not overlook the fact that when he actually cites the C-propositions, that his philosophy most agrees with (and the philosophy of the materialist most disagrees with) the only propositions cited are some of those in set C. Further, agreement with all C-propositions will hardly serve Berkeley's interests. To see why, imagine that the class of all C-propositions amounts to some ten thousand propositions—probably a conservative number. It is likely that Berkeley and the materialist will agree on the vast majority of these propositions, and that their respective philosophical doctrines will be in conflict with none of the propositions on which they agree. Propositions such as that trees are different from bushes, and that red is different from green will be C-propositions likely included in the ten thousand; but, nothing in either Berkeley's philosophy or in that of the materialist will require denying these. Neither will either deny practically any other C-proposition. Disagreements will center on just a few. If this is right, and Berkeley's philosophy agrees with all but four of the ten thousand, and the materialist's philosophy agrees with all but six, this does

3. The passage actually contains more than I have intimated. Berkeley also says that an object acting causally on a mind or spirit is opposed to common sense, as is the claim that matter is infinitely divisible. This is, in effect, to say that set C contains, as well, the propositions that objects do not causally operate on minds, and that matter is at most finitely divisible, so that there are minimum particles. I find both of these claims suspicious. If anything is a matter of common sense, and should be included in set C, it is the proposition that objects *do* causally operate on minds, not its contrary. I would think, too, that common sense has no view on the question about divisibility.

not count as much of an advantage for Berkeley's philosophy, not relative to the total numbers involved. Moreover, a difference in degree of agreement with all C-propositions does not distinguish between ordinary C-propositions ("Trees are different from bushes.") and more important ones ("There are physical objects.") Sheer numerical difference in degree of agreement allows for both Berkeley and the materialist to agree with *all* of the important C-propositions, and to disagree only over a few not so important ones. This, again, would accord no theoretical advantage to Berkeley's philosophy.

We should, then, take Berkeley to be concentrating on a small sub-group of C-propositions, and when we look at the ones he actually cites, we note that he includes nearly all of the members of C. Others which I have added to C (e.g., "Objects exist independently of perception," and "Objects do not have phenomenal individuals as constituents" and "There is genuine causation between physical events") were included because they seem to deserve inclusion as much as the members of CSR favored by Berkeley, and partly because their exclusion would be somewhat unfair to the materialist.

But is this all? That is, is degree of agreement with set C the only factor on which the fate of Berkeley's philosophy or that of the materialist is based? The answer is given forcefully by Berkeley in a series of most interesting comments in which he sets out a number of other parameters on which the acceptability of materialism or his philosophy rests. For instance, he claims in *Principles* 50 that his philosophy is at least as good in explaining various items in need of explanation:

> You will say there have been a great many things explained by matter and motion; take away these and you destroy the whole corpuscular philosophy and undermine those mechanical principles which have been applied with so much success to account for the phenomena. In short, whatever advances which have been made, either by ancient or modern philosophers, in the study of nature do all proceed on the supposition that corporeal substance or matter does really exist. To this, I answer that there is not any one phenomenon explained on that supposition which may not as well be explained without it, as might easily be made appear by induction of particulars. (Berkeley 1948–57, 2:62)

Berkeley also maintains that his philosophical doctrines make up a *simpler* theory than materialism. Rejection of materialism brings with it rejection of the thesis that external physical objects are causes of immediately perceived ideas, and Hylas asks:

> And, in consequence of this, must we not think there are no such things as physical or corporeal causes, but that spirit is the immediate cause of all

the phenomena in Nature? Can there be any thing more extravagant than this?

Philonous replies for Berkeley:

Yes, it is infinitely more extravagant to say a thing which is inert operates on the mind, and which is unperceiving is the cause of our perception. (Berkeley 1948–57, 2:236)

Actually, Berkeley's simplicity claim is complex: it includes not only the claim of numerical simplicity (one entity as cause versus a multiplicity of causes), but also explanatory simplicity. It is easier to understand how a spirit might cause ideas, Berkeley insists, because we all have first-hand introspective access to such causation in our own cases. In contrast, it is difficult to understand how something such as a physical object can act to produce an idea in a spirit, especially if the physical object consists partly in an inert material substance. That a thing which is " . . . stupid, thought-less and inactive, operates on a spirit" (*Ibid.*, p. 244) is most difficult to conceive if one assumes a mind-body dualism, as the materialists gener-ally (though not exclusively) did.

Berkeley also claims that certain scientific, religious, and philosophical issues are relevant to deciding between materialism and his philosophy. The strategy is nearly the same for all three: first, we ask whether materi-alism or Berkeley's philosophy is consistent with scientific, religious, and philosophical doctrines that are agreed on all sides to be true. He recog-nizes that there may be no *philosophic* truths of this sort. Next we ask whether there are some standing problems within any of these three areas that either materialism or Berkeley's philosophy helps to solve or avoids. Last, we ask whether materialism or Berkeley's philosophy raises any new scientific, religious, or philosophical problems, and if so whether they are solvable or intractable. To illustrate in the case of religion, con-sider this exchange:

HYLAS: . . . there remains one great difficulty which I know not how you will get over. And, indeed, it is of such importance that if you could solve all others without being able to find a solution for this, you must never expect to make me a proselyte to your principles.

PHILONOUS: Let me know this mighty difficulty.

HYLAS: The Scripture account of creation is what appears to me utterly ir-reconcilable with your notions. Moses tells us of a creation—a cre-ation of what? of ideas? No, certainly, but of things, of real things, solid corporeal substances. Bring your principles to agree with this and I shall perhaps agree with you.

Philonous then launches into an elaborate account of how his (Berkeley's) philosophy is to be consistent with the creation story found in the *Bible*.[4] He then goes over to the offensive, and charges that materialism is perhaps inconsistent with the creation story. Philonous says:

> Is it not . . . evident the assertors of matter destroy the plain obvious sense of Moses, with which their notions are utterly inconsistent, and instead of it obtrude on us I know not what, something equally unintelligible to themselves and me? . . . Moses tells us of a creation. A creation of what? Of unknown quiddities, or occasions, or *substratum*. No, certainly, but of things obvious to the senses. You must first reconcile this with your notions if you expect I should be reconciled with them.

Philonous does not quite say outright that materialism is inconsistent with the biblical creation story; he merely strongly suggests that it is. Instead of dwelling on this point, though, he goes on to another:

> But allowing matter to exist and the notion of absolute existence to be as clear as light, yet, was this ever known to make the creation more credible? Nay, has it not furnished the atheists and infidels of all ages with the most plausible arguments against creation? (Berkeley 1948–57, 2:250, 256)

Philonous goes on to explain that materialism makes it plausible to maintain that matter is co-eternal with God and thus was never created. This gives people reason to hold that there never was a creation of the physical world and raises embarrassing questions about how matter can be co-eternal with God. All of these questions are said to be avoided by Berkeley's philosophical theory (immaterialism, as he calls it), and this fact is taken to count in favor of immaterialism and against materialism.

Berkeley deals with science in much the same way. First, he tries to secure the consistency of immaterialism with science, particularly physics; this is done by accepting an instrumentalist account of scientific theories and scientific explanation.[5] But this is not all; for, as Philonous says,

> In Natural Philosophy, what intricacies, what obscurities, what contradictions has the belief in matter led men into? To say nothing of the numberless disputes about its extent, continuity, homogeneity, gravity, divisibility, etc . . . do they not pretend to explain all things by bodies operating on bodies, according to the laws of motion? And yet, are they able to compre-

4. This consistency question, concerning creation, was addressed briefly in chapter 5 in connection with the EIP principle in its "actual perception" form. I here assume that Berkeley's account of creation is consistent with the other core elements of his philosophy.

5. On Berkeley's scientific instrumentalism, see Karl Popper 1953.

hend how any one body should move another? Nay, admitting there was no difficulty in reconciling the notion of an inert being with a cause, or in conceiving how an accident might pass from one body to another, yet, by all their strained thoughts and extravagant suppositions, have they been able to reach the mechanical production of any one animal or vegetable body? Can they account, by the laws of motion, for sounds, taste, smells, or colours, or for the regular course of things? Have they accounted, by physical principles, for the aptitude and contrivance of even the most inconsiderable parts of the universe?

Materialism, Berkeley is saying, raises numerous problems in science which it cannot solve, and fares badly at helping to solve important standing problems. In contrast, he says that immaterialism fares much better on these counts.

But laying aside matter and corporeal causes and admitting only the efficiency of an All-perfect Mind, are not all the effects of nature easy and intelligible? If the *phenomena* are nothing else but *ideas*; God is a *spirit*, but matter an unintelligent, unperceiving being. If they demonstrate an unlimited power in their cause; God is active and omnipotent, but matter an inert mass. If the order, regularity, and usefulness of them can never be sufficiently admired; God is infinitely wise and provident, but matter destitute of all contrivance and design. These surely are great advantages in *physics*.

Philosophy is accorded a similar treatment as in science and religion, except that Berkeley does not ask whether materialism or immaterialism best accords with some standing truths in philosophy, maybe because there are so few agreed on truths of that sort. But he does ask the question of whether materialism or immaterialism best helps to avoid or solve various problems in philosophy.

Then in *metaphysics:* what difficulties concerning entity in abstract, substantial forms, hylarchic principles, plastic natures, substance and accident, principles of individuation, possibility of matter's thinking, origin of ideas, the manner how two independent substances so widely different as *spirit* and *matter* should mutually operate on each other? What difficulties, I say, and endless disquisitions concerning these and innumerable other the like points do we escape by supposing only spirits and ideas? (Berkeley 1948–57, 2:257, 257–58)

There is also the matter of scepticism which may be added to this list. That is, Berkeley holds that scepticism of a certain sort is either implied or otherwise strongly supported by materialism, and this he takes as another disadvantage for that theory, counting against it. He also seems to hold that immaterialism avoids scepticism, in the sense that it neither implies it nor strongly supports it; indeed, he may also hold that immaterialism outright refutes scepticism. If he is right about these points, however, he does not count that fact as decisive against materialism. Rather, he treats it as one more mark of evidence against the theory, one which could be counter-balanced by other advantages enjoyed by that theory.[6]

In all these passages we may note a methodology that Berkeley is utilizing. Two philosophical theories, materialism and immaterialism, he regards as competitors for our attention and acceptance. He seems, as well, to regard these as the only competitors in the field. Each of these theories is internally consistent, but they are inconsistent with one another. Each purports to give a complete theory of perception and the external world, among other things. In the passages we have noted, Berkeley is indicating a general method for adjudicating between rival theories. One principle he uses in this endeavor can be stated this way:

Where two philosophical theories compete with each other relative to a subject matter, S, then if one of these theories is simpler than the other, that simpler theory is more acceptable than its rival, all else being equal between the two theories.

In this case, as noted earlier, simplicity is to be taken as both numerical and explanatory simplicity. Subject matter S, of course, will vary; in the context of Berkeley's philosophy, S is concerned primarily with perception, the external world, and our knowledge of it. In principle, however, S could range over many different theories within philosophy.

Other principles have essentially the same form. Here is one stated just for religious truths:

Where two philosophical theories compete with respect to subject matter S, if one theory is consistent with more agreed upon religious truths than the other, then the first theory is more acceptable than the other, all else being equal.

A similar principle could easily be stated for agreed upon truths of science and philosophy, if there are any of the latter. There is also a principle that highlights problem-solving:

Where two philosphical theories compete with respect to subject matter S, if one theory helps to solve problems in S while the other theory does not,

6. Scepticism and Berkeley's response to it are taken up in the next chapter.

or one theory solves more problems in S than the other theory, then the first theory is more acceptable than the second, all else being equal.

In the case of the latter principle, again, subject matter S can be variable. For Berkeley, as we have seen, the different subject matters are religion, science, and philosophy. A similar principle could easily be devised for problem-avoidance, a criterion suggested by the passages lately quoted. Also suggested by Berkeley's comments is a principle concerning problems which the theories do *not* solve. The theory with the fewest of those problems is preferrable, all else being equal than any other theory.

Then, finally, Berkeley suggests a principle concerning *new problems* which may be raised by a theory, even by one which solves many other standing problems. The principle might be:

> Where two philosophical theories compete with respect to subject matter S, if one theory raises fewer new problems than the other, then that theory is more acceptable than the other, all else being equal.

This principle could reasonably be calibrated to deal not just with numbers of new problems but also with their seriousness and relative intractability.

The method suggested here for deciding between philosophical theories is familiar to us today, no doubt due in part to the strong influence of Willard Quine and other pragamtically oriented philosophers. Quine, in particular, has stressed that philosophical theories are just that, theories, which differ from scientific theories mainly in their degree of comprehensiveness and scope. However, he says, philosophical theories are to be evaluated by means of the same criteria used to evaluate any other non-mathematical theory: explanatory fecundity, simplicity, conservativeness of principle, and the like, factors Quine holds will apply in this evaluative enterprise.[7] Berkeley's method in the *Dialogues* is Quineian insofar as he uses pragmatic criteria for evaluating and deciding between philosophical theories, and in this way his method has a modern ring. It departs from what would be familiar today only insofar as Berkeley's methodology includes a parameter—degree of comportment with religious truths—that is not now generally regarded as a mark of a good theory, in either science or most areas of philosophy.

Another salient feature of Berkeley's set of parameters is that it disappointingly gives us no indication of how we are to weight the various factors. We do not know, for example, whether agreeing with selected religious truths is to count equally with helping to solve standing problems

---

7. See particularly W. V. Quine and J. Ullian 1968 for the account of the theoretical virtues.

in science. Lacking this information, it is difficult to determine whether one theory, such as immaterialism, fares better by these criteria than does its rival materialist theory. We could solve this problem on Berkeley's behalf by resolving to count all factors equally. Doing so would help, but some problems would remain if we wanted to determine how the materialist and the immaterialist fare by these criteria. Probably the biggest problem would be deciding how we are to understand the notion of explanation when we say that one philosophical theory explains some items not explained by another theory, or does so better than the other theory.

Fortunately, these large issues need not be examined here, for the present concern is merely to bring the method to light. In that regard, one additional factor needs to be raised, namely agreement with common sense. Immediately following presentation of the various parameters surveyed above, Berkeley has Philonous say:

> After all, is there any thing farther remaining to be done? You may remember you promised to embrace that opinion, which upon examination should appear most agreeable to common sense, and remote from *scepticism*. This by your own confession is that which denies matter, or the absolute existence of corporeal things. Nor is this all; the same notion has been proved several ways, viewed in different lights, pursued in its consequences, and all objections against it cleared. Can there be a greater evidence of its truth? or is it possible it should have all the marks of a true opinion, and yet be false? (Berkeley 1948–57, 2:259)

How shall we understand this passage? According to one reading, Berkeley is letting everything ride on agreement with common sense because he feels this factor is of overriding importance. In effect, to take this line is to hold that the other factors identified above are important, though agreement with common sense counts for more than any one of those other parameters. Agreement with common sense has the greatest weight. Berkeley could even be read as claiming that such agreement trumps the combined effect of all the other factors. Another possibility is that Berkeley feels, or (more likely) is willing to concede for purposes of argument, that all else is equal on all of the above parameters. In that case, this one factor—degree of agreement with common sense—is called upon to decide the issue. Doing this does not relegate agreement with common sense to a mere tie-breaking role in special circumstances. Berkeley could be thinking of agreement with common sense as one additional factor, more or less equally weighted with the others noted above. It just happens, we might say, that all else *is* equal on the other parameters, so agreement with common sense is called upon, in this one case, to be the deciding factor. This does not imply that being a tie-breaker is the *only* role, in general, for agreement with common sense.

I doubt that Berkeley's point is that agreement with common sense is of overriding importance. This is because in the passage above he attaches importance as well to all of the other factors, over and above agreement with common sense. This suggests, rather, that agreement with common sense is just one additional factor to be taken into account. Moreover, many of the above factors are gone over in the *Principles*, and it would be odd for Berkeley to take the time in two books to use a fair bit of space setting out how immaterialism fares relative to these factors, if he thought they paled in importance to agreement with common sense. If he thought the latter, we would expect him to proceed directly to such agreement, and to either leave out altogether or to downplay the matter of these other factors. This is not what happens; the other factors are given the lion's share of attention, and agreement with common sense is brought in at the end. The most reasonable interpretation of this would be that such agreement is allowed to be a tie-breaker, in this particular case. Were the two theories in equal agreement with common sense, but one theory came out better on some other parameter, then that theory would be most acceptable. That is, the role of agreement with common sense is not to merely be a tie-breaker; it just happens that this is how matters play out in the situation of materialism pitted against immaterialism.

Scorekeeping

How do things fare, then, with Berkeley's philosophy and common sense? This is really more than one question, because we have to look as well at how things go with materialism relative to the same question. With regard to Berkeley's philosophy this question has already been considered and answered. He consistently accepts seven of the elements in set C, and thus his philosophy is consistent with seven elements of C. There is no question, however, that Berkeley thinks the materialist philosophy scores much worse relative to common sense. He puts the words in Hylas' mouth:

> I own myself entirely satisfied for the present in all respects. But what security can I have that I shall still continue the same full assent to your opinion, and that no un-thought of objection or difficulty will occur hereafter?

This passage comes immediately after Philonous has reminded Hylas of the promise to side with the theory which agrees most with common sense. So, Berkeley thinks immaterialism wins the competition relative to agreement with common sense.

Materialism, of course, includes and is consistent with the statement that there are physical objects. It also accepts metaphysical realism, the thesis that physical objects exist independently of perception. This thesis, indeed, helps to define the materialist position. The materialist may well hold, too, that objects have some of the sensible qualities they are perceived to have. If we think of Locke as one paradigm materialist, then of course he holds that objects actually have the primary qualities they are perceived to have. So, there is partial agreement at least with common sense on this metaphysical point.

Berkeley reads the materialist position differently on this issue. He takes the materialist to be committed to holding that *all* of the primary and secondary qualities are actually *insensible*. This is because he is thinking of representative realism as Locke's theory of perception, and on that theory no object and no quality of an object is ever immediately perceived. In *that* sense, even the primary qualities would be insensible. In his catalog of the ways in which the materialist position diverges from common sense, and so is either a "novelty" or a "paradox," Philonous says,

> That the qualities we perceive, are not on the objects; that we must not believe our senses.

He also characterizes the materialist position in a contrast with his own:

> It is likewise my opinion, that colours and other sensible qualities are on the objects. I cannot for my life help thinking that snow is white and fire hot. You indeed, who by *snow* and *fire* mean certain external, unperceived, unperceiving substances, are in the right to deny whiteness or heat, to be affections inherent in them.

He also puts the point in Hylas' terms:

> I tell you, that colour, figure, and hardness, which you perceive, are not the real natures of those things, or in the least like them. The same may be said of all other real things or corporeal substances which compose the world. They have none of them any thing in themselves, like those sensible qualities by us perceived. (Berkeley 1948–57, 2:259, 244, 229–30, 227)

The middle passage quoted concerns only secondary qualities, but it is clear from the other passages between which it is placed that Berkeley's point is more general than that.

Berkeley's point, I think, depends on one or both of two further theses. The first is that for Locke no sensible quality is itself immediately perceived. From this, though, I do not think that Berkeley has any ground for inferring that the qualities are insensible—at least, not if that means that objects lack the qualities they are perceived to have. For it is still true for the representative realist who holds that we never immediately perceive anything but ideas, that in immediately perceiving ideas we perceive objects to have some qualities. Locke's theory then goes on to tell us that we are mistaken in some of these cases; the objects do not have the secondary qualities as they are perceived by us.

However, Berkeley's has another reason to hold that for the representative realist, objects lack the sensible qualities they are perceived to have. He would argue, that is, that the likeness principle *commits* the representative realist to this conclusion. His point is not that the realist *actually holds* the thesis in question, but rather that the realist cannot avoid holding to it. The likeness principle, as it has come to be called, is the thesis that an idea can be like only another idea.[8] Hence, ideas of primary qualities cannot be like, or resemble, actual qualities in bodies. Since, *ex hypothesi* for the representative realist, ideas of secondary qualities do not resemble actual qualities in bodies, it follows that for this realist, objects do not have qualities they are perceived to have, despite the fact that the realist *says* something quite different on this point.

It is not clear that this argument is decisive. To see why, we can contrast the way the two sides argue. First the representative realist:

(1) In perception, we perceive objects to have sensible qualities.
(2) Immediately perceived ideas of primary qualities actually resemble real qualities in objects.
(3) Hence, objects have some of the qualities we perceive them to have.

Berkeley's counter-argument is this:

(4) In perception we perceive objects to have sensible qualities.
(5) No immediately perceived ideas resemble, or are like, actual qualities of bodies.
(6) Hence, objects do not have the sensible qualities we perceive them to have.

Statement (6), Berkeley will claim, is one to which the representative realist is committed, given (4) and (5). Thus, representative realism (or, for

8. The term comes from Phillip Cummins 1966, 63–69. K. Winkler 1989 has a good discussion of this principle, and an interpretation of it opposed to Cummins 1966, 141–48.

Berkeley, materialism) is committed to the denial of one of the propositions in set C, and in that sense is inconsistent with that element of C.

Berkeley's argument depends squarely on (5), which is denied by the
realist. Berkeley's basis for (5), in turn, is the likeness principle; but, of
course, the realist will deny that, too. So, to be conclusive, Berkeley's argument requires that the likeness principle be a necessary truth. Representative realism, conjoined with that necessary truth, entails (6), and in
that sense realism is inconsistent with the C-proposition that objects have
the sensible qualities we perceive them to have.

The realist, however, need not acquiesce, for he need not concede that
the likeness principle is a *necessary* truth. In defense of this point he would
remind us of how Berkeley argues for the likeness principle. The argument is that in order to justify or establish a resemblance thesis holding
between ideas and qualities in bodies, one needs to compare both items.
But, in order to make the comparison both items, ideas and qualities,
would have to be immediately perceived. *Ex hypothesi*, only the ideas are
immediately perceived. Hence, one cannot make the requisite comparison, and so cannot establish the resemblance thesis.[9]

The realist strategy here would be to attack the first step in Berkeley's
argument, and to do so in a specific way. Even if it is contingently true
that in order to establish a resemblance thesis, one needs to compare the
two allegedly resembling items (a thesis the realist would also deny, of
course), this is not a *necessary* truth. We can see that it is not necessary by
noticing that a resemblance thesis can be established in another manner.
For instance, we postulate that objects have qualities resembling those in
some immediately perceived ideas; and, this postulation is justified on the
grounds that it helps to explain other data; thus, the resemblance thesis is
justified on broadly explanatory grounds. One can cavil about this argument. The point of giving it is just to show that it makes perfect sense; and,
since it does, Berkeley's claim about establishing a resemblance thesis
only on the basis of a comparison is not a necessary truth. Hence, the realist would say, Berkeley has given us no reason to believe that the likeness
principle is a necessary truth, and so no reason to think that the realist
would be *inconsistent* in claiming that objects have *some* of the sensible
qualities we perceive them to have.

In fact, we can say a bit more. Suppose that Berkeley need not hold the
likeness principle to be a necessary truth, but only that he have a good argument in its favor. Presumably that argument would be based on the
need to make a comparison if one is to establish a likeness, as indicated

9. Berkeley gives this argument in *Commentaries* 378.

above. The foregoing counter-argument in terms of the explanatory fecundity of a postulated likeness shows that one need not make, or even be
in a position to make, a comparsion in order for one to be justified in
thinking that a relevant likeness holds. The materialist, or realist, has an
effective reply on this point, then, even if the likeness principle is at best
contingently true.

To show a difference between his position and materialism over this
point, then, Berkeley would need to stress that the common sense position
is that objects possess *all* of the sensible qualities we typically perceive
them to have. Such an insistence would produce a wedge between his position and that of the materialist; but it is not as big a split as Berkeley
makes it seem.

There can be little doubt about materialism and the C-proposition that
objects do not have phenomenal individuals, or ideas, as constituents.
This proposition, like metaphysical realism, is a staple of the materialist
theory. Nor can we doubt that for the materialist physical objects are public entities. It is true that the representative realist cannot say of physical
objects that different people *immediately* perceive the same physical object.
In this respect the materialist position differs from Berkeley's. However,
the difference does not matter to the *public character* of objects; they can be
public insofar as different people do mediately, or indirectly, perceive objects. The publicity of objects, then, is perfectly consistent with materialism.

It is true that the materialist position as Berkeley conceives of it is not
consistent with the thesis that objects are typically immediately perceived.
This is because the only materialist position Berkeley considers is that of
the representative realist, and on that theory all perceived physical objects
are indirectly perceived. On this point, immaterialism agrees with common sense and materialism does not, just as Berkeley supposes. Neither
can the materialist accept a further element of PDR,— the proposition that
when physical objects are immediately perceived, they are typically perceived as they are. The reason is obvious: materialism, as here conceived,
does not agree that objects are immediately perceived. Further, materialism is not even in the position to accept the somewhat weaker proposition
(arguably another C-proposition) that when objects are perceived they are
typically perceived as they are. In this case the reason is different: generally the materialist, or representative realist, accepts some version of the
primary-secondary quality distinction, and so denies that objects actually
have a fair number of secondary qualities. But in perception of objects,
they are perceived to have secondary qualities, so they are not *typically*
perceived as they are, even though they are sometimes so perceived in
virtue of their having primary qualities.

Within set C there remain just the two elements of EDR, and the thesis that there is genuine causation between physical events. Certainly the latter is consistent with the materialist position, though it is not consistent with immaterialism. In that case, then, to this point immaterialism, or Berkeley's theory, accepts and is consistent with seven propositions in set C. That is its degree of agreement with the crucial C-propositions on which, I have proposed, Berkeley's adjudication argument rests. So far we have seen that materialism, however, agrees with or is consistent with five of these C-propositions, and "partially"agrees with a sixth. By this I mean not that it is partly consistent with the sixth, but rather that it is consistent with part of what is designated by the sixth proposition: some of the sensible qualities that objects are perceived to have are actually possessed by the objects according to the materialist, and this contention, I have argued, is perfectly consistent. The difference in degree of agreement with common sense is thus quite small as measured by degree of agreement with set C. The crucial difference, if Berkeley is to be found correct, will have to be over epistemic items in set C.

We can start with that part of EDR which concerns certain knowledge: the proposition is that we typically gain certain perceptual knowledge of physical objects. We have seen that Berkeley consistently accepts this proposition. Moreover, we know that in his view the materialist is in no position to accept it.

> N.B. I am more for reality than any other Philosophers, they make a thousand doubts & know not certainly but we may be deceiv'd. I assert the direct contrary.

Here it is clear Berkeley is referring to Descartes, one of the philosophers he has in mind as a materialist. Later he mentions Malebranche, for Berkeley also a materialist:

> On second thoughts I am, on t'other extream I am certain of that wch Malbranch seems to doubt of. Viz the existence of Bodies. (Berkeley, 1948–57, 1:64, 84)

There is also his attack on the representative realism which he finds in Locke. This theory, he thinks, rules out perceptual knowledge of bodies altogether, and so rules out certain knowledge of bodies:

> But though it were possible that solid, figured, moveable substances may exist without the mind, corresponding to the ideas we have of bodies, yet how is it possible for us to know this?

If materialism, or representative realism, were to *entail* that we lack perceptual knowledge of objects, then of course it would be inconsistent with our having certain knowledge of objects. This is exactly the situation Berkeley thinks obtains.

> Either we must know it by sense, or by reason. As for our senses, by them we have the knowledge only of our sensations, ideas, or those things that are immediately perceived by sense, call them what you will: but they do not inform us that things exist without the mind, or unperceived, like to those which are perceived. It remains therefore that if we have any knowledge at all of external things, it must be by reason, inferring their existence from what is immediately perceived by sense. But what reason can induce us to believe the existence of bodies without the mind, from what we perceive, since the very patrons of matter do not pretend, there is any necessary connexion between them and our ideas?. . . In short, if there were external bodies, it is impossible we should ever come to know it. (Berkeley 1948–57, 2:48, 48–49)

It is clear that if Berkeley's argument is correct, then the other element of EDR is also ruled out by materialism. That is, if materialism implies that we lack perceptual knowledge of bodies, then of course it implies that we lack immediate, non-inferential knowledge of bodies. So on this point, too, materialism would be inconsistent with EDR, and thus to that extent inconsistent with common sense. The historical tradition has sided with Berkeley on this question, though seldom by bringing in agreement with common sense. Hume and Kant, for example, agreed with Berkeley that representative realism (materialism) rules out knowledge of physical objects, and many later philosophers followed them in this.

If we grant that Berkeley's arguments on these epistemic points are quite strong, as I propose to do in this book, then they are sufficient to make a case for the claim that materialism is inconsistent with EDR.[10] In that respect, then, immaterialism comes out in a better position, for it is consistent with EDR, as noted earlier (chapter 7). Further, it is in virtue of this superior position relative to these epistemic points that immaterialism may be said to win the competition over agreement with common sense, though the margin of victory is overall quite slim.

Berkeley's success in this competition, though, depends on his having correctly isolated all of the important C-propositions on which to conduct the competition. This is what has been identified here as set C. If some C-propositions which belong in C have been overlooked, matters might

10. Actually, I think much more can be said in behalf of the representative realist on this point, but I defer that to my *Empiricist Epistemology* (in preparation).

be somewhat different, and the scales might tip in the direction of the materialist, even granting the superiority of immaterialism with respect to EDR. For example, a materialist might well argue that it is eminently commonsensical to believe that atomism is true, and thus that objects are composed of micro-particles. This proposition is consistent with materialism, he might argue, but not with immaterialism. If atomism is added as an element of C, the overall "score" of the materialist would increase at the expense of immaterialism.

Further, in order for this competition relative to common sense to have any purchase, degree of agreement with common sense has to have some epistemic weight. It has to contribute to the confirmation of a theory, or to acceptability of a theory to some degree. In this respect, Berkeley's competition demands that the elements of common sense which he identifies, namely set C, should have some special status relative to all other C-propositions. The propositions in C have to all be elements of reflective common sense, and settled, universally believed and basic, if agreement with C is to increase the likelihood of truth in a theory. The elements of C have to be distinguished from the run of the mill C-propositions in some such way; for, agreement with a great many of the latter carries no special epistemic weight in favor of a theory.[11]

11. Dan Garber once noted, in conversation, that it is odd that Berkeley bothers with this methodology, since he (Berkeley) thinks that he has a priori arguments which suffice to establish the core elements of his philosophy—indeed, that most of those core elements are established by such arguments in the first thirty-three sections of the *Principles*. Garber's point is very well taken. I suspect that part of the reason Berkeley engages this methodology is that he notices the *possibility* that the EIP principle is false, just as he notices that it is possible that matter exists. See my comments on these points in chapter 5. However, my claim here is purely conjectural; Garber's question stands as a general problem for the Berkeley commentator.

CHAPTER 9

Scepticism

Besides bringing people back to common sense and away from meta-physical obscurity and excess, Berkeley says that his aims are to un-cover the doctrines that lead to scepticism and atheism. He is interested not only in showing what these doctrines are, but also in refuting the doc-trines and thereby undercutting the principal supports for scepticism and atheism. This is not all, however, for he also aims to refute scepticism and atheism outright, and not merely to criticize arguments which lead to those conclusions.

In this chapter I will focus on Berkeley's treatment of scepticism rather than atheism. The chapter has three main targets: (1) to understand just what Berkeley means by 'scepticism'; (2) to discover which principles he thinks lead to scepticism; and, (3) to explicate Berkeley's answer to scepti-cism. The latter topic is complex, involving both an examination of his criticism of arguments which supposedly lead to scepticism, and also his attempted refutation of scepticism itself.

Types of Scepticism

In the beginning of the first *Dialogue*, Berkeley characterizes scepticism in terms of doubtfulness. He has Hylas say that a sceptic is " . . . one that doubts of everything." (Berkeley 1948–57, 2:173). Presumably the doc-trine, as opposed to the person, would then be that every proposition is doubtful. But this possibly self-refuting thesis is not what Berkeley takes scepticism to be. Following Hylas' admission that his initial statement of scepticism is in error, Hylas remarks:

> What think you of distrusting the senses, of denying the real existence of sensible things, or pretending to know nothing? Is this not sufficient to denominate a man a *sceptic*?

Philonous accepts this suggestion. He says,

> Shall we therefore examine which of us it is that denies the reality of sensible things, or professes the greatest ignorance of them; since, if I take you rightly, he is to be esteemed the greatest *sceptic*? (Berkeley 1948–57, 2:173)

These two passages actually suggest three distinct notions of scepticism

(1) We do not gain knowledge by means of the senses, i.e., we do not gain any perceptual knowledge.
(2) There is no knowledge, i.e., no person knows any proposition.
(3) There are no sensible things, i.e., no sensible qualities (shape, color, and the like) or sensible objects (tables, chairs, and so on).

The first two notions are properly epistemic notions of scepticism, the first being a local form pertaining just to perceptual knowledge and the latter global, encompassing all putative knowledge. The third notion we may think of as ontological scepticism, denying existence to a whole category of entities.

Ontological scepticism of this sort can be thought of as derivatively a sceptical doctrine. Statement (3) is just a negative existential, making no claims about knowledge. Still, it entails some important epistemic ideas. If there are no sensible things or sensible qualities, then of course we have no knowledge of such entities, nor do we acquire such knowledge in perception. In the first instance, though, it is the denial of knowledge (or of justified belief) which is the sceptical doctrine. Denial of the existence of some types of entities is a sceptical thesis only insofar as it entails that there is no knowledge of such entities.

While properly sceptical on any account, neither (1) nor (2) can be taken as Berkeley's targets. Hylas pretty much represents the views of Berkeley's opponents, principally Locke and Descartes, and neither of them denies that we have knowledge of individually perceived ideas. So (1) does not express a view that Berkeley's opponents accept and he denies. Nor, therefore, does (2). Instead, it is scepticism regarding ordinary physical objects that is at issue, a much more restricted doctrine than (2). Berkeley represents it in the preface to the *Dialogues* this way:

> Upon the common principles of philosophers, we are not assured of the existence of things from their being perceived. And we are taught to distinguish their real nature from that which falls under our senses. Hence arise *scepticism* and *paradoxes*. It is not enough, that we see and feel, that we smell and taste a thing. Its true nature, its absolute external entity, is still concealed.

This suggests that we should amend the first two statements:

(1.1) We do not gain knowledge, by means of perception, of either the nature or the existence of ordinary physical objects.

(2.1) We do not know any propositions concerning the nature or existence of ordinary physical objects.

Berkeley also talks about certainty in our beliefs about physical objects. For instance, in another exchange with Hylas, Philonous says,

> I . . . assert that I am as certain as of my own being, that there are bodies or corporeal substances (meaning the things I perceive by my senses), and that granting this, the bulk of mankind will take no thought about, nor think themselves at all concerned in the fate of those unknown natures, and philosophical quiddities, which some men are so fond of. (Berkeley 1948–57, 2:167, 238)

Armed with such an idea we could amend (1.1) to talk of *certain* perceptual knowledge, and change (2.1) so that it concerns certain knowledge of ordinary physical objects. That Berkeley has such theses in mind is indicated by his allegation that on his views, one does have such certain knowledge and that it is gained in perception. Still, there are important differences to be observed. First, and most obviously, the two scepticisms with respect to certain knowledge are very narrow, much more so than (1.1) and (2.1). They are, as well, much more difficult to refute, since one would then have to show that we do have certain knowledge in this domain. Perhaps most important, (1.1) and (2.1) express sceptical theses that Berkeley's opponents might want to reject, while the amended versions concerning certain knowledge of physical objects they would surely accept. Berkeley then needs to be seen as maintaining that his opponents are committed to holding (1.1) and (2.1), not that they openly do so. Scepticism about certain knowledge of physical objects, however, they would accept outright.[1]

Berkeley's Project

Berkeley has three aims with regard to scepticism: First, to uncover those principles or doctrines which lead to scepticism; second, to refute those principles; and, third, to refute scepticism itself. Regarding the first point he says,

> My purpose therefore is, to try if I can discover what those principles are, which have introduced all that doubtfulness and uncertainty, those absurdities and contradictions into the several sects of philosophy.

In the same passage he addresses the second point:

> There may be some grounds to suspect that those lets and difficulties, which stay and embarrass the mind in its search after truth, do not spring from any darkness and intricacy in the objects, or natural defect in the understanding, so much from false principles which have been insisted on, and might have been avoided.

As for the third part of his project, he says in the preface to the *Dialogues:*

> If the principles, which I here endeavor to propogate, are admitted for true; the consequences which, I think, evidently flow from thence, are, that

1. There are some complications here. Descartes does maintain in the sixth *Meditation* that we have knowledge of the general truth that there are material objects, and that they have the primary (geometrical) properties. But he concedes that even with God's help in the best of circumstances, we do sometimes fall into error with respect to *individual* physical object propositions. So, perhaps Descartes would be willing to allow acceptance of (1.1) and (2.1), restricted to individual physical object propositions, while he would reject both taken in full generality.

Locke's rejection of (1.1) and (2.1) comes in his account of sensitive knowledge in book 4 of the *Essay*. I take sensitive knowledge, for Locke, to amount to genuine knowledge, despite the fact that it falls short of the certainty attending intuitive and demonstrative knowledge.

The matter of certain knowledge is also complex. If we understand this notion as ruling out the logical possibility of error, as both Descartes and Locke do, then of course they would be sceptical about certain knowledge of objects. But then in *this sense* of certainty, even Berkeley would be sceptical about such knowledge. However, as we have already seen, Berkeley utilizes a much weaker concept of certainty appropriate to physical object beliefs, one which requires merely the absence of grounds for doubt. In this sense, while Berkeley can claim to be certain of the existence of physical objects and their qualities, it may be that Descartes and Locke could make the same claim.

atheism and *scepticism* will be utterly destroyed, many intricate points made plain, great difficulties solved, several useless parts of science retrenched, speculation referred to practice, and men reduced from paradox to common sense. (Berkeley 1948–57, 2:26, 168)

In the first part of the project, Berkeley says there are four main principles that lead to scepticism: (*A*) the thesis that there are abstract ideas; (*M*) the thesis that objects consist in material substance with inherent sensible qualities; (*RE*) that is, realism regarding the existence of ordinary physical objects and at least some of their qualities, a thesis which is the denial of the EIP principle; and, (*RR*) the theory which we would call the representative realist theory of perception. Each is worth some consideration.[2]

In the Introduction to the *Principles*, Berkeley says that he will take notice of

what seems to have had a chief part in rendering speculation intricate and perplexed, and to have occasioned innumerable errors and difficulties in almost all parts of knowledge. And that is the opinion that the mind hath a power of framing *abstract ideas* or notions of things. (Berkeley 1948–57, 2:27)

This passage comes on the heels of one, quoted above, in which Berkeley tells us that his aim is to uncover those principles which lead to scepticism. So, part of what he means by saying that the abstract ideas thesis makes speculation difficult and leads to errors is that the thesis engenders scepticism. How is this supposed to come about?

I assume that Berkeley cannot mean merely that if there are abstract ideas, it would be difficult to have much knowledge about *them*. For that, by itself, contributes nothing to the sceptical doctrines noted earlier. To see what he might have in mind, consider what he says about time.

Beside the external existence of the objects of perception, another great source of errors and difficulties, with regard to ideal knowledge, is the doctrine of *abstract ideas*, such as hath been set forth in the Introduction. The plainest things in the world, those we are most intimately acquainted with, and perfectly know, when they are considered in an abstract way, appear strangely difficult and incomprehensible. Time, place, and motion, . . . are what everybody knows; but having passed through the hands of a metaphysician, they become too abstract and fine, to be apprehended by men of ordinary sense.

2. Thesis A is identified as yielding scepticism in the Introduction to the *Principles*, section 6, as well as at *Principles* 97 and *De Motu* 43. For principle M having the same implication, see the first of the *Dialogues*, in Berkeley 1948–57, 2:172. Principle RE is implicated at *Principles* 88, and RR in sections 8 and 18–20.

Undoubtedly Berkeley holds that the external existence of objects of perception is a principle that leads to scepticism. So, in coupling the abstract ideas thesis with that concerning external objects, his point is to implicate them in the same "error."

But it is not clear that Berkeley shows that the abstract ideas thesis actually leads to scepticism. To see this, consider how he completes the passages just partly quoted:

> Bid your servant meet you at such a *time*, in such a *place*, and he shall never stay to deliberate on the meaning of those words: in conceiving that particular time and place, or the motion by which he is to get thither, he finds not the least difficulty. But if *time* be taken, exclusive of all those particular actions and ideas that diversify the day, merely for the continuation of existence or duration in the abstract, then it will perhaps gravel even a philosopher to comprehend it. (Berkeley 1948–57, 2:83)

What the servant would fail to know, given what Berkeley says, is the correct *analysis* of the concept of time. In this respect, the servant would not know what time is and neither, perhaps, would even the best philosophers. But this is not scepticism, or if it is it is not the sort that Berkeley officially aims to attack. For ignorance concerning the correct analysis of the concept of time is perfectly consistent with one having all manner of knowledge of propositions which temporally locate physical objects. Thus, one might know that the refrigerator was in this room yesterday, despite being in the dark about the correct analysis of time. So, the thesis of abstract ideas does not appear to lead to scepticism in the way that Berkeley claims.

It is possible, though, that Berkeley's point in the last-quoted passage is not about the analysis of the concept of time. His point may be, instead, that if there is a concept of time, abstracted from one's experience of the passage of time, then practically no person would understand the concept of time. The concept of time, being abstract, would also be "rarefied" in a way that would impede understanding by all but the most acute and learned philosopher. If this is what he means, scepticism may be a result at least for some temporal propositions. The reason would be that one cannot come to know a proposition one does not fully understand; and, one would not understand these temporal propositions because one would not understand, or not fully understand, the concept of time. Hence, with perhaps the exception of the acute philosopher, nobody would know these temporal propositions.

This reasoning could then be extended. Nobody would understand propositions about triangular shapes, or things having colors, or the creatures over there being people, if there were abstract ideas of triangularity, color, and person. Thus, nobody would know propositions in which terms for those abstract ideas were essentially used.

It is possible that the passage quoted is to be read along these lines. However, I think Berkeley has another reason for thinking that the abstract ideas thesis leads to scepticism, one which I bring out below. It does this because it implies the falsity of the EIP principle, i.e., the *esse is percipi* principle.

The thesis that physical objects consist in material substance in which qualities inhere, or *M*, is also supposed to lead to scepticism. Hylas points out that he has heard rumors that Philonous denies the existence of matter, something Hylas regards as extravagant. Philonous agrees that the rumors are correct, but he denies that scepticism results. To this, Hylas says:

> What! Can anything be more fantastical, more repugnant to common sense, or a more manifest piece of scepticism, than to believe that there is no such thing as *matter*?

And Philonous responds:

> What if I should prove, that you who hold there is, are by virtue of that opinion a greater *sceptic*, and maintain more paradoxes and repugnancies to common sense, than I who believe no such thing? (Berkeley 1948–57, 2:172)

We know that for Berkeley the notion of matter is supposed to be incoherent or at least to make no sense. Moreover, Berkeley holds that the notion of qualities inhering in matter is unintelligible. So, as with abstract ideas, the supposition of matter has the result that no person would know the correct analysis of the concept of an object. In this respect, Berkeley is right to say that given matter and inherence, nobody would know the *nature* of objects, perhaps not even the *essential natures* of objects.[3] But the material substance thesis does not rule out knowing many other things about objects. It does not rule out, for example, knowing that there is a chair in the corner, that it has a certain shape, that it is made of wood, nor even that it has a brown color. The assumption of matter, by itself, does not rule out knowledge of any of these things, nor even rule out that such knowledge is gained by means of perception of the object. In this respect, one can perceptually acquire a great deal of knowledge about the nature of objects even if the material substance and inherent qualities thesis is true.

3. For discussion of this sort of sceptical doctrine see Margaret Atherton 1991, 238ff. Also relevant is Daniel Garber 1982, 174–193.

One might think that if sensible qualities inhere in a material substance, then these qualities would not be perceiveable, and hence we would not have any means of acquiring knowledge of them. Thus, scepticism of precisely the sort which concerns Berkeley would result after all from the thesis of matter and inherent qualities. However, this line of reasoning, too, is not quite right.

To see why, notice that the material substance and inherent qualities thesis is consistent with a naive form of direct realism, according to which perceived sensible qualities actually exist on or in the objects, and the objects are immediately perceived by immediate perception of some of their sensible quailities. According to such a view, sensible qualities are perfectly perceiveable, despite their being inherent in matter. And again, although we would know nothing about matter itself or about the mysterious relation of inherence, we would know plenty about objects.[4] Of course, direct realism is not an option that any philosopher took very seriously before Thomas Reid (perhaps excepting Arnauld) and certainly Berkeley never entertains the position as viable. So we could argue in Berkeley's behalf that the view that objects consist in material substances with inherent sensible qualities, tacitly conjoined with the assumption that no form of direct realism is correct, implies that objects are not immediately perceiveable, and neither are any of their sensible qualities. *This* position, Berkeley would urge, surely does imply scepticism regarding objects. On this point Berkeley is on firmer ground, we may assume, at least if we grant Berkeley that inferences from propositions about immediately perceived entities to propositions about objects are suspect. But notice what carries the inference to the sceptical result. It is not the supposition of matter and inherent qualities by itself that does this work. Instead, it is the denial of direct realism regarding objects and their qualities (together with the assumption that the inductive inferences needed for inferential knowledge of objects are not cogent) that has the unwanted sceptical consequence.

Yet maybe there is still something to be said in support of the claim that the material substance thesis leads to scepticism. For Berkeley takes that thesis to imply that objects exist unperceived, or have what Berkeley calls a real absolute existence. The supposition of matter, in other words, implies the third of the four principles that Berkeley thinks lead to scepticism. If this third principle, which is just the denial of the EIP principle favored by Berkeley, implies scepticism, then so does the material substance

4. Compare the remarks made by Turbayne in his edition of the *Three Dialogues* (Indianapolis: Bobbs-Merrill) 1954, xiii, particularly what he there calls the "first version of materialism."

thesis. And indeed, this is just how Berkeley thinks of the matter. Here is a representative passage:

> So long as we attribute a real existence to unthinking things, distinct from their being perceived, it is not only impossible for us to know with evidence the nature of any real unthinking thing, but even that it exists.

Moreover, we know that Berkeley holds that the material substance thesis implies that objects exist unperceived. He says,

> But why should we trouble ourselves any farther, in discussing this material *substratum* or support of figure and motion, and other sensible qualities? Does it not suppose they have an existence without the mind? And is not this a direct repugnancy, and altogether inconceiveable?

In fact, with these materials at hand, Berkeley can easily reply to the comments made earlier about abstract ideas and scepticism. At *Principles* # 5 he says:

> If we thoroughly examine this tenet, it will, perhaps, be found at bottom to depend on the doctrine of *abstract ideas*. For can there be a nicer strain of abstraction than to distinguish the existence of sensible objects from their being perceived, so as to conceive them existing unperceived? (Berkeley 1948–57, 2:79, 35, 42)

If we take this passage to contain the claim that if there are abstract ideas, then the EIP principle is false, as was maintained in chapter 4, then it is easy to see why Berkeley thinks that the abstract ideas thesis leads to scepticism. The denial of the EIP principle has this consequence, and the abstract ideas thesis implies the denial of the EIP principle.

Seen in this way, both the material substance thesis and the abstract ideas thesis imply scepticism and for the same reason: each individually implies that the EIP principle is false, and the latter, Berkeley assures us, leads directly to the sceptical consequences noted earlier.

While I think these comments accurately reflect Berkeley's reasoning, we should also ask whether the reasoning is correct. One reason to think it is not was already supplied regarding matter and can be noted again: all forms of direct realism are perfectly consistent with the denial of the EIP principle; indeed, direct realism incorporates that denial. But on a direct realist theory, physical objects and their qualities are typically immediately perceived, and this fact eliminates Berkeley's reason for holding that we would lack knowledge of such objects if we granted that they exist unperceived. For, being immediately perceivable, physical objects and their qualities would qualify as things about which immediate knowledge can be had. As before, it would only be by tacitly assuming that direct realism is not an option that scepticism results. Rejecting direct realism but accepting that objects exist unperceived leads straight to indirect realism, which under Locke's influence Berkeley treats as representative realism, and it is this which would have sceptical consequences. Hence, strictly speaking, Berkeley is wrong: neither the abstract ideas thesis, nor the material substance thesis, nor indeed the denial of the EIP principle, *taken alone*, implies scepticism. Each needs to be conjoined with another premise in which direct realism and thus the immediate perception of physical objects is ruled out.

Even so, we should remind ourselves that Berkeley never seriously considers the option of direct realism since, as he might put it, it is "agreed on all hands" that direct realism is false. So there is a good sense in which he is not guilty of any error. Nevertheless, in no case is the inference an immediate one as Berkeley's texts would have us believe, and so none of the first three putative scepticism-producing principles unearthed by Berkeley *by itself* implies that we lack knowledge of physical objects.[5]

There can be little doubt that Berkeley thinks that representative realism leads to scepticism. Here is how Philonous characterizes Hylas' views:

> It is your opinion, the ideas we perceive by our senses are not real things, but images, or copies of them. Our knowledge therefore is no farther real, than as our ideas are the true representations of those originals. But as these supposed originals are in themselves unknown, it is impossible to know how far our ideas resemble them; or whether they resemble them at all. (Berkeley 1948–57, 2:246)

The problem Berkeley sees for this view is straightforward: one never immediately perceives physical objects, but only ideas, some of which represent the objects and some of their qualities. In order to know whether one is in the perceptual presence of an object one has to be able to compare the object's qualities with the manifest qualities of the immedi-

5. But what of that comment in *Principles* 86 where Berkeley says that if objects exist unperceived, how would we know that they are when unperceived as they are when perceived? This suggests that even if *direct* realism were true, Berkeley would urge that scepticism threatens. On this view it would be realism *per se* and not indirect realism, which would lead to scepticism, and it would have this result because it allows objects to exist unperceived. Although relevant to the question of scepticism here considered, it is clear that even if correct the sceptical doctrine supported by this line of reasoning falls short of (1.1) and (2.1). The claim that we do not know what objects are like when they are not perceived does nothing to show that we lack knowledge of *perceived* objects.

ately perceived ideas. But given the theory, one can never accomplish this; Hence, given the theory, one has no means of gaining perceptual knowledge of objects or their qualities, which is (2.1), and presumably from this it follows that one has no knowledge of objects, which is just (1.1). Of course, if one has no knowledge of objects, one also has no *certain* knowledge of them; so, the amended versions of scepticism earlier referred to would likewise follow from this fourth principle.[6]

A great many philosophers from Berkeley's time to our own have supposed that this argument is sound. We can readily see why once we note that the argument Berkeley has given is an instance of a more general argument he gives elsewhere:

> . . . though it were possible that solid, figured, moveable substances may exist without the mind, corresponding to the ideas we have of bodies, yet how is it possible for us to know this? Either we must know it by sense, or by reason. As for our senses, by them we have the knowledge only of our sensations, ideas, or those things that are immediately perceived by sense . . . but they do not inform us that things exist without the mind, or unperceived, like to those which are perceived. It remains therefore that if we have any knowledge at all of external things, it must be by reason, inferring their existence from what is immediately perceived by sense. (Berkeley 1948–57, 2:48)

Berkeley's argument is thus that if physical objects and their qualities are not immediately perceived, then they are not entities about which one gains immediate knowledge. If this is so, then any perceptual knowledge one has of physical objects and their qualities is inferential, and thus would be based upon whatever immediate perceptual knowledge one has. The latter is restricted to immediately perceived ideas. However, neither deductive nor inductive inferences from propositions about immediately perceived ideas to propositions about physical objects or their qualities are successful. Hence, there is no inferential perceptual knowledge of physical objects, and thus no perceptual knowledge of them at all. Since there is no *non*-perceptual knowledge of such objects, we reach the fully general sceptical result that there is no knowledge of physical objects, given the truth of any form of indirect realism, including representative realism.

Though there are elements in this argument that are open to question, for present purposes we will assume that it is sound. We may accordingly summarize the results reached thus far. Of the four doctrines Berkeley singles out, only the last—indirect representative realism—has sceptical

6. See *Principles* 87 for this argument.

consequences. The other three doctrines—the abstract ideas thesis, the thesis of material substance, and metaphysical realism—taken individually or jointly do not imply scepticism.

Why, then, is Berkeley so confident that scepticism does follow from these theses? The correct answer, I think, is the same for each thesis. Berkeley thinks that each implies indirect or representative realism and *it*, as we have noted, implies scepticism. The thesis of abstract ideas, he seems to hold, implies the denial of the EIP principle, as does the supposition of material substance. The denial of the EIP principle is just the affirmation of metaphysical realism, the view that physical objects and some of their qualities exist unperceived. Now Berkeley, along with nearly every other philosopher in the period, takes for granted the theory of ideas. In his hands, this amounts to the view that in every perceptual experience some ideas are immediately perceived (= thesis *I*). Hence, if physical objects and their qualities are perceived at all, they are indirectly perceived. Whence, given the argument in *Principles* 18, scepticism can exist about the objects and their qualities. But it is clear that the assumption of thesis *I* does major work in Berkeley's argument. It is this thesis which effectively rules out direct realism.[7] Succinctly stated, here is the argument that scepticism results from each of the four principles, A, M, RE and RR, which we have been discussing:

(1) The abstract ideas thesis and the thesis of material substance each implies the denial of the EIP principle.
(2) The denial of the EIP principle implies metaphysical realism about objects.
(3) Hence, since principle I is true about perception, all perceived physical objects are indirectly perceived. That is, given principle I and metaphysical realism, indirect realism must be true.
(4) Hence, perceived physical objects are not things about which we gain immediate knowledge.
(5) Hence, any knowledge we have of physical objects is inferential.
(6) Arguments from propositions about immediately perceived ideas to propositions about physical objects, whether they be deductive or inductive, are not satisfactory. (*Principles* 18–20)
(7) Hence, we have no inferential knowledge of physical objects.
(8) Hence, we have no knowledge of physical objects. (from 4 and 7)

---

7. One can hold the theory of ideas in some form and still hold on to direct realism. The trick is to interpret ideas so that they are not *perceived* entities, even though they are constituent elements in every perceptual experience. Arnauld seems to have held such a view. For illuminating discussion see Steven Nadler 1989.

This cannot be said to show that the abstract ideas thesis, or the thesis of material substance, or metaphysical realism, *individually*, implies scepticism. The abstract ideas thesis implies the denial of the EIP principle, and thus implies metaphysical realism. The same may be said of the thesis of material substance. Metaphysical realism, together with principle I, implies some form of indirect realism, and it is this which implies scepticism. These comments capture the respect in which the theses concerning Berkeley lead to scepticism, in all cases via indirect (for Berkeley representative) realism.

Rejecting the Principles

As we noted earlier, Berkeley's second aim is to refute the principles which he thinks lead to scepticism. This means refuting the four principles examined above. We have already looked closely at the arguments Berkeley gives against the abstract ideas thesis (chapter 3), and against metaphysical realism, the latter in the discussion of the arguments for the EIP principle (chapter 5). Those arguments need no repeating here.

The argument Berkeley gives against matter is quite complex, because the concept of matter is, as Kenneth Winkler nicely puts it, a "moving target" in Berkeley's writings.[8] However, I think the main argument is that matter as a substratum requires that sensible qualities inhere in matter. Berkeley would claim, though that sensible qualities have been shown to be ideas and thus entities that can only exist in a thing that perceives. So, since matter qua substratum is certainly a non-perceiving entity, sensible qualities do not inhere in it. There is no matter if it is to be a material substratum with inherent sensible qualities. Here is the argument in Berkeley's words:

> It is worth while to reflect a little on the motives which induced men to suppose the existence of material substance;.... First ... it was thought that colour, figure, motion, and the rest of the sensible qualities or accidents, did really exist without the mind; and for this reason, it seemed needful to suppose some unthinking *substratum* or *substance* wherein they did exist, since they could not be conceived to exist by themselves. Afterwards ... men being convinced that colours, sounds, and the rest of the sensible secondary qualities had no existence without the mind, they stripped this *substratum* ... of those qualities, leaving only the primary ones ... which they still conceived to exist without the mind, and consequently to stand in need of a material support. But it having been shewn, that none, even of these, can possibly exist otherwise than in a spirit or mind which perceives them, it follows that we have no longer any reason

8. K. Winkler 1989, 178.

to suppose the being of *matter*. Nay, that it is utterly impossible there should be any such thing, so long as the word is taken to denote an *unthinking substratum* of qualities or accidents, wherein they exist without the mind. (Berkeley 1948–57, 2:72–73)[9]

Berkeley's argument against the representative realist theory is sometimes said to be that the theory leads to scepticism, and so the theory is not true. In the present context, however, it is clear that Berkeley needs a different argument against representative realism. The argument he actually gives depends on the likeness principle—the principle that asserts that an idea can be like nothing but another idea. Representative realism holds that at least some ideas, those of the primary qualities, resemble actual qualities in bodies. It requires, therefore, a resemblance between an idea and a non-idea. Here is how he states the argument at *Principles* 8:

> Though the ideas themselves do not exist without the mind, yet there may be things like them whereof they are copies or resemblances, which things exist without the mind, in an unthinking substance. I answer, an idea can be like nothing but an idea; a colour or figure can be like nothing but another colour or figure. If we look but ever so little into our thoughts, we shall find it impossible for us to conceive a likeness except only between our ideas. (Berkeley 1948–57, 2:44)

Earlier (chapter 8) I explained how the representative realist could argue that the likeness principle is not a necessary truth. However, here its necessity is not at issue, but only its truth. And Berkeley would argue that surely the principle is *true*. Or, at the least, the representative realist is never in a position to accept the denial of the likeness principle, because in order to justify that denial one needs to compare an idea and a non-idea and find a resemblance. Given representative realism, however, one is never able to do this, and thus the representative realist has no basis for denying the likeness principle.

Supposing the four principles which Berkeley holds lead to scepticism have each been shown to be false, we may conclude that the arguments for scepticism have been undermined, and thus that scepticism itself is left without support. This is what Berkeley claims, though only of three of the four principles here discussed. In *Principles* 87 he says that if ideas are

> looked on as notes or images, referred to *things* or *archetypes* existing without the mind, then are we involved all in *scepticism*. . . . All this scepticism

---

9. K. Winkler (1989) discusses five other concepts of matter which Berkeley discusses and argues against, 180–81.

follows, from our supposing a difference between *things* and *ideas*, and that the former have a subsistence without the mind, or unperceived.

In this passage Berkeley is linking representative realism and also metaphysical realism to scepticism. He then goes on to say in section # 88,

> But all this doubtfulness, which so bewilders and confounds the mind, and makes *philosophy* ridiculous in the eyes of the world, vanishes, if we annex a meaning to our words, and do not amuse our selves with the terms *absolute, external, exist,* and such like, signifying we know not what.

Strictly speaking, Berkeley's point here is that all this doubtfulness vanishes if we give up metaphysical realism. But as that would also require one to give up representative realism, we can reasonably take him to be saying that the doubtfulness vanishes if these two theses, metaphysical and representative realism, are dropped. How shall we interpret the point overall? We could say that Berkeley means that dropping these two principles would show that scepticism is false, but such an interpretation would have Berkeley inferring the falsity of a consequent (scepticism) from having denied the antecedents (representative and metaphysical realism). A more charitable reading of the above passages is that Berkeley is saying that the support for scepticism has been swept away, so that there is no remaining reason to accept it.

In connection with atheism, Berkeley says in *Principles* 92 that,

> How great a friend material substance hath been to *atheists* in all ages, were needless to relate. All their monstrous systems have so visible and necessary a dependence on it, that when this cornerstone is once removed, the whole fabric cannot choose but fall to the ground; insomuch as it is no longer worth while, to bestow a particular consideration on the absurdities of every wretched sect of *atheists*

Here I think the last clause shows that he takes the rejection of matter to undermine the case for atheism, and not to show that atheism is false. But in this very section, he had said that there is a close parallel between his treatment of atheism and scepticism.

> For as we have shewn the doctrine of matter or corporeal substance, to have been the main pillar and support of *scepticism*, so likewise upon the same foundation have been raised all the impious schemes of *atheism* and irreligion. (Berkeley 1948–57, 2:79, 81)

Given the parallel he is drawing, we should treat his case against both of these doctrines in the same way: in each he is showing that the support for the doctrine has been undermined, and that we no longer have any reason to take the doctrine seriously.

Overall, then, Berkeley's argument is that all of the four identified doctrines, the abstract ideas thesis, the thesis of material substance, metaphysical realism, and representative realism, are false or at least implausible. Further, the arguments by which these results are established themselves should not presume the *falsity* of scepticism, lest Berkeley's arguments here be hollow indeed.

Refuting Scepticism

Refuting arguments which lead to scepticism, though of great importance, does nothing by itself to show that scepticism is false, any more than a related strategy would show that atheism is false. But Berkeley does want to refute scepticism; he is not content just to refute principles which lead to it. Recall how he writes in the preface to the *Dialogues:*

> If the principles, which I here endeavor to propogate, are admitted for true; the consequences which, I think, evidently flow from thence, are that atheism and scepticism will be utterly destroyed, many intricate points made plain, great difficulties solved, several useless parts of science retrenched, speculation referred to practice, and men reduced from paradox to common sense.

Here he is not saying that there are some principles, accepted by other philosophers, which lead to scepticism or atheism. Instead, his point is that there are some principles which he accepts and which will suffice to show that atheism and scepticism are false. Leaving atheism aside, we may ask which principles does Berkeley think have this interesting result?

Berkeley himself makes it seem as though it is the EIP principle that does the work of showing scepticism to be false. He says:

> I can as well doubt of my own being, as of the being of those things which I actually perceive by my senses: it being a manifest contradiction, that any sensible object should be immediately perceived by sight or touch, and at the same time have no existence in Nature, since the very existence of an unthinking thing consists in being perceived.

> I deny that I agreed with you in those notions that led to scepticism. You indeed said, the reality of sensible things consisted in an *absolute existence* out of the minds of spirits, or distinct from their being perceived. And pur-

suant to this notion of reality, you are obliged to deny sensible things any real existence; that is, according to your own definition, you profess your-self a *sceptic*. But I neither said nor thought the reality of sensible things was to be defined after that manner. To me it is evident, for the reasons you allow of, that sensible things cannot exist otherwise than in a mind or spirit. (Berkeley 1948–57, 2:168, 88, 211–12)

These passages seem to suggest that the EIP principle itself suffices to show that scepticism is false.[10]

If this interpretation is correct, then Berkeley endorses the proposition that if the EIP principle is correct, then we have perceptual knowledge of objects. We can think of a way to support this proposition, as well. Entities which are said to exist only within the mind, in accord with the EIP principle, are all perceived by a mind. Hence, physical objects are perceived by a mind, since they exist only within a mind. Being perceived by a mind, however, is sufficient for that mind gaining knowledge of the object perceived. So, the truth of the EIP principle implies that we have perceptual knowledge of objects.

I think there is something right and important in this argument, namely, that perception of objects is what Berkeley takes to be the factor which facilitates knowledge acquisition. The foregoing argument, though, does not motivate perception of objects in quite the right way. True, objects are said to exist only in minds, and so are perceived. From this we cannot derive that any object is perceived by some person, some individual finite mind. Indeed, we cannot even derive this if we add to the EIP principle the proposition, endorsed by Berkeley, that physical objects exist. It is consistent with those two propositions that all perceived physical objects are perceived only by the infinite spirit, and never by finite ones. And in connection with scepticism, it is only the epistemic condition of finite spirits or persons that is at issue.

Of course, this fact about the EIP principle not implying that we have perceptual knowledge of objects does not imply that this is how *Berkeley* conceived of things. *He* may well have supposed the implication goes through. Some reason to think that Berkeley did *not* conceive of matters in this way, however, can be found in other passages where he talks of scepticism, passages in which he says that it is perception of objects which does the work in refuting scepticism, but where he makes no mention of the EIP principle. Here are two such passages:

Is it not a sufficient evidence to me of the existence of this *glove*, that I see it, and feel it, and wear it? Or if this will not do, how is it possible I should

10. Richard Popkin (1980, 309–11) interprets Berkeley's refutation of scepticism along these lines.

be assured of the reality of this thing, which I actually see in this place, by supposing that some unknown thing which I never did see or can see, exists after an unknown manner . . .

I assure you Hylas, I do not pretend to frame any hypothesis at all. I am of a vulgar cast, simple enough to believe my senses, and leave things as I find them. To be plain, it is my opinion, that the real things are those very things I see and feel, and perceive by my senses. These I know. . . . (Berkeley 1948–57, 2:224, 229)

In chapter 6, I gave reasons to think that when Berkeley speaks of perceiving physical objects, he generally means that they are immediately perceived. So, the last quoted passages are making two points: (1) that physical objects are immediately perceived; and, (2) that *by* immediately perceiving objects we come to acquire knowledge of these objects. Here we have Berkeley's answer to scepticism: we have knowledge of objects in virtue of the fact that the objects are immediately perceived.

Earlier we noted (chapter 7) that what allows Berkeley to claim that physical objects are immediately perceived is the collections account of objects, together with the assumption that in every perception some ideas are immediately perceived. These are the principles which Berkeley accepts and which allow for perceptual knowledge of objects. We have noted above passages in which Berkeley links perception of objects and perceptual knowledge. Here are passages that show that, for him, the collections account is also of importance if we are to have such knowledge:

I am not for changing things into ideas, but rather ideas into things; since those immediate objects of perception, which according to you, are only appearances of things, I take to be the real things themselves.

What you call the empty forms and outside of things, seems to me the very things themselves. Nor are they empty or incomplete otherwise, than upon your supposition, that matter is an essential part of all corporeal things. We both therefore agree in this, that we perceive only sensible forms: but herein we differ, you will have them to be the empty appearances, I real beings. In short you do not trust your senses, I do. (Berkeley 1948–57, 2:244–45)

The collections account of objects of itself has no implication regarding knowledge of objects and no bearing on the issue of scepticism. It is because the collections account of objects facilitates the result that physical objects are immediately perceived that it is connected to scepticism and to the refutation of scepticism.

There is actually one other point which Berkeley is relying upon in this refutation of scepticism. Recall that Berkeley also holds, in accord with common sense, that when physical objects are perceived, they are gener-

ally perceived as they are. It is this which, along with the collections account of objects and the thesis that objects are immediately perceived, allows him to hold that we gain perceptual knowledge of the *nature* of objects, and not merely of their existence. That objects are perceived as they
are, however, is a thesis which rests on Berkeley's account of sensible
qualities (discussed in chapter 7), and thus that account of sensible qualities is also implicated as lying behind and helping shore up his refutation
of scepticism.

We thus see that the immediate perception of physical objects is important to Berkeley not merely because it is an element of common sense—
though there is that. It is also the most important ingredient in his refutation of scepticism, another topic on which we know he puts great store.
We can also see more clearly another relationship between common sense
and the refutation of scepticism. Berkeley does not argue that since the
sceptical hypothesis is inconsistent with common sense, therefore that hypothesis is false. That is, he does not argue that because a proposition is a
element of common sense that therefore that proposition is true. Rather,
he argues that because he has been able to show, on independent
grounds, that we immediately perceive physical objects, we thus have
knowledge of objects. Of course, that we immediately perceive objects is a
matter of common sense, and this fact is of importance to Berkeley, as we
have seen. The point made here is that it is not *because* this proposition is
an element of common sense that Berkeley thinks he has refuted scepticism.

The refutation of scepticism, of course, is of great value to Berkeley. He
holds that scepticism is a great support for freethinking in religious matters, and this is something he opposes and even finds threatening to the
faith. However, the work that the refutation of scepticism does in Berkeley's philosophy overall is something else. It counts as one of the marks of
evidence in favor of his overall philosophical theory. In this respect the
refutation of scepticism is like the degree of agreement with common
sense. It is one of the parameters by which one judges the level of acceptability of one's philosophical theory relative to its competition. On this parameter, too, Berkeley claims to have won the competition.

The question of scepticism touches upon all of the major themes with
which this book has been concerned. Berkeley thinks that the abstract
ideas thesis leads to scepticism, though in this chapter some reason to
doubt this connection has been provided. At the same time, we have
noted how Berkeley probably conceived of this connection and, given his
assumptions, it is not implausible to think that acceptance of abstract
ideas supports scepticism. Scepticism is also related to the concept of immediate perception and its objects in a direct way. Berkeley aims to refute

scepticism, and not merely to undercut arguments that can be used to support scepticism. To achieve that aim, he argues that physical objects are among the entities that are immediately perceived. It is this, and not his defense of the *esse is percipi* principle on which his proposed refutation of scepticism is based. Then, finally, there is the relationship between scepticism and common sense. Scepticism is itself directly opposed to common sense, since it is an element of common sense to maintain that we have non-inferential knowledge of physical objects. This conflict with common sense, however, is not used by Berkeley either as a reason to reject scepticism, or as a decisive reason to reject the theory which he thinks leads to scepticism. It is just one additional factor to be considered when one weighs the different pieces of evidence counting for and against the rival positions of materialism and immaterialism.

Bibliography and Cited Works

Primary Sources

Aristotle. 1941. *The Basic Works of Aristotle*. Edited by R. McKeon. New York: Random House.
Berkeley's Philosophical Works. 1975. Edited by Michael Ayers. London: Dent.
The Works of George Berkeley. 1948–57. Edited by A. A. Luce and T. E. Jessop. 9 vols. Edinburgh: Thomas Nelson and Sons.
Locke, John. 1975. *An Essay concerning Human Understanding*. Edited by Peter Nidditch. Oxford: Clarendon Press.

General Works

Aaron, Richard. 1955. *John Locke*, 2d ed. Oxford: Clarendon Press.
Alexander, Peter. 1970. "Inferences About Seeing." In *Knowledge and Necessity*. Royal Institute of Philosophy Lectures, vol. 3. London: Macmillan.
Allaire, Edwin. 1963. "Berkeley's Idealism."*Theoria* 29: 229–244.
Alston, William. 1991. *Perceiving God*. Ithaca: Cornell University Press.
Armstrong, David. 1960. *Berkeley's Theory of Vision*. Melbourne: Melbourne University Press.
——. 1968. *A Materialist Theory of the Mind*. New York: Humanities.
Atherton, Margaret. 1987. "Berkeley's Anti-Abstractionism." In *Essays on the Philosophy of George Berkeley*, edited by Ernest Sosa. Dordrecht: Reidel.
——. 1991. *Berkeley's Revolution in Vision*. Ithaca: Cornell University Press.
Ayers, Michael. 1993. *Locke: Epistemology and Ontology*. London: Routledge.
Belfrage, Bertil. 1992. "The Constructivism of Berkeley's New Theory of Vision." In *Minds, Ideas and Objects*, vol. 2, edited by Phillip Cummins and Guenter Zoeller. Atascadero, Calif.: Ridgeview.

Bennett, Jonathan. 1971. *Locke, Berkeley, Hume: Central Themes*. Oxford: Clarendon Press.

Bolton, Martha. 1987. "Berkeley's Objection to Abstract Ideas and Unconceived Objects." In *Essays on the Philosophy of George Berkeley*, edited by Ernest Sosa. Dordrecht: Reidel.

Bracken, Harry. 1965. *The Early Reception of Berkeley's Immaterialism*. The Hague: Nijhoff.

Brykman, Geneviève. 1993. *Berkeley et le Voile des Mots*. Paris: J. Vrin.

Chappell, Vere. 1994. "Locke's Theory of Ideas." In *The Cambridge Companion to Locke*, edited by Vere Chappell. New York: Cambridge University Press.

Chisholm, Roderick. 1942. "The Problem of the Speckled Hen." *Mind* 51:368–73.

——. 1957. *Perceiving*. Ithaca: Cornell University Press.

Cornman, James. 1975. *Perception, Common Sense, and Science*. New Haven: Yale University Press.

Craig, Edward. 1968. "Berkeley's Attack on Abstract Ideas." *Philosophical Review* 77:425–37.

Cummins, Phillip. 1963. "Perceptual Relativity and Ideas in the Mind." *Philosophy and Phenomenological Research* 24:204–14.

——. 1966. "Berkeley's Likeness Principle." *Journal of the History of Philosophy* 4:63–69.

——. 1975. "Berkeley's Ideas of Sense." *Nous*, 9:55–72.

——. 1995. "Berkeley's Manifest Qualities Thesis." In *Berkeley's Metaphysics*, edited by Robert Muehlmann. University Park: Pennsylvania State University Press.

Dancy, Jonathan. 1985. *Contemporary Epistemology*. London: Blackwell.

Dicker, Georges. 1982. "The Concept of Immediate Perception in Berkeley's Immaterialism." In *Berkeley: Critical and Interpretive Essays*, edited by Colin Turbayne. Minneapolis: University of Minnesota Press.

——. 1992. "Berkeley on the Immediate Perception of Objects." In *Minds, Ideas and Objects*, vol. 2, edited by Phillip Cummins and Guenter Zoeller. Atascadero, Calif.: Ridgeview.

Donagan, Alan. 1978. "Berkeley's Theory of the Immediate Objects of Vision." In *Studies in Perception*, edited by Peter Machamer and Robert Turnbull. Columbus: Ohio State University Press.

Downing, Lisa. 1995. "Berkeley's Case Against Realism about Dynamics." In *Berkeley's Metaphysics*, edited by Robert Muehlmann. University Park: Pennsylvania State University Press.

Dretske, Fred. 1969. *Seeing and Knowing*. New York: Humanities.

Flage, Daniel. 1986. "Berkeley on Abstraction." *Journal of the History of Philosophy* 24 (October): 483–501.

Gallois, Andre. 1974. "Berkeley's Master Argument." *Philosophical Review* 83:55–69.

Garber, Daniel. 1982. "Locke, Berkeley, and Corpuscular Scepticism." In *Berkeley: Critical and Interpretive Essays*, edited by Colin Turbayne. Minneapolis: University of Minnesota Press.

Gibson, James. 1966. *The Senses Considered as Perceptual Systems*. New York: Houghton Mifflin.

Graham, Jody. 1997. "Common Sense and Berkeley's Perception by Suggestion." *International Journal of Philosophical Studies* 5:397–423.

Hausman, Alan. 1984. "Adhering to Inherence: A New Look at the Old Steps in Berkeley's March to Idealism." *Canadian Journal of Philosophy* 14:421–43.

Hausman, Alan, and David Hausman. 1995. "A New Approach to Berkeley's Ideal Reality." In *Berkeley's Metaphysics*, edited by Robert Muehlmann. University Park: Pennsylvania State University Press.

Jesseph, Douglas. 1993. *Berkeley's Philosophy of Mathematics*. Chicago: University of Chicago Press.

Jessop, T. E. *Berkeley:* 1953. *Philosophical Writings.* Austin: University of Texas Press.

Kim, Jaegwon. 1993. *Supervenience and Mind.* Cambridge: Cambridge University Press.

Lowe, E. J. 1995. *Locke on Human Understanding.* London: Routledge.

Luce, A. A. 1963. *The Dialectic of Immaterialism.* London: Hodder and Stoughton.

——. 1966. "Berkeley's New Principle Completed." In *New Studies in Berkeley's Philosophy,* edited by Warren Steinkraus. New York: Holt, Rinehart.

Mackie, J. L. 1976. *Problems from Locke.* Oxford: Clarendon Press.

Macrae, Robert. 1965. " 'Idea' as a Philosophical Term in the Seventeenth Century." *Journal of the History of Ideas* 26:175–84.

Malcolm, Norman. 1964. *Knowledge and Certainty.* Englewood Cliffs, N.J.: Prentice-Hall.

McCracken, Charles. 1983. *Malebranche and British Philosophy.* Oxford: Clarendon Press.

Metz, Rudolf. 1925. *George Berkeley, Leben und Lehre.* Stuttgart: Fr. Frommanns Verlag.

Muehlmann, Robert. 1992. *Berkeley's Ontology.* Indianapolis: Hackett, 1992.

——, ed. 1995. *Berkeley's Metaphysics.* University Park: Pennsylvania State University Press.

Nadler, Steven. *Arnauld and the Cartesian Philosophy of Ideas.* Princeton: Princeton University Press, 1989.

Pappas, George. 1980. "Ideas, Minds and Berkeley." *American Philosophical Quarterly* 17:181–94.

——. 1982a. "Berkeley, Perception and Common Sense." In *Berkeley: Critical and Interpretive Essays,* edited by Colin Turbayne. Minneapolis: University of Minnesota Press.

——. 1982b. "Non-Inferential Knowledge." *Philosophia* 12:81–98.

——. 1983. "Adversary Metaphysics." *Philosophy Research Archive* 9:571–85.

——. 1985. "Abstract Ideas and the *'esse is percipi'* Thesis." *Hermathena,* 139:47–62.

——. 1987. "Berkeley and Immediate Perception." In *Essays on the Philosophy of George Berkeley,* edited by Ernest Sosa. Dordrecht: Reidel.

——. 1991. "Berkeley and Common Sense Realism." *History of Philosophy Quarterly* 8:27–42.

——. 1996. "Theories of Perception." In *Encyclopedia of Philosophy: Supplement Volume,* 1996. Edited by Donald Borchert, 394–396. New York: Macmillan.

——. 1998. "Epistemology in the Empiricists." *History of Philosophy Quarterly* 15:285–302.

——. 1999. "Berkeley and Scepticism." *Philosophy and Phenomenological Research* 59: 133–149.

Pitcher, George. 1969. "Minds and Ideas in Berkeley." *American Philosophical Quarterly* 6:198–207.

——. 1977. *Berkeley.* London: Routledge.

——. 1986. "Berkeley and the Perception of Objects." *Journal of the History of Philosophy* 24:99–105.

Popkin, Richard. 1980. *The High Road to Pyrrhonism.* San Diego: Austin Hill.

Popper, Karl. 1953. "Berkeley as a Precursor of Mach and Einstein." *British Journal for the Philosophy of Science* 4:26–36.

Prior, Arthur. 1955. "Berkeley in Logical Form." *Theoria* 21:117–22.

Quine, Willard, and Joseph Ullian. 1968. *The Web of Belief,* 2d ed. New York: Random House.

Sartorius, Rolf. 1969. "A Neglected Aspect of the Relationship Between Berkeley's Theory of Vision and His Immaterialism." *American Philosophical Quarterly* 6:318–23.

Sellars, Wilfrid. 1981. "Foundations for a Metaphysics of Pure Process." *Monist* 64:37–65.

Steinkraus, Warren, ed. 1966. *New Studies in Berkeley's Philosophy.* New York: Holt, Rinehart.

Sosa, Ernest, ed. 1987. *Essays on the Philosophy of George Berkeley*. Dordrecht: Reidel.

Thomas, George. 1976. "Berkeley's God Does Not Perceive." *Journal of the History of Philosophy* 14:163–68.

Tipton, Ian. 1974. *Berkeley: The Philosophy of Immaterialism*. London: Methuen.

——. 1987. "Berkeley's Imagination." In *Essays on the Philosophy of George Berkeley*, edited by Ernest Sosa. Dordrecht: Reidel.

Turbayne, Colin, ed. 1982. *Berkeley: Critical and Interpretive Essays*. Minneapolis: University of Minnesota Press.

Urmson, James. 1982. *Berkeley*. Oxford: Oxford University Press.

Van Iten, Richard. 1968. "Berkeley's Alleged Solipsism." *Revue Internationale de Philosophie* 16:447–52.

Watson, Richard. 1966. *The Downfall of Cartesianism*. The Hague: Nijhoff.

Weinberg, Julius. 1965. *Abstraction, Relation and Induction*. Madison: University of Wisconsin Press.

Winkler, Kenneth. 1983. "Berkeley on Abstract Ideas." *Archiv für Geschichte der Philosophie* 65:63–80.

——. 1989. *Berkeley: An Interpretation*. Oxford: Clarendon Press.

Yandell, David. 1995. "Berkeley on Common Sense and the Privacy of Ideas." *History of Philosophy Quarterly* 12:411–23.

Index